Elusive Peace

Elusive Peace: International, National, and Local Dimensions of Conflict in Colombia

Edited by
Cristina Rojas and Judy Meltzer

palgrave
macmillan

First published in 2005 by
PALGRAVE MACMILLAN™
175 Fifth Avenue, New York, N.Y. 10010 and
Houndmills, Basingstoke, Hampshire, England RG21 6XS
Companies and representatives throughout the world.

PALGRAVE MACMILLAN is the global academic imprint of the Palgrave Macmillan division of St. Martin's Press, LLC and of Palgrave Macmillan Ltd. Macmillan® is a registered trademark in the United States, United Kingdom and other countries. Palgrave is a registered trademark in the European Union and other countries.

ISBN 1–4039–6744–X

Library of Congress Cataloging-in-Publication Data

Elusive peace : international, regional and local dimensions of conflict in Columbia / edited by Cristina Rojas and Judy Meltzer.
    p.cm.
Includes bibliographical references and index.
ISBN 1–4039–6744–X (cloth)
    1. Columbia—Politics and government—1974– 2. Drug traffic—Government policy—Columbia. 3. Political violence—Columbia—History. 4. Counterinsurgency—Columbia—History. 5. Narcotics, control of—International cooperation. 6. Columbia—Relations—Foreign countries. 7. Military assistance, American—Columbia. 8. Economic assistance, American—Columbia. I. Rojas, Cristina. II. Meltzer, Judy.

F279.E48 2004
986.106'34—dc22   2004053372

A catalogue record for this book is available from the British Library.

Design by Newgen Imaging Systems (P) Ltd., Chennai, India.

First edition: January 2005
10 9 8 7 6 5 4 3 2 1

Printed in the United States of America.

Contents

List of Contributors

Bruce Bagley is Professor of International Studies at the University of Miami, United States.

Jackeline Barragán is Program Coordinator at Black Creek Community Health Centre, Toronto, Canada.

Albert Berry is Professor Emeritus of Economics and Research Director of the program on Latin America and the Caribbean at the Centre for International Studies at the University of Toronto, Canada.

Álvaro Camacho Guizado is the Director of the Centre for Socio Cultural and International Studies at Los Andes University, Bogota, Colombia.

Adam Isacson is Senior Associate at the Center for International Policy, Washington D.C., United States.

Jean E. Jackson is Professor of Anthropology at the Massachusetts Institute of Technology (MIT), United States.

Judy Meltzer is a Senior Analyst at the Canadian Foundation for the Americas (FOCAL), Ottawa, Canada.

Cristina Rojas is Associate Professor at the School of International Affairs, Carleton University, Ottawa, Canada.

Ana María Sanjuán is Director of the Center for Peace and Human Rights at the Central University of Venezuela.

Francisco Thoumi is Visiting Professor, Department of Economics, University of El Rosario, Bogota, Colombia.

Juan Gabriel Tokatlian is Professor of International Studies at the University of San Andrés, Argentina.

List of Abbreviations

Agency for International Development (AID)
Asamblea Nacional Constituyente (ANC)
Asociación Nacional de Instituciones Financieras (ANIF)
Asociación Nacional de Usuarios Campesinos (ANUC)
Autodefensas Unidas de Colombia (AUC)
Autodefensas Unidas de Venezuela (AUV)
Autoridades Indígenas de Colombia (AICO)
Canadian Foundation for the Americas (FOCAL)
Center for Socio-cultural and International Studies (CESO)
Central Intelligence Agency (CIA)
Centro de Investigación y Educación Popular (CINEP)
Cost, Insuránce, and Freight (CIF)
Comisión Colombiana de Juristas (CCJ)
Comptroller General of the Republic (CGR)
Consejería para los Derechos Humanos y el Desplazamiento (CODHES)
Consejo Regional Indígena del Cauca (CRIC)
Departamento Administrativo Nacional de Estadísticas (DANE)
Departamento Nacional de Planeación (DNP)
Drug Enforcement Administration (DEA)
Economic Commission for Latin America and the Caribbean (ECLAC)
Ejército de Liberación Nacional (ELN)
Ejército Popular de Liberación (EPL)
Fiscal Year (FY)
Foreign Military Financing (FMF)
Frente Bolivariano de Liberación (FBL)
Fuerzas Armadas Revolucionarias de Colombia (FARC)
General Accounting Office (GAO)
Instituto Colombiano de Reforma Agraria (INCORA)
Internally displaced populations (IDP)
International Crisis Group (ICG)

International Development Research Centre (IDRC)
International Military Education and Training (IMET)
International Organization on Migration (IOM)
North Atlantic Treaty Organization (NATO)
Norwegian Refugee Council (NRC)
Observatory on Security and Defense in Latin America, University Institute Ortega y Gasset (OSAL)
Organización Nacional Indígena de Colombia (ONIC)
Organization for Economic Development Cooperation (OEDC)
Organization of American States (OAS)
Program for Development and Peace in the Magdalena Medio Region (PDPMM)
Project Counselling Service (PCS)
Rehabilitation and Consolidation Zones (RCZ)
The Center for International Policy (CIP)
The Inter-American Treaty of Reciprocal Assistance (ITRA)
The People's Revolutionary Army (ERP)
The United Nations Development Programme (UNDP)
Unión Patriótica (UP)
United Nations High Commission for Human Rights office for Colombia (UNHCHR)
United Nations International Drug Control Programme (UNDCP)
United States Institute of Peace (USIP)

CHAPTER 1

Elusive Peace: International, National, and Local Dimensions of Conflict in Colombia

Judy Meltzer[*] and Cristina Rojas[**]

Introduction

Peace remains elusive in Colombia. After four decades of fighting and a multitude of failed attempts at negotiating peace, Colombia remains home to the largest conflict in the Western Hemisphere; a conflict that has killed hundreds of thousands of civilians, and displaced millions of people. Although disproportionately impacting the poorest and most vulnerable Colombian citizens, all spheres of society have been affected by the violence that the conflict has entailed. The conflict has also had impacts beyond Colombia's borders, spilling into the region with consequences for migration, borders, regional relations, as well as international policy and engagement.

Over the course of four decades, the nature and spatiality of conflict have changed. From the leftist rebellion of the 1950s rooted in economic, social, and political exclusion, the conflict diversified in the 1980s and 1990s, giving rise to multiple forms of violence (Sánchez 2001, 3), occupying new spaces within and beyond Colombia's borders. Internally, two disjointed guerrilla groups fight the state as well as paramilitary forces. Political identities have fragmented, and distinctions between actors blurred. There are no "good guys"—the guerrillas, far-removed from their ideological roots, perpetrate human rights atrocities financed through kidnapping, extortion, and the illegal drug industry. The paramilitary, emerging in the 1980s with funding from wealthy landowners to protect elite assets from the guerrilla, represent a privatization of the conflict, and continue to be responsible for horrendous human rights atrocities. The drug economy has shifted economic frontiers further into areas inhabited by indigenous people in the Vaupés, Guania, the Putumayo, the Sierra Nevada, and other regions. The state, historically absent and exclusionary, continues to be characterized by institutional weakness. As such, Colombia remains a paradox, by minimal procedural measures one of the oldest democracies in the region, yet caught in a cycle of violence, lawlessness, poverty, and inequality.

Regional and international dimensions of the conflict have also changed over the course of the war. Colombia's monopoly over drug traffic in the Western Hemisphere by the 1980s not only provided inexhaustible economic fuel for all protagonists, but it focused international attention on the conflict. By the 1990s, Colombia's conflict had internationalized. While the United States concentrated on waging a "war on drugs," "alternative development" and "negotiated peace" became the focus for other countries and multilateral actors. Reaching the "pinnacle" of inter-American attention, Colombia received its own Summit Declaration in support of peace at the Summit of the Americas in Quebec City 2001.

The contemporary search for peace in Colombia is defined by two distinct stages. From 1982 to 2002 the search for a negotiated settlement was the singular focus of successive administrations (Bejarano 2003). This disjointed process collapsed under President Pastrana (1998–2002) in 2002, giving rise to a new framework for understanding and addressing the conflict under President Álvaro Uribe (2002–2006) who came to power later that year. Although negotiations were retained as an option, the new policy centered on empowering the state by strengthening the military.

This book analyses the culmination of the first stage of attempts at negotiated settlement under Pastrana's government, in order to shed light on the post-2002 transition and contextualize the shift in tactics of President Uribe.

Under President Pastrana negotiated peace took on new dimensions domestically and internationally. Not only was a demilitarized zone granted to the largest of guerrilla forces, the Fuerzas Armadas Revolucionarias de Colombia (FARC), but the international community was mobilized to support and fund the incipient negotiating processes. Perhaps most significantly, this period gave rise to the controversial Plan Colombia, a framework for U.S.–Colombian engagement in the war against drugs. With the demise of Pastrana's peace process in February of 2002, public support for negotiated peace crumbled, thus setting the stage for a new chapter in the Colombian conflict, under the leadership of President Álvaro Uribe.

In 2002 the impetus to dialogue disappeared. Peace negotiations had collapsed, transborder repercussions of the conflict on Colombia's politically fragile neighbors, including regional militarization, were increasingly harder to ignore, and the implementation of the U.S.-led Andean Regional Initiative was an early indicator of a new kind of interventionism in the Andes. The watershed events of September 2001, the aggressive unilateralism of the hemispheric hegemon in its "war against terrorism" and escalating human rights abuses, contributed to new discourses and doctrines of security within Colombia.

The book presents analyses of the significant transition between two distinct models in Colombia's elusive search for peace, and its local, national, and international dimensions. It represents a dialogue between Latin American and North American scholars, based on research presented at a workshop on Colombia held as national and international politics were changing course. The workshop was organized by the Universidad de los Andes; The Norman Paterson School of International Affairs and The Centre for Security and Defense Studies at Carleton University; the Canadian Foundation for the Americas (FOCAL); and the International Development Research Centre (IDRC).

The book is unique in its interdisciplinary and multiscalar approach to understanding the conflict and the ongoing search for peace in Colombia. It draws upon scholarship from political science, economics, anthropology, and international relations, to look at the connections, consequences, and contradictions of the conflict in local, regional, and international spaces. In doing so, it not only contextualizes the transition to a new model for conflict resolution, but highlights the often overlooked impacts of national and international policies at local and regional levels, from Plan Colombia's impact on indigenous communities to regional spillover and local identities.

The Current Context

A Discourse of Democratic Security

Three years of attempts at negotiating peace between the government and guerrilla forces came to an end under the Pastrana government in early 2002. Presidential elections in May of that year swept independent candidate (dissident Liberal) Álvaro Uribe to power. His victory was unprecedented: not only did it rupture the long-standing two-party system, whose exclusionary nature has often been cited as one of the root causes of the conflict, but he came to power with unparalleled support, winning over 50 percent of the vote on a hardliner platform of military crackdown, in stark contrast to his forbearers' promises of negotiated peace, marking a historic break with past politics around the conflict. The enormous level of support for his "law and order" campaign was attributed to several factors including: disillusionment with the decades of failed peace negotiations, an urbanization of violence which threatened populations that had previously felt insulated from the conflict, and a global shift in the discourse on terrorism and its counterpart: security.

Uribe's presidency has been characterized by a sustained popularity for his focus on a strong state, the deepening of ties to the United States, and a discourse of "democratic security," which underlies a range of controversial policies. The state of emergency implemented in wake of violence immediately following his inauguration was the most potent that Colombia's constitution allowed, and set the stage for the policy shift to come. New powers were granted to the police and military, including increased power of search and to arrest without warrant; and with them growing concerns that they would be used against opposition within civil society and the media. With the powers of decree granted by the state of emergency, Uribe also created zones of "rehabilitation and consolidation," entailing even greater powers for the military including restricted movement, curfews, and mandatory identification in conflict hotspots of Sucre, Bolívar, and Arauca. One of the most controversial of Uribe's policies was his creation of a network of paid civilian informants to transmit information on insurgent groups. Equally contentious has been the strategy to arm peasant populations to act as soldiers in areas of the country with little state presence. These policies have had the potential effect of further blurring the lines between civilian and combatant, making civilians more likely to be targeted by insurgents, in contravention of international humanitarian law.

As Eduardo Cifuentes, former Public Ombudsman, stated,

> soldiers are trained to act collectively. They belong to units under a commander, they have protected institutional living quarters, and they have permanent systems of prevention. If these peasant soldiers are going to be in their homes, it will be very difficult to organize an effective response in the case of an attack [. . .] (Hagen 2003, 68)

These policies are particularly unsettling in light of the persistent failure of the government to put a stop to collusion with paramilitary forces and lessons from Uribe's own political history in this regard. The Colombian government's program of "democratic security" is contingent on its ability to leverage funds and military support from the United States. This has not proved too problematic thus far. Presidents Uribe and George W. Bush have brought bilateral relations between Colombia and the United States to their highest level yet (Godoy 2003), manifest in unprecedented military counternarcotic aid under the rubric of the "war on terror." From the outset, Uribe positioned himself as a close ally of the United States, and as such became the only country in South America to support the U.S. war on Iraq. More compliant than his predecessors, Uribe has embraced the controversial aerial spraying of coca crops advocated and undertaken with the United States, and has been more lenient in allowing Colombians to be extradited to the United States on drug charges, a priority in the U.S.' original bilateral focus on the "war against drugs."

More recently, President Uribe initiated negotiations with perhaps the most unlikely of the armed insurgents—the paramilitary. In July 2003, following a year of quiet talks, the government signed an unprecedented agreement with three right-wing paramilitary organizations to begin formal negotiations for their demobilization and reintegration. The Ralito Accord marked the official beginning of negotiations to demobilize and reintegrate paramilitary forces. The Accord includes conditions of ceasefire; the demobilization of approximately 13,000 Autodefensas Unidas de Colombia (AUC) troops by the end of December 2005; the designation of an area of the country where paramilitary signatories will congregate; reintegration programs for former paramilitary, and most controversially, amnesty for demobilized paramilitary, largely at the discretion of the president himself (International Crisis Group 2003, 23).

From Uribe's perspective, the accord represents an important step toward ending the conflict, opening the door to negotiations with guerrillas, who have consistently set paramilitary demobilization as a prerequisite (and who remain unwilling to negotiate with Uribe's administration). However the agreement has been beset by problems. The paramilitary are without political status—a previous prerequisite for the government to negotiate, forcing the government to make legislative changes allowing for negotiations with armed actors without a recognized political dimension. They are increasingly fragmented, and even successful demobilization of the AUC would leave numerous other paramilitary organizations intact. Moreover, the paramilitary forces are responsible for the worst human rights atrocities in the conflict, targeting civilians in massacres, tortures, and forced displacement to consolidate territorial control. The notion of impunity for these crimes particularly for the leaders of the paramilitary is unacceptable, not only to the millions of Colombians affected but also by the broader international community. Provisions for truth, and reparation—incompatible with the agreement as it currently stands—are crucial to any post-conflict scenario in Colombia.

There also exists the danger that "reintegrating" paramilitary will entail their quiet absorption by the military, with whom they continue to collude. Although Colombia's prosecutor general has initiated investigations into collusion against officials in the Army, Police, and Department of Security (International Crisis Group 2003, 15),[1] the persistence of complicity has been condemned by human rights organizations and the international community. In their *World Report 2003*, Human Rights Watch stated that

> paramilitary groups operating with the tolerance and often support of units within Colombia's military were linked to massacres [. . .] selective killings and death threats. There were numerous and credible reports of joint military–paramilitary operations and the sharing of intelligence and propaganda [. . .] Throughout Colombia, paramilitaries continued to move uniformed and heavily armed troops unhindered past military operations. (2003b, 1)

The weakness of the justice system and persistence of near total impunity in Colombia create a particularly problematic backdrop. President Uribe's focus on strengthening state security has not been accompanied by a concomitant focus on institutions of justice. Both the UN Commission on Human Rights and Human Rights Watch have recently drawn attention to the declining ability of the Attorney General's office to investigate and prosecute reports of human rights abuses (Human Rights Watch 2002; International Crisis Group 2003, 17).

Despite these pitfalls, public support for Uribe in Colombia remains exceptionally high; and even those wary of his tactics admit to an increased feeling of "everyday security" in urban centers that his presidency seems to have catalyzed. The elusiveness of peace despite successive negotiations by previous administrations sheds light on the high level of support for the hard-line security doctrine. Support for strong state institutions as the only means to end conflict is accepted across the political spectrum. However unless institutions safeguarding justice and civil rights are simultaneously strengthened, Colombians risk having the doctrine of "democratic security" result in the rollback of citizen rights and democratic norms.

U.S. Intervention: From the "War on Drugs" to the "War on Terror"

It is now impossible to separate the current "war on terror" from the "war on drugs" out of which it evolved. The nature of U.S. current engagement with

Colombia developed when Colombia assumed the role of leading producer and exporter of cocaine and heroin in the 1990s (ironically as a direct result of a balloon-effect crackdown on drug cultivation in other Andean countries); it became viewed as the key protagonist in the U.S. battle against domestic drug consumption and bilateral relations were shaped accordingly.

Since the late 1990s until 2001, U.S.–Colombian relations have been defined by the national strategy set out in Plan Colombia and its regional sequel, the Andean Regional Initiative. The emergence and evolution of these initiatives are analyzed in detail in subsequent chapters. Broadly, these documents outlined a U.S.–Colombian strategy to first and foremost combat drug cultivation and second to support alternative social and economic development initiatives. Within this framework, the United States has provided more than US$2 billion in aid since 1999, of which more than 80 percent has been allocated to military and policy forces (U.S. Institute for Peace May 12, 2003)—the United States has funneled more than US$755 million into Colombia in 2003 alone. (The Center for International Policy (CIP) statistical index at the end of the book provides a comprehensive breakdown of U.S. funds disbursed to Colombia.)

After 9/11, the U.S. conceptualization of the Colombian "problem" shifted from that of a "war on drugs" to a "war on terror." Whereas U.S. military aid had been previously restricted to counternarcotics efforts, in September 2002 the U.S. Congress authorized the direct use of U.S. military aid in the conflict itself; the number of military personnel remained limited to 400, although this limit has been perpetually bypassed via private contracts and presidential authority (in February 2003 Bush authorized sending in an additional 150 U.S. troops to take direct military action in seeking three kidnapped Americans) (Forero February 21, 2003).

In 2003, the largest insurgent organizations, the AUC, FARC, and Ejército de Liberación Nacional (ELN), had been included on the U.S. Department of State's list of terrorists, as well as those of other Western countries. In March 2003, in a statement to the U.S. Congress by Secretary of State Colin Powell, Colombia was listed with only three other countries—Afghanistan, Philippines, and Pakistan—as urgently needing U.S. investment to counter terrorist activities outside of the Middle East (*Revista Cambio* March 30, 2003).

Given Colombia's dependence on economic and military assistance, the United States has been well situated to apply pressure on the Colombian government to take action to stop human rights violations by its own forces. To this effect, since the implementation of Plan Colombia, human rights–related conditions were established upon which the disbursement of security assistance was meant to be contingent. The most critical condition was that of severing the links between military and paramilitary forces. In theory, the Colombian government had to receive "certification" based on meeting these conditions prior to receiving at least portions of aid. The consistent failure of the U.S. Department of State to take advantage of this opportunity to effect progress on human rights has been particularly disappointing. Despite compelling evidence from credible human rights organizations including Amnesty International, Human Rights Watch, and the Washington Office on Latin America showing the failure of the Colombian government to break is ties with paramilitary groups, Colombia has been consistently "certified" to receive aid, undermining the supposed safeguard and reaffirming that the United States is willing to turn a blind eye to these violations.

As Human Rights Watch pointed out, although

the Colombian armed forces are arresting more paramilitaries than in years past, this has yet to translate into effective action that includes the arrest of top leaders and the breaking of ties between the military and paramilitary groups. In short, the links between the military and para-military groups remain as strong as ever. (2003a)

Recently, in spite of strong evidence that the Colombian government had failed to sufficiently comply with the conditions, in February 2003 the U.S. Congress certified Colombia to receive an additional US$523 million in aid, of which approximately US$368 million is allocated for drug eradication and "antiterrorism" with nearly US$110 million to the Colombian military; and the remaining US$164 million toward alternative development, strengthening of democracy and protection of human rights. Again on July 8, 2003, US$32 million in additional funding was released.

Often pointed to as evidence of direct U.S. involvement in "counter-insurgent" activities is the increase in U.S. aid funneled directly toward protecting the 500-mile-long Caño Limón oil pipeline, co-owned by U.S. company Occidental Petroleum and Colombia's state oil company, Ecopetrol. Included in the 2003 Congressional budget for Colombia were US$99 million for a new program to train Colombian soldiers to protect the pipeline. Oil pipelines have long been an infrastructure target for Colombian guerrillas, notably the ELN. In 2001 alone, attacks on the pipeline cost approximately US$500 million in revenue (Washington Office on Latin America 2003). Colombia is Latin America's third largest exporter of oil to the United States. Critics argue that the above actions not only indicate direct

U.S. involvement in the conflict, but also the prioritizing of U.S. corporate interests over civilian protection (Miller 2003). For 2004, Bush has requested additional funding for Colombia nearing 600 million, also to be heavily weighted toward security initiatives, making Colombia the second largest recipient of U.S. military aid after Israel, outside the Middle East.

As a recent International Policy Report points out, there is a persistent paradox in U.S.–Colombian relations. The deeper the United States becomes involved, the less political and public debate there is about Colombia, the conflict, and U.S. involvement (Vaicius and Isaacson 2003, 2). In spite of increasing "end game"/"exit strategy" rhetoric, the United States continues to vest significant military and financial resources in Colombia. In addition to the material changes brought about by the "war on terror" there are less tangible repercussions resulting from this new lens. As in the Middle East, the Bush administration's version of the "war on terror," with its stark division between friends and foe, has further simplified the Colombian conflict and its multiple social, economic, and political underpinnings, making it less likely that U.S. policy will respond to these challenges.

The transformation and deepening of U.S. engagement with Colombia and the role of other international actors is the focus of the first section of the book. In chapter 2, Bruce Bagley shows that, on balance, Colombian and U.S. drug-control policies during the 1990s have failed to curb drug production and trade, or to reduce political violence. On the contrary, by 2000, Colombia faced the possibility of growing political instability—manifested in the proliferation of organized crime, intensification of political violence, and guerrilla warfare—as well as the spreading of the conflict across borders. Accordingly, Colombia has become crucial within the U.S. agenda in the Western Hemisphere. This chapter shows that as the conflict becomes more complex, not only has the U.S. involvement in Colombian affairs increased, but it has also changed. It concludes that the U.S. response to the conflict is flawed and is likely to worsen Colombia's ongoing problems of spiraling violence and insecurity.

Chapter 3 in this section, by Juan Gabriel Tokatlian, reminds us that the conflict is characterized by a long-standing struggle for inclusion into a closed sociopolitical system. He explores how the internationalization of the conflict, particularly U.S. involvement, shapes the policy options of the actors involved and the ways in which this will be exacerbated by the transition to a "war on terror" including the risk that Colombia becomes a laboratory for foreign intervention and new type of war. He puts forward innovative ideas for regional actors, particularly in the Southern Cone, to become more involved in diplomatic initiatives for peace and thus serve as a counterbalance to the direction that international intervention has taken.

International, and particularly U.S. engagement in the conflict has not only had an impact on Colombia, but has affected the entire region. It is well known that the conflict in Colombia has had tremendous repercussions beyond its own borders—the so-called "spillover effects." The second section of the book focuses on the region, analyzing some of the predicted and unpredicted impacts of the conflict on the neighborhood, including political consequences and regional perceptions.

Ripples through the Region

Panama, Ecuador, Peru, Bolivia, Venezuela, and Brazil experience disparate humanitarian, economic, and political repercussions as a result of the neighboring conflict, relative to their respective geographies and domestic politics. Not only have these countries directly felt the brunt of the conflict, but they have inevitably become caught up in a new foreign policy toward the region on the part of the United States, which concretized with the transformation of Plan Colombia into the Andean Regional Initiative.

The human costs have been the greatest for bordering countries—particularly for Ecuador, Venezuela, and Panama. Incursions by both guerrillas and paramilitaries have become more frequent, used both as bases for drug trafficking, and initiating attacks against each other and local civilians. These countries also bear the brunt of transnational displacement, with Ecuador and Panama in particular receiving a growing influx of Colombians displaced by the conflict. Although only a minute fraction of them apply for official refugee status, the International Crisis Group (2003, 4) reported that the Project Counselling Service (PCS) estimated that up to 100,000 Colombians have sought refuge in a neighboring country since 2001.

The spillover of the conflict has also had high political and economic costs, as a divisive political issue in domestic politics (such as the case of Venezuela), diverting precious funds to military and border-control budgets and reshaping interregional as well as bilateral relations with the United States in each case. This materialized in concrete terms in 2001 with the U.S.-led Andean Regional Initiative, billed as a follow-up to Plan Colombia. The Andean Initiative, which has been used strategically by countries in the region to leverage U.S. funds, had an equally significant focus on drug eradication and military build-up. The CIP cites five key problems with the Andean Regional Initiative: its persistent, overriding military focus; the balloon effect of drug cultivation and production it was likely to produce; its potential to escalate conflict; its reliance on private contractors; susceptibility to augment human rights violations; and lack of multilateral support for the Initiative (CIP Colombia Project 2001). The chapters in the section look at Plan Colombia and the Andean Regional Initiative in detail and key regional and country-specific impacts in turn.

Álvaro Camacho Guizado (chapter 4) provides insight into the evolution of Plan Colombia and the Andean Regional Initiative, and the military industrial complex within which they are embedded. He highlights the disconnect between the context upon which they were based and the radical changes in the structure of the drug trade and the reconfiguration of social alliances among and around the various armed actors. This failure to recognize and adapt to a changing situation is part of the same logic that has consistently failed to take into account the development issues at the root of the conflict.

The heterogeneity among countries in the region vis-à-vis Colombia reflects divergent experiences of the "spillover" and the domestic political and economic differences. In terms of specific countries, Ecuador, Venezuela, and Panama have faced similar problems: inflows of tens of thousands of refugees (though not necessarily with formal refugee status), cross-border incursions and outbreaks of violence by armed insurgents.

Ecuador's inability to prevent the cross-border spillover of the conflict returned security to the top of their foreign policy agenda. Ecuador and the United States have mutually developed their relationship in this area, through increased investments in military infrastructure, including the construction of a U.S. airbase on the Ecuadorian coastal city of Manta. Despite increasing allocation of U.S. funds for security, cross-border incursions have worsened. By 2002, it was estimated that at least 3,000 members of insurgent organizations were operating in northern Ecuador, including using the northeastern city of Lago Agrio as a supply point (Giugale, Lafourcade, and Luff 2003, 43). Although a shift in Ecuador's position vis-à-vis the Colombian conflict was anticipated in 2002, when the current president, Lucio Gutiérrez, assumed power with support from a largely left-leaning coalition that included indigenous organizations, it never materialized. At the expense of coalition unity, Gutiérrez has spent significant political capital in preserving friendly relations with the United States, and, in line with this, has consistently maintained support for Uribe's approach to dealing with the conflict.

Both Panama and Venezuela have also experienced the blurring of borders and overflow of the conflict. Panama, has felt particularly vulnerable to a spreading of the conflict, without its own security forces and under the watchful eye of its primary partner, the United States. However, Venezuela has a very different political relationship with Colombia. President Hugo Chávez, who came to power in 1999, has maintained uneasy relations with the Colombian government and Uribe himself. Despite offers to host peace negotiations between the government and the guerrilla, Chávez has been more critical of Plan Colombia and U.S. intervention than other leaders in the region. However, he continues to balance the conflicting needs of a stable relationship with Colombia (as each other's largest trading partner and potential ally, particularly given the political instability he has faced in recent years) with contradictions posed by Uribe's and U.S. positions to the ideological underpinnings of Chávez's "Bolivarian Revolution."

Chapter 5 by Ana María Sanjuán looks specifically at the precarious relationship between Colombia and Venezuela, and its oscillation between stability and tension through history. Venezuela is one of the countries that has been most affected by the conflict, having been subjected to guerrilla incursions, kidnapping, and high levels of violence along the frontier. The election of Hugo Chávez, the subsequent shift in foreign policy, and violent political polarization that has ensued, have given rise to new tensions between the two countries. Sanjuán, in this chapter, evaluates the impact of the conflict on the redefinition of civil–military relations in Venezuela, which is also dealing with its own political–institutional crisis exacerbated by extreme political polarization. She underscores the need for conflict prevention and resolution mechanisms and simple spaces for dialogue through which to manage their bilateral relationship, which have previously existed but have been dismantled in recent years.

Peruvian and Bolivian experiences with "spillover" are also distinct in the region. Their concerns are less for incursions of armed insurgents, or inflows of refugees than they are for its impact on their respective drug industries. Not surprisingly, both Peru and Bolivia experienced an increase in coca and opium poppy cultivation in 2002, as a result of the attempted crackdown on cultivation in Colombia, testament to the so-called "balloon effect" whereby a decrease in cultivation and production in one area consequently leads to an increase in other areas, if the demand for the product persists. This "balloon-effect" is well documented and has contributed to increasing political instability in the region. However there is less understanding of the current structure and political economy of the drug industry, or the impact that recent changes in the industry have had on the Colombian conflict, its economy and development in general. It is these questions that the chapters in the third section of the book seek to address.

New Perspectives on Drugs

It is impossible to understand Colombia's conflict, and broader social, political, and economic development in the latter half of the twentieth century without careful attention to the production and trafficking of illegal drugs, and their evolution over the past decade. The drug industry is inextricably linked to issues of employment, land redistribution, political alignments, displacement, and violence. Since assuming the dubious title of primary producer/exporter of cocaine and more recently heroine in the Western Hemisphere, the conflict in Colombia entered the international public sphere as a debate about the elimination of illegal drug production and drug trafficking. The inexhaustible economic fuel for the conflict provided by the industry not only shaped international aid, but undermined international leverage in resolving the conflict, which has historically been contingent on degrees of economic dependency in other contexts.

In July 2003, it was reported that massive crop fumigation (with relatively minimal investments in alternative development and livelihoods) had resulted in significant drug eradication in Colombia. In a debriefing from his trip to Colombia in July 2003, U.S. Drug Czar John Walters proclaimed that over 150,000 hectares of coca had been eliminated, with 97 percent reduction of production in the Putumayo, one of the largest growing areas in the country (*Infobrief* July 28, 2003). The Central Intelligence Agency (CIA) reported an apparent 35 percent decrease in the number of metric tons of cocaine exported in 2003 (*Infobrief* July 28, 2003).

However, critics persistently point to the tremendous health, environmental, and economic costs of drug eradication with little implementation of alternative development and livelihood strategies. They also highlight problems in simple calculations of eradication—although coca production may have dropped in some areas of Colombia it more accurately reflects the dispersion of production within Colombia and throughout the region. Since the 1980s total cultivation in South America appears to have remained relatively steady, shifting only in spatiality, as evidenced by recent increases in production in Bolivia and Peru.

Although there is a clear connection between earlier antidrug initiatives in Peru and Bolivia and the exponential growth of the drug industry in Colombia over the past decade, there has been inadequate analysis of the development of the drug industry—its ebb and flow over time, how it affects and reflects violence in Colombia, and the factors that determine the success or failure of policies designed to combat it.

Chapter 6 provides an analysis of the political economy of the drug industry and its overall impact on Colombia's economy. This chapter by Albert Berry and Jackeline Barragán represents a unique analysis of quantitative evidence on the "gains and losses" resulting from the drug industry in Colombia, over a span of more than 20 years. Berry and Barragán's analysis traces illicit drug production beyond its cultivation and trafficking to the investment of returns in productive sectors ranging from financial and construction to service sectors. The research represents an important step toward better understanding the role of illicit drug industry in the highly inequitable distribution of income in Colombia. The study finds that, in addition to the high levels of violence that accompany the illegal drug industry, the bulk of the revenues from drug-related activities are concentrated in the hands of a few, and have ultimately led to a concentration of assets and diminishing incentives to invest in other productive sectors.

Chapter 7 by Francisco E. Thoumi in the third section of the book takes up these questions in an innovative reexamination of drug production and counternarcotic policies in Colombia. The production of drugs, and the violence it entails, have often been explained by the presence of poverty, income inequality, economic crises, and state corruption. Through a comparative analysis, Thoumi assesses these explanations and finds that although these variables may influence the development of illegal crops, they do not constitute the main reasons for their existence. Rather, he points to the weakness of social and political institutions and absence of social capital that have enabled the development of this industry in Colombia.

This pervasive inequality in income and the corresponding inaccessibility of social services or political resources moves us to the human crisis which is at the center of the conflict.

Cultural and Local Consequences

It is in connecting the national and transnational dimensions of the conflict with human costs at the local level that the chapters in the final section of the book make a unique contribution, linking the regional issues with local and cultural experiences. Although analysis of the impact of the conflict on communities and individuals has been well documented in recent years, the social stories they tell are rarely combined with macrolevel analyses. In contrast to the political–economic analyses that precede them, these chapters show how the multiscalar conflict is played out, and contested, in the everyday.

The human costs of the conflict are immense, and continue to rise. In 2002, over 2,700 people were kidnapped, and more than 4,000 civilians were killed as a direct result of the conflict (Amnesty International 2003). Trade unionists, journalists, and human rights defenders were disproportionately targeted in political killings—in 2002 over 170 trade unionists and 17 human rights defenders were killed. These figures do not adequately convey the degree of violence that pervades Colombia beyond the strict parameters of conflict, including 32,000 homicides in 2002 alone. More than 3 million Colombians have been displaced by the conflict, of a population of approximately 44 million, the second highest in the world behind Sudan (*El Tiempo* May 29, 2003). Over 1.2 million have permanently left the country, according to the International Organization on Migration (IOM), and the Consejería para los Derechos Humanos y el Desplazamiento (CODHES)—a Colombian NGO—reported an estimated 412,553 people were displaced in 2002 alone. According to the UN Commission for Human Rights, it is estimated that approximately 30 percent of displacements in 2002 were a result of paramilitaries assuming control over "guerrilla territories." In approximately half of the cases it was reported that a combination of military activity by paramilitaries and government troops was to blame. That displacement attributed to state agents seems to have decreased while those attributed to paramilitary groups increased, also points to military–paramilitary collusion (UNHCHR February 24, 2003). It was also estimated that guerrillas were responsible for approximately 14 percent of displacements (Benetti 2003).

Many Colombians have also been displaced by coca crop fumigations, although they tend to go uncounted as they are excluded from official registers, referred to by the government as "migrants"—thus overlooking the context within which fumigation occurs. It is increasingly well documented that fumigations have deprived peasants of their livelihoods, indiscriminately destroying food crops, leaving lands infertile, killing farm animals, and polluting water sources (CODHES April 28, 2003).

Displacement most affects marginalized populations—in 2002 Afro-Colombians and indigenous populations represented a third of the total displaced, despite constituting only 11 percent of the national population (CODHES April 28, 2003). Afro-Colombian and Indigenous communities, vulnerable in part due to the resource-rich territory they cultivate on, continue to be caught in a deadly cross fire between armed insurgents—killed by guerrilla if not cooperative, and by paramilitary if perceived to be cooperating with guerrilla forces.

This level of violence has devastating consequences for Colombian society and its social fabric. It has eroded social networks, institutions, and bonds of trust among communities, household, and individuals. Indigenous populations have both suffered from the conflict more than any other community in Colombia, but they have also contested it. Chapter 8 by Jean E. Jackson looks at the emergence of indigenous actors in the national political arena in recent years, and their surprising success in gaining recognition despite relatively small numbers and the disproportionate impact of the conflict on indigenous communities. She looks specifically at political participation in the Constituent Assembly and the 1991 Constitution, and the impact that the inclusion of notions of plurality in the new Constitution had on increasing respect for indigenous autonomy, territoriality, and self-determination. However, the inadequate implementation of constitutional reforms, combined with the escalation of violence, particularly in the vast sections of the country with little state presence, and the failure of the neoliberal economic model to equalize the distribution of wealth, have served to undermine political gains achieved. Her chapter ends with a warning—that the escalation of the conflict based on notions of "counterterrorism" will have escalating costs for indigenous populations, rendering them even more vulnerable to violence, poverty, displacement—and a plea, to continue searching for a solution to the conflict that will not involve such high costs.

In the final chapter, Cristina Rojas relates conflict in Colombia to the process of identity construction, and dynamics of recognition. She links the disproportionate impacts of violence along lines of race, ethnicity, and gender to the historical construction of depreciatory images of particular identitites/communities, and argues that it is only upon the recognition and reconstruction of identities that peace can be based. Rojas underscores that a focus on identity does not mean that the political and material aspects of violence are ignored; rather, they are intertwined. Not only is violence more prevalent among indigenous and Afro-Colombian communities, for example, but their demands for social, civil, and economic rights, including justice, are not recognized as legitimate and are often criminalized and met with force, contributing to impunity and making cause or attribution of responsibility for violence, elusive.

In this chapter, Rojas also uses identity as a tool to understand the dynamics of the conflict and the domestic and regional consequences of its monological construction as a "war on drugs." Ultimately, it has transformed a political problem into a criminal one, with the effect of silencing dissident voices and constraining alternate forms of political organization.

More than a source of violence, however, Rojas shows that the processes of identity formation and recognition are fundamental to a solution. The creation of public spaces, where marginalized groups are recognized as legitimate political actors, generates potential opportunities to resolve disagreement.

This volume explores the contemporary evolution of the conflict in Colombia, and the shifts at local, national, and international levels over the past decade that contributed to the transition to a new politics of conflict and the primacy of military and state strength over negotiations. The chapters in this book are part of an ongoing dialogue between scholars in Latin America and North America. The editors are indebted to the authors for their contributions, and to Adam Isacson of the CIP and Colleen Duggan of the International Development Research Centre's Peace Building Program for their support. Much credit must be given to others who worked behind the scenes whose insight, support, and dedication were invaluable including Olga Abizaid, Eleanor Douglas, Anthony Tillett and Catherine LeGrand. We are grateful for the financial support for this project from the Centre for Security and Defence Studies, at Carleton University, the Canadian International Development Agency, the Canadian Foundation for the Americas, the International Development Research Centre, and the Social Science and Humanities Research Council of Canada.

Notes

* Senior Analyst, Canadian Foundation for the Americas (FOCAL).

** Associate Professor, School of International Affairs, Carleton University.

1. The Report states that "from July 2001 to March 2003, the Prosecutor General's Office opened 33 files against members of the army, policy and Department of Administrative Security to investigate their links with the paramilitaries" (International Crisis Group 2003, 15).

References

Amnesty International. 2003. *Report: Colombia*. London: Amnesty International.

Bejarano, Ana María 2003. Protracted Conflict, Multiple Protagonists, and Staggered Negotiations: Colombia 1982–2002. *Canadian Journal of Latin American and Caribbean Studies* 28: 223–47.

Benetti, Cathy. 2003. Colombia IDP crisis worsens (May 15). Norwegian Refugee Council. http://www.reliefweb.int/w/rwbnsf/0/fb6a21e49279092cc1256d27 00309a31?OpenDocument (consulted on November 4, 2003).

Center for International Policy (CIP). 2001. Colombia Project: "Why we oppose the Andean Regional Initiative." http://www.ciponline.org/colombia/092401.htm (consulted on November 4, 2003).

Consejería para los Derechos Humanos y el Desplazamiento (CODHES) April 28, 2003. In *Colombia IDP Crisis Worsens*, edited by *Cathy Benetti* (May 15, 2003), Norwegian Refugee Council. http://www.idpproject.org/publications/reports/ colombia.pdf (consulted on November 4, 2003).

El Tiempo (Colombia). May 29, 2003. Colombia es el segundo país del mundo con más desplazados, dice Comité en EU para refugiados. http://www.eltiempo.com (consulted on July 15, 2003).

Forero, J. February 21, 2003. Rebels Keeping Colombia on Edge. *The New York Times*.

Giugale, Marcelo, O. Lafourcade, and Connie Luff, eds. (2003). *Colombia: The Economic Foundation of Peace*. Washington: The World Bank.

Godoy, H. 2003. *Plan Colombia's Strategic Weakness*. Mar. Dallas: Latin American Studies Association.

Hagen, Jason. 2003. Uribe's People: Civilians and the Colombian Conflict. *Georgetown Journal of International Affairs* (Winter/Spring): 65–71.

Human Rights Watch 2002. *A Wrong Turn: The Record of the Colombian Attorney General's Office* (November). Washington: Human Rights Watch.

———. 2003a. Colombia: Human Rights Certification Under Public Law 108–7. In *Background Briefing* (July). Washington: Human Rights Watch.

———. 2003b. Colombia: Human Rights Developments. In *World Report 2003* (January 14). Washington: Human Rights Watch.

Infobrief. July 28, 2003. Washington: U.S. Office on Colombia.

International Crisis Group (2003). *Colombia: Negotiating with Paramilitaries. Latin America Report* N.5. September 16. Bogota/Brussels: ICG.

Miller, Scott. 2003. U.S. is Committed to Helping Colombia Defeat Narcoterrorism, Says Diplomat. *The Washington File.* Office of International Information Programs. March 5. Washington: U.S. Department of State. http://usinfo/state.gov (consulted on November 4, 2003).

Revista Cambio. March 30, 2003. La cuenta de cobro. http://www.revistacambio. com/ html/pais/articulos/829 (consulted in November 4, 2003).

Sánchez, G. 2001. Prospects for Peace. In *Violence in Colombia 1990–2000 Waging War and Negotiating Peace*, edited by Charles Berquist, Ricardo Peñaranda, and Gonzalo Sánchez. Delaware: SR Books.

UN High Commission on Human Rights (UNHCHR). February 24, 2003. *Chairperson's Statement.*

United States Institute for Peace. 2003. US Involvement Deepens as Armed Conflict Escalates in Colombia. *Newsbte*, May 12. http://www.usip.org/newsmedia/ releases/2003/0512_bcolombia.html (consulted on November 4, 2003).

Vaicius, Ingrid and Adam Isacson. 2003. The War on Drugs Meets the War on Terror. *International Policy Report* (February). Washington, D.C.: Center for International Policy.

Washington Office on Latin America. 2003. Protecting the Pipeline: the US Military Mission Expands. *Colombia Monitor. WOLA Briefing Series* (May).

PART 1

U.S. Intervention: From the "War on Drugs" to the "War on Terror"

CHAPTER 2

Drug Trafficking, Political Violence, and U.S. Policy in Colombia under the Clinton Administration

*Bruce Michael Bagley**

Introduction

This chapter examines the impact of U.S. and Colombian government drug control policies on the evolution of drug cultivation, drug trafficking, and political violence in Colombia during the 1990s. Its central thesis is that the Washington/Bogota-backed war on drugs in Colombia over the decade did not merely fail to curb the growth of the Colombian drug trade and attendant corruption, but actually proved counterproductive. Among the most important unintended consequences were the explosion of drug cultivation and production activities; the dispersion and proliferation of organized crime; and the expansion and intensification of political violence and guerrilla warfare in the country. As a result, Colombia at the outset of 2000 faced more serious threats to its national security and political stability than it had in 1990. It concludes that the massive escalation of the flawed anti-drug strategies of the past decade proposed by the Clinton administration in January 2000 is more likely to worsen Colombia's ongoing problems of spiraling violence and insecurity than to resolve them.

Drug Cultivation and Production in Colombia[1]

Despite the U.S. Government's provision of almost 1 billion dollars in counternarcotics aid to Colombia over the decade of the 1990s, by 1999 Colombia had become the premier coca-cultivating country in the world, producing more coca leaf than both Peru and Bolivia combined (GAO 1999a, 4–5). Between 1989 and 1998, Colombian coca leaf production increased by 140 percent, from 33,900 to 81,400 metric tons. Even more remarkable, 1999 coca leaf production levels more than doubled the 1998 totals, reaching an estimated 220 tons. These dramatic increases in overall production reflected the fact that between 1996 and 1999, the total number of hectares of coca leaf under cultivation in Colombia rose by almost 100 percent, from 68,280 to 120,000 hectares. This explosive expansion occurred in spite of a permanent Colombian National Policy Eradication Program that sprayed a record 65,000 hectares of coca in 1998 alone (approximately 50 percent more than the total for 1997). The increase in coca-growing lands in Colombia between 2000 and 2002 was 8,200 hectares (+6.0 percent) (see the appendix). Concomitantly, Colombia also maintained its status as the world's principal cocaine-refining nation, supplying some 80 percent (220 metric tons) of the total cocaine imports (approximately 300 metric tons) smuggled into the United States in 1999.

During the 1990s Colombian production of opium poppy (the raw material for heroin) also skyrocketed from zero in 1989 to 61 metric tons in 1998. While these production totals meant that Colombia still ranked only as a relatively minor player in the world heroin market (less than 2 percent of total global supply), they did enable it to become the major heroin supplier to the eastern part of the United States by the end of the decade, exporting an estimated 6 metric tons of pure heroin yearly.

With approximately 5,000 hectares under cultivation, Colombia also continued to be an important producer of marijuana over the decade. In both 1998 and 1999 Colombia supplied about 40 percent (4,000 metric tons) of total annual cannabis imports into the U.S. market.

A study by Colombia's National Association of Financial Institutions (Asociación Nacional de Instituciones Financieras, ANIF) reported that worldwide street sales of Colombian cocaine, heroin, and marijuana totaled US$46 billion in 1999. Based on the assumption that less than 10 percent of total sales are repatriated to Colombia each year, ANIF estimated that the country's total earnings from the illicit drug trade amounted to approximately US$3.5 billion in 1999. This figure placed drug earnings close to the US$3.75 billion made from oil—the country's top export—and more than two and one half times earnings from coffee exports in 1999 (ANIF 2000).

Drug Cultivation and Production in the Andes

These dismaying statistics notwithstanding, it would be inaccurate to conclude that the U.S.-sponsored "war on drugs" in the Andean region as a whole was a total failure during the 1990s. In contrast to the Colombian situation, in Peru coca cultivation decreased by 27 percent between 1996 and 1997 alone, dropping from 96,000 hectares to 70,000 hectares. In 1999, fewer than 50,000 hectares of coca were cultivated in Peru. As a direct result, total Peruvian cocaine production also declined precipitously over the 1990s, from a high point of 606 metric tons in 1992 to 264 tons in 1998. Since March 1998, however, resurgence in the price of Peruvian coca leaf threatened to rekindle the growth of cultivation in that country (Krauss August 19, 1999; U.S. Department of State 1999).

Bolivia also registered substantial declines in coca cultivation during the decade, dropping from 48,800 hectares in 1996 to 46,000 in 1997, and down to 38,000 hectares in 1998, while total cocaine production declined from 248 metric tons in 1992 to 77 tons in 1999 (Cabrera Lémuz December 19, 1999; U.S. Department of State 1999).

Much of the success of the U.S.-backed coca eradication and alternative development programs in Peru and Bolivia in the late 1990s is attributable to the disruption of the "air bridge" that had permitted Colombian trafficking organizations earlier in the decade to transport coca paste or "base" from these two central Andean countries into Colombia, where it was subsequently refined into cocaine and then smuggled into the United States. The air bridge effectively collapsed in late 1995 after the Peruvian air force, under orders from President Alberto Fujimori, began to shoot down suspected trafficker airplanes flying between Peru and Colombia. Indeed, during 1995, the Peruvians shot down 25 planes and forced many other suspect aircraft to land for inspection. As a result, between April and August 1995 demand for coca leaf in Peru plummeted and leaf prices dropped by more than 60 percent. Combined with the more aggressive eradication efforts undertaken by both the Peruvian and Bolivian governments (with U.S. financial backing) in 1996 and subsequent years, alternative development programs began to enjoy considerable success among the coca-cultivating peasants in both countries. With the air bridge down, however, the Colombian traffickers rapidly expanded coca cultivation in Colombia, thus leading to Colombia's progressive displacement of Peru and Bolivia as the major coca-cultivating country in the world during the late 1990s (Krauss August 19, 1999; *The Economist* March 4, 2000).

In 1999, the continued success of Peru's highly lauded coca eradication program was in serious jeopardy as the price of coca leaf in the country shot back up over the year to two-thirds of its previous 1995 high, thereby stimulating renewed peasant cultivation. Several factors appear to account for this reactivation of coca growing in Peru. First, Peruvian traffickers gradually found ways to reopen some air routes to Colombia and to replace others with road, river, and sea routes, thus raising international demand for Peru's coca crop and making coca cultivation in the country more profitable. The decision by the U.S. government in May 1998 to suspend Awac and P-3 Orion surveillance flights over Peru in order to increase aerial spying over Colombia as trafficking activities increased there clearly reduced the Peruvians capacity to intercept drug flights over their national territory. The ability of the Peruvian police to carry out interdiction operations was further diminished when *El Niño* hit Peru in early 1998 and obliged the country's security forces to transfer helicopters and planes normally used in anti-drug operations to the flooded Pacific coast for emergency aid duty. Similarly, a renewed outbreak of tensions between Peru and Ecuador in 1998 led the Peruvian military to send some planes to the border area temporarily, thereby reducing the availability of aircraft for interdiction activities. In late August 1999 the Clinton administration once again agreed to resume surveillance flights over Peru to help the Peruvian air force intercept smuggling planes (Krauss August 19, 1999; *The Economist* March 4, 2000).

Second, more Peruvian traffickers began processing coca paste into refined cocaine within their own country, thereby increasing domestic demand for coca leaf in Peru. Third, cocaine consumption in Peru's major urban centers rose substantially in the late 1990s (as it did in major urban centers throughout the region over the decade), thereby increasing the profitability of the local market. Finally, the continued decline of coca leaf availability in Bolivia placed an additional premium on coca cultivation in Peru (and Colombia), especially in light of rising demand for cocaine in Europe, where street prices often ran twice as high as those current in the United States (Krauss August 19, 1999; *The Economist* March 4, 2000).

Interdiction of Drug Trafficking Routes

Some 13 million U.S. drug users spent approximately US$67 billion on illicit drugs in 1999, making the U.S. market the most lucrative one in the world for Colombian traffickers. Washington spent roughly two-thirds of its US$17.8 billion 1999 anti-drug budget on interdiction and related activities to curb the flow of illicit drugs from Colombia and elsewhere in the hemisphere into the United States. Indeed, throughout the 1990s the U.S. government placed heavy emphasis on interdiction activities as a key tactic in its overall strategy in the war on drugs (Office of National Drug Control Policy 1998, 42–52; GAO 1999b).

During most of the 1980s, the Medellin cartel dominated the Colombian drug trade and its principal trafficking routes passed through (or over) the

Caribbean into the United States via South Florida and elsewhere along the U.S. Atlantic seaboard. As these "traditional" smuggling routes came under increasing pressure from U.S. drug enforcement over the second half of the decade, a gradual shift away from the Caribbean routes to new ones passing through Central America and Mexico and across the U.S. southwest border took place. By the early 1990s, 70–80 percent of the cocaine smuggled out of Colombia entered the United States from Mexico while only 20–30 percent continued to come in via the Caribbean (GAO 1996; Office of National Drug Control Policy 1997, 49–62).

This dramatic shift in contraband routes was undoubtedly bought about by the heightened interdiction efforts of U.S. law enforcement agencies, reinforced by the growing involvement of the U.S. military (especially the Navy and Air Force). U.S. "success" on this front in the war on drugs did not, however, result in a reduction in the availability of cocaine (or heroin) in the U.S. market, much less a rise in street prices, over the 1990s. In practice, the Medellin and Cali traffickers proved highly adaptable, quickly establishing new contraband routes to replace the older and riskier ones. Rather than curtailing drug trafficking from Colombia into the United States, increased interdiction in the Caribbean merely "ballooned" Colombian smuggling activities into Central America and Mexico, along with the attendant corruption and violence that typically accompanies large-scale drug trafficking activities (Lupsha 1995; Golden July 11, 1997).

Initially, the Colombian drug cartels arranged for existing Mexican drug organizations to smuggle their "product" across the U.S.–Mexican border on a simple fee-for-service basis. By the mid-1990s, however, as first the Medellin and then the Cali trafficking rings were partially dismantled by U.S. and Colombian law enforcement authorities, the Mexican drug *mafiosi* began to demand drugs rather than cash in return for their services. Commonly, they received as much as 40–50 percent of any shipments they handled. The Mexicans' expanded role in the Colombian cocaine trade over the 1990s increased their illicit profits exponentially and led to the consolidation of several Mexican cartels (e.g. the Juarez cartel, the Tijuana cartel, and the Gulf cartel) that soon rivaled the Colombian organizations in size, profitability, and violence. Indeed, during the second half of the decade the emergence of these powerful new Mexican criminal organizations unleashed an unprecedented wave of drug-related violence and corruption in Mexico that seriously threatened the country's fledgling process of democratization (Dillon August 22, 1997; Golden January 9, 2000; Waller n.d.).

Over the decade, Washington responded to the increase in drug trafficking activity along the U.S.–Mexican border by bolstering U.S. drug enforcement throughout the southwest and by pressuring Mexico City to cooperate more fully with U.S. authorities in joint drug control operations on the border and in Mexico. Although only partially successful in enlisting Mexican collaboration because of the extensive drug-related corruption in that country, by the end of the 1990s enhanced U.S.–Mexican border interdiction had begun to make significant progress in reducing the flow of Colombian cocaine and heroin across the border. U.S. and Mexican drug control efforts were given a real boost by the rift that opened up in the late 1990s between Colombian and Mexican trafficking organizations over the exorbitant size of the Mexican share of the cocaine trade. The outbreak of internecine violence among rival Mexican mafia families, especially after the death of Juarez drug lord Amado Carrillo Fuentes (a.k.a. *El Señor de los Cielos*) in 1997, also contributed to declining Colombian use of Mexican routes and, thus, to greater U.S. drug enforcement success along the border (Riley January 26, 2000; Sandoval January 17, 2000).

Once again, however, this U.S. interdiction "success" was more apparent than real. At the end of the decade there was clear evidence that the Colombian traffickers had begun to shift back to smuggling routes in the Caribbean. Increasingly, reports surfaced indicating that Colombian cocaine and heroin were transiting through the Dominican Republic, Haiti, Cuba, and Puerto Rico into the United States. There was also mounting evidence of increased use of shipboard containers for cocaine smuggling into U.S. east coast ports and of a reversion to "swallowers" or "mules" traveling on commercial air transportation and cruise ships for the transport of heroin. As of late 1999 perhaps as much as 50 percent of the Colombian cocaine trade and 80–90 percent of the heroin traffic was routed across the Caribbean rather than through Mexico. This return to the more traditional routes was made possible, in part, by Washington's decision earlier in the decade to transfer some U.S. Custom's personnel from South Florida to the southwestern border, leaving the Caribbean/South Florida routes exposed once again. The severe recessions suffered by many Caribbean island economies over the latter half of the decade unquestionably made them more vulnerable to drug smuggling and related corruption as well (Rohter October 27, 1998; Associated Press February 11, 2000; Kidwell February 13, 2000; Reuters February 10, 2000).

The May 1999 closure of Howard Air Base in Panama in fulfillment of Washington's 1977 treaty obligations to return control of the Panama Canal Zone to Panama by the end of the century further reduced U.S. air surveillance capabilities over Colombian drug smuggling activity. Throughout the 1990s, the U.S. Air Force had used Howard as a base of AWAC operations to monitor the gaps not covered by the three U.S.-run ground radar stations located in southern Colombia. With the loss of Howard, drug contraband flights, especially along Colombia's pacific coast, began to surge in late 1999. Requests from the Miami-based U.S. Southern Command to the Pentagon for surveillance flights over Central and South America and the Caribbean were satisfied only 43 percent of the time during 1999. The U.S. government negotiated rights to upgrade an air base in Manta, Ecuador to replace Howard (Johnson February 5, 2000).

Starting in 1998, the Colombian Air Force, like its Peruvian counterpart, began to force or shoot down suspected drug smuggling aircraft. In 1998 and 1999, 36 planes were intercepted; 6 were shot down and another 30 were destroyed after landing. In early February 2000, Colombian Defense Minister Luis Fernando Ramírez announced that the Pastrana government intended to step up its air interdiction activities over 2000 with the help of the new equipment to be provided by the Clinton administration (Johnson February 11, 2000).

The Decline of the Colombian Cartels

In Colombia, although cultivation and smuggling expanded exponentially over the decade, the combined efforts of the U.S. and Colombian governments did succeed in partially disrupting the drug trafficking activities of the country's two most notorious drug trafficking rings—the Medellin and Cali cartels—during the 1990s. In the early 1990s, following the August 1989 assassination of the leading Liberal Party presidential candidate Luis Carlos Galán by hitmen (*sicarios*) on the payroll of the Medellin drug lord Pablo Escobar, first the government of President Virgilio Barco (1986–1990) and then of César Gaviria (1990–1994) mounted concerted attacks against this cartel. By 1994, after the 1993 death of Pablo Escobar in a rooftop gun battle in Medellin, the Medellin cartel had been largely dismantled. Similarly, in 1995–1996 the government of Ernesto Samper (1994–1998) went after and effectively dismantled most of the Cali cartel (Bagley 1989–1990; Clawson and Lee III 1998).

The dismemberment of these two powerful and violent transnational drug trafficking organizations over the early and mid-1990s constituted important achievements for the U.S. and Colombian drug enforcement authorities.

The undeniable significance of the Colombian government's successful assaults on the Medellin and Cali cartels over the decade should not, however, obscure the underlying reality of the ongoing explosion of drug cultivation and drug trafficking in Colombia over the second half of the 1990s. Nor should it distract attention from the accelerating political corrosion that flowed from the country's still-flourishing illicit drug trade. In practice, rather than curbing the nation's booming drug traffic, the deaths, extradition, or incarcerations of the two principal cartels' "bosses" created only temporary and relatively minor disruptions in the contraband flow of drugs from Colombia to the U.S. and European markets. Indeed, the vacuum left by partial demise of the Medellin and Cali cartels was quickly filled by the rise and proliferation of scores of smaller, less notorious (but equally violent) trafficking organizations or *cartelitos* throughout Colombia that engaged in both cocaine trafficking and the even more lucrative and rapidly expanding heroin trade. Unlike the Medellin and Cali cartels, however, these new, smaller trafficking groups have maintained relatively lower profiles, often operating from bases located in Colombia's many "intermediate" or secondary cities and small towns where they could bribe and intimidate local officials to gain "protection" for their activities in relative anonymity (Colombia. Presidencia de la República 1997, 24–25; *Revista Semana* November 1, 1999a; Thompson November 29, 1999).

While unlikely to pose direct challenges to Colombian national security similar to those mounted by the Medellin and Cali cartels in the late 1980s and early 1990s, the advent of these new "boutique" cartels presented both Colombian and U.S. drug enforcement officials with major new challenges that they have not been able to overcome effectively. Despite some, highly publicized "coups" against the traffickers, such as the capture of drug lord Alejandro Bernal (a.k.a. *Juvenal*)—the successor of Pablo Escobar and his Medellin organization—during "Operation Milenio" in October 1999, the drug trade in Colombia continued to flourish. Its violent and corrosive effects continue to permeate Colombia's political and judicial institutions virtually unabated, severely undermining possibilities for effective democratic reform in the country (*Revista Semana* October 25, 1999; Semple October 14, 1999).

Political corruption in Colombia certainly pre-dated the advent of large-scale drug trafficking in the country. Drug trafficking and the attendant phenomena of criminal violence and political corruption that it spawns first emerged in Colombia in the late 1960s and 1970s in a context of a weakly institutionalized state already rife with political corruption and patronage politics. The rise and expansion of powerful transnational criminal organizations involved in the international drug trade during the 1970s and 1980s were a result of, and subsequently greatly exacerbated, the underlying institutional weaknesses of the Colombian political system. In the 1980s and early 1990s the huge profits earned by Colombia's cartels from the illicit drug trade enabled them to organize and equip their own private armies (paramilitary groups) and to bribe and intimidate Colombian politicians and government officials at all levels. As a result, Colombia's system of justice virtually collapsed in the late 1980s and early 1990s, key elements of the police and the military were routinely bought off, and an estimated 60 percent of the Colombian Congress received illicit campaign contributions to guarantee their cooperation on critical issues like extradition.[2]

The country's business elite or private sector also proved vulnerable and complicitous, often accepting payments in cash, facilitating money laundering operations through legitimate businesses, selling properties at exorbitant prices and so forth. Indeed, during the 1990s clear distinctions between legitimate and illegitimate private sector activities were often virtually impossible to make. Illustrating the depths of the problem, a February 2000 report of the so-called "Truth Commission" (composed of investigators from various state agencies) on corruption in the state banking sector revealed that over the 1990s $7.2 billion pesos had been systematically siphoned off from six different state-owned banks. Over the 1990s, under considerable pressure from the United States, Bogota did manage to rein in, at least partially, the rampant corruption and escalating criminal violence emanating from the Medellin and Cali cartels. Nonetheless, Colombia's relatively successful campaigns against these two major criminal organizations did not by any means extirpate drug-related corruption in the country.

The FARC and the Colombian Drug Trade

The problems faced by drug enforcement agents working in Colombia were compounded over the decade by the growing involvement of Colombia's principal guerrilla organization—the Fuerzas Armadas Revolucionarias de Colombia (FARC)—in drug cultivation and drug trafficking activities. The eclipse of the major cartels opened up greater opportunities for FARC's 20,000 man-strong guerrilla army to profit from the country's booming drug industry. They did so mainly by taxing peasant growers in their zones of influence and by contracting out their services to the trafficker organizations to protect crops, processing laboratories, and landing strips (*Revista Semana* March 8, 1999a). In the late 1990s, admittedly spotty evidence hinted that some FARC "fronts" may even have begun to operate their own processing facilities in remote areas of the country. There was, however, no indication that FARC personnel engaged in international drug smuggling activities outside of Colombia (*Newsweek* June, 1999; Reuters July 29, 1999).

By the end of the decade, Colombian government estimates placed the FARC's total earnings from the drug trade as high as US$400 million per year. Added to the estimated US$500 million per year that the FARC were believed to earn from their more "traditional" guerrilla activities (e.g. collection of revolutionary "taxes" on landowners, kidnapping, extortion, robbery, "commissions" collected from local governments and businesses, and their own business investments), FARC's total annual income in 1999 may have amounted to as much as US$900 million.[3]

While income from the drug trade has certainly bolstered the FARC financially, it would be a mistake to conclude that drug money was in the past, or is now, essential to the continuation of the FARC's war against the Colombian government. In the first place, there are a number of FARC "fronts" that have never depended on either coca or opium poppy "rents" to sustain their activities. Second, declines in income from drug sources could, and in all likelihood would, be made up by increasing earnings from kidnappings, extortion, and revolutionary "taxes" on peasants, landowners, businessmen, and foreign multinationals. Hence, elimination of the underground drug economy in Colombia, if it were ever to occur, would not automatically nor inevitably end the country's 40-year old guerrilla war (Reyes October 17, 1999).

Nonetheless, fueled in no small part by drug-related earnings, the FARC grew steadily in numbers and firepower over the 1990s. By the second half of the decade, they frequently proved able to defeat or severely punish the Colombia armed forces in combat. The Clinton administration's 1996 and 1997 decisions to "decertify" Colombia (mainly because of President Samper's alleged acceptance of US$6.1 million in campaign contributions from the Cali cartel during his 1994 presidential race) led to a substantial reduction in U.S. aid to Colombia. Predictably, these reductions contributed to the Colombian military's deteriorating capacity to fight the FARC effectively. The growing size and strength of the FARC was, in turn, a key factor behind President Andrés Pastrana's decision to sponsor an ambitious new peace initiative.

Pastrana's Peace Process and the Zona de Despeje

While progress in these peace negotiations proved excruciatingly slow during the first 18 months of his administration, President Pastrana and FARC guerrilla chieftain Manuel Marulanda Vélez (a.k.a. *Tirofijo*) did agree in November 1998 to establish a 42,000 square kilometer demilitarized zone (*zona de despeje*) in the southeastern Department of Caquetá. In effect, the accord obliged the government's security forces to withdraw completely from this Switzerland-sized territory in the country's eastern plains (*llanos orientales*) region and banned them from conducting military operations or even gathering intelligence in the area. The rationale behind the Pastrana government's creation of the *zona de despeje* was to demonstrate Bogotá's peaceful intentions and to facilitate peace talks with the FARC by creating a neutral area in which the negotiations could physically take place.[4]

In practice, the *zona de despeje* quickly became a kind of sanctuary for the FARC. Some 5,000 FARC troops were permanently stationed there and became the *de facto* government in the area. Pastrana's growing legion of critics both inside and outside Colombia (including many in the U.S. Congress) repeatedly denounced the creation of the *zona de despeje* as a sign that Pastrana was "surrendering" the country to the FARC while permitting the consolidation of a "narcoguerrilla" state within Colombian national territory. Since 1999, FARC forces that were operating in the zone were frequently accused of violating both the letter and spirit of the accord by carrying out selective assassinations, harboring kidnap victims, threatening local mayors and judges, conducting illegal searches and seizures, detaining innocent civilians, improperly rerouting public moneys, forcibly recruiting children into their ranks, training new troops and terrorist commandos, and constructing anti-aircraft batteries and other military fortifications to strengthen their defenses. They were also accused of exploiting some 35,000 hectares of coca within the zone, of buying up coca leaf from peasant farmers in surrounding departments (e.g. Meta, Guaviare, Caquetá, Putumayo) and selling it directly to the drug cartels, and of utilizing the 37 landing strips at their disposal inside the demilitarized zone to fly processed cocaine to virtually any part of the country (Ambrus and Contreras November 29, 1999).

Colombian and U.S. intelligence sources also believed that the FARC utilized the *zona de despeje* and their coca and other illicit earnings to undertake a major rearmament program since 1999. In mid-January 2000, General Tapias estimated that since 1999 the FARC had acquired more than 20,000 East-German assault rifles along with grenade launchers, mortars, SAM-12 surface-to-air missiles, sophisticated electronic communications equipment, and their own small but growing air force.

The Paramilitaries, Human Rights, and the Drug Trade

Like their leftist FARC rivals, Colombia's approximately 7,000 rightist paramilitary forces (Autodefensas Unidas de Colombia, AUC) also finance themselves at least in part by taxing the drug trade in the areas they control.

In a televised interview conducted with national paramilitary chief Carlos Castaño Gil in early January 2000, Castaño openly admitted for the first time that his "self-defense" forces based in northwest Colombia routinely charged a 40 percent tax on peasants who produced coca. Indeed, the bloodiest conflicts between Colombia's guerrillas and paramilitaries since the 1990s have taken place in regions rich in natural resources (e.g. oil, gold, or emeralds) or drug crops (*Revista Semana* April 26, 1999; Associated Press January 10, 2000).

Supported by many large landowners, drug traffickers, and segments of the army, the virulently anti-Communist paramilitaries have been primarily responsible for the waves of civilian massacres that have swept Colombia since the 1990s. Despite the "paras" brutality, fear of the leftist rebels has become so widespread that 60 percent of Colombians surveyed in a 1999 poll declared that they did not favor disbanding the self-defense groups. Moreover, a majority interviewed in the same poll stated that they wanted U.S. troops to intervene because their own government was incapable of protecting them (Robinson 1999–2000, 64).

The FARC, along with most human rights groups in and outside of Colombia, have repeatedly denounced instances of collusion between the self-defense groups and government security forces. According to FARC's leader Marulanda: "The paramilitary groups are an official expression of state policy." When the paramilitaries enter a zone, army units in the area routinely overlook their activities. On multiple occasions, the army has reportedly provided communications and logistical support for paramilitary operations. To refute the high command's contention that there are no close ties between the "paras" and the army, in 1999 the FARC distributed lists of paramilitary base locations, radio frequencies used to communicate with army units and the names of army officers who act as go-betweens (Human Rights Watch 1996; *Revista Cambio* November 29–December 6, 1999; Robinson 1999–2000).

Such military–paramilitary linkages unquestionably constitute major impediments to any future progress in Bogotá's current peace negotiations with the FARC. Cognizant of this, in 1999 President Pastrana removed four generals from active military service for their links to the paramilitaries and put one of them on trial. He also completed the disbanding of the infamous *Brigada XX* (Intelligence Brigade) that had been closely connected to rightist paramilitary bands for years and began the process of reorganizing and modernizing military intelligence units with U.S. assistance. Nonetheless, the linkages persist and army–paramilitary confrontations remained extremely rare (Martínez December 20, 1999; Reuters April 9, 1999).

In recognition of the paramilitaries growing involvement in the drug trade and their record as the worst human rights abusers in Colombia, in mid-January 2000 U.S. government officials called upon the Pastrana administration to move more forcefully to suppress paramilitary activities throughout the country. According to Washington's public statements, the elimination of these self-defense groups remains an essential step along the path toward peace and the reestablishment of law and order in the country (Agence France Presse January 15, 2000).[5]

The ELN, the EPL, the ERP, and the Quest for Peace

The Pastrana administration's quest for a negotiated peace settlement was further complicated by the presence of three additional, leftist armed insurgent movements in Colombia. These include the National Liberation Army (ELN), the Popular Liberation Army (EPL), and the People's Revolutionary Army (ERP). With some 5,000 combatants, the Castroite ELN is the second largest leftist rebel group in the country. Like the FARC, it operates throughout the national territory. Unlike the FARC, however, the ELN does not appear to have engaged systematically in drug trafficking activities during the 1990s.[6] Instead, it has financed its operations mainly by extorting money from multinational companies operating Colombia's oil fields and by blowing up (50–100 times a year) the 900-kilometer pipeline that transports crude from fields along the Venezuelan border to port facilities on the north coast and relied heavily on ransoms from kidnappings (*Revista Semana* June 14, 1999; June 21, 1999; and December 20, 1999).

From the outset of Pastrana's negotiations with the FARC, the ELN sought to participate in the peace process on an equal footing. Rather than including the ELN in the government's dialogue with the FARC, however, President Pastrana—at the FARC's request—opted to deal with the ELN separately in a parallel set of peace talks. While these negotiations proceeded fitfully over the first 18 months of the Pastrana government, no substantive progress was achieved. Moreover, Pastrana consistently refused to concede to the ELN's demand for the creation of a *zona de despeje* in northern Colombia (in the Department of Bolívar) similar to, albeit smaller than, that he had granted to the FARC in southern Colombia (*El Espectador* February 8, 2000; *El Tiempo* January 8, 2000).

In mid-January 2000, the ELN launched a week-long series of attacks that destroyed 28 electrical pylons in the northwestern Departments of Antioquia and Chocó and left the country's power grid on the verge of collapse. Colombian military spokesmen frankly admitted that it would be virtually impossible for the armed forces to protect the 15,000 electrical transmission towers spread throughout the nation. In the wake of these damaging bombing attacks, the Pastrana government reopened negotiations with the ELN and accepted, in principle, the ELN's demand for the creation of a demilitarized zone in southern Bolívar where the ELN could hold its national convention and begin peace talks with the government. Adamantly opposed to this concession to the ELN and determined to control the profitable coca and gold mining activities in the area, in mid-February 2000 the AUC paramilitaries carried out a series of brutal massacres in ELN-linked peasant communities designed to prevent the consolidation of an ELN *zona de despeje* in the region. The intensity and extreme cruelty of the AUC military campaign in southern Bolívar reflected both the depths and bitterness of their rivalry with the ELN and the high economic stakes that underlie the guerrilla–paramilitary struggle in the region.

The EPL, with fewer than 500 combatants, was far smaller than either the FARC or the ELN at the end of the 1990s. Its principal bases of operation are located in the northeastern departments of César, Santander, and Norte de Santander near the Venezuelan border. Like the ELN, the EPL appears to have stayed out of the drug trade, concentrating instead on extortion, kidnapping, and assassination activities to finance itself. In the 1980s, the EPL gradually abandoned its radical Maoist ideology and, in the early 1990s, negotiated a peace settlement with Bogota that led the bulk of its members (almost 3,000) to lay down their arms and reenter civil society. The remaining splinter elements of the EPL, led by Hugo Carvajal (a.k.a. *El Nene*), steadfastly refused to enter into peace negotiations with the Pastrana government. With the death of Carvajal on January 12, 2000 their capacity to insert themselves in the peace process became unclear (Agence France Presse January 2, 2000; Reuters January 29, 2000).[7]

With only 150 combatants, the ERP was the smallest and least well known of the four guerrilla groups still active in Colombia at the outset of 2000. Its origin lies in a split within the ELN that occurred in August 1996 during the ELN's Third Ideological Congress. Its principal base of operations was located in northern Colombia in the border areas of the Departments of Antioquia, Sucre, and Bolívar. Under constant siege from AUC paramilitary forces, especially in southern Bolívar, in 1998 the ERP guerrillas, with the backing of *Frente 37* of the FARC, sought refuge in the remote Montes de María region in central Bolívar Department along the Sucre border. Given its small size and inability to hold its territory against AUC pressure, the ERP has not been a significant factor in drug cultivation or trafficking (*Revista Semana* February 28, 2000b).

After a prolonged period of quiescence, the ERP resurfaced in late when it launched a highly publicized series of *pescas milagrosas* (random kidnappings) along the Sucre-Bolívar border. In mid-February 2000, the AUC renewed their attacks on the ERP with assaults on various small rural communities (*corregimientos*) near Ovejas, Sucre, in which some seventy people died. In late February 1999 reports of intense fighting between AUC and ERP forces in the Montes de María region indicated that the AUC offensive continued to escalate.

Kidnappings for ransom unquestionably became one of the main sources of financing for all four guerrilla groups over the 1990s. At the start of 2000, the FARC held 850 kidnapping victims hostage. The ELN had another 702, the EPL 200 and the ERP a few dozen. During 1999, the AUC paramilitary groups kidnapped 120 people, reflecting a sixfold increase in their kidnapping activity over the previous year. In 1999, the total number of abductions reported in Colombia rose to 2,945 cases, compared to 2,216 the year before (a 33 percent increase over 1998 levels), breaking Colombia's own kidnapping world record (Associated Press January 28, 2000; Reuters March 4, 2000).

This rising wave of kidnappings not only complicated Pastrana's peace efforts, but also contributed to a growing exodus of professional upper middle and upper class Colombians fleeing from their troubled country to the United States. According to Colombian government estimates, 800,000 people—2 percent of Colombia's total population of 40 million—left Colombia since 1996. In 1999 alone, 366,423 Colombians applied for nonimmigrant visas to the United States, up from 150,514 in 1997. About three-quarters of the nonimmigrant and just over half of the 11,345 immigrant applications were granted in 1999. In addition, while still small in absolute terms (only 334 over the 12 months stretching from the last quarter of 1998 through the first three-quarters of 1999), political asylum requests from Colombians also rose substantially (396 in the last quarter of 1999). The U.S. approval rate for asylum requests has also risen, from 19 percent in 1998 to 46 percent by the end of 1999 (Rohter March 5, 2000). Nevertheless, escalating violence and insecurity in both rural and urban areas have led growing numbers to opt for emigration.

Violence, Internal Migration, and Social Catastrophe

In the 15 years between 1985 and 2000 Colombia's internal wars displaced some 1.7 million Colombians from their places of origin. In 1999 alone at least 225,000 people were driven from their homes, communities, and livelihoods by political and drug-related violence. Of these, approximately 53 percent were women and children. In contrast to the privileged few from the wealthier strata of Colombian society that have managed to emigrate to the United States, the vast impoverished majority of displaced Colombians have found themselves condemned to roam the country as internal migrants in search of work, food, shelter, and safety. In mid-1999 the United Nations reported that current aid and other efforts by the Colombian government to help the displaced "have proven absolutely insufficient, causing a deplorable situation of human suffering" (Kovaleski August 11, 1999; Reuters November 25, 1999).

A 1999 study of Colombia's displaced population found that paramilitary groups were responsible for 47 percent of all forced displacements in recent years. The guerrillas—especially the FARC and the ELN—were held responsible for 35 percent; state security forces accounted for 8 percent, unknown criminal groups for 7 percent and drug traffickers for 1 percent (CODHES 1999).

Indeed, many observers contend that both the right-wing groups and the Marxist insurgents alike employ strategies of systematic regional "cleansing" to rid areas of people who do not support them and then turn over the abandoned lands to their followers or family members. Colombian air force anti-guerrilla bombings and army raids have, nonetheless, also been significant complicating factors in many rural areas as has the U.S.-backed anti-drug campaign—particularly aerial spraying of the coca and opium poppy crops—carried out by the Colombian government (Kovaleski August 11, 1999).

The few government-established refuge camps available are typically overcrowded and frequently vulnerable to violent reprisals from one side or the other in the ongoing conflicts convulsing the nation's rural areas. Tens of thousands have been left no alternative but to swell the ranks of rural migrant laborers working in the illicit coca or opium fields as *raspachines* or "scrapers" harvesting coca leaves or collecting opium gum from poppy flowers—the only gainful employment remaining in many violence-torn rural areas (Kovaleski August 11, 1999).

Hundreds of thousands of others migrated from the countryside to Colombia's urban areas where housing, schooling, health care, and jobs are scarce, especially given the country's deep economic recession in the late 1990s (*El Tiempo* March 8, 2000). Consequently, begging, prostitution, and violent crime in Colombia's urban centers skyrocketed over the 1990s. Medellin, for example, following the demise of the Medellin drug cartel in the early 1990s, witnessed the proliferation of criminal youth gangs often affiliated with major criminal organizations (Johnson January 23, 2000). Bogota, Cali, and other major cities have all suffered similar dramatic increases in migration, delinquency, and common criminality over the 1990s (Rohter October 21, 1999; *Revista Semana* March 27, 2000a,b).

The spiraling violence and massive population displacements in the countryside have also driven thousands of dispossessed peasants into the ranks of either the guerrillas or the paramilitaries. Although all sides deny that they pay their troops regular wages, they do admit to payments of irregular stipends to impoverished rural youths (or their families) as part of their efforts to recruit new combatants into their organizations. Children as young as eight to ten years of age are often used as spies or scouts and teenagers (both boys and girls) are routinely trained and deployed as fighters. Some are simply kidnapped and others are taken, often against their will, in lieu of payment of "taxes" or repayment of family debts. But many of Colombia's displaced youth find joining up with one side or the other to be their only viable life-option (Johnson January 23, 2000).

The Marxist guerrillas often stage "consciousness-raising" political sessions in the peasant communities where they hold sway to attract new adherents to their groups and they routinely furnish food, shelter, uniforms, weapons, and even basic education to the young people who enlist. Marxist ideological indoctrination is an integral part of the training for new arrivals. The paramilitaries espouse anti-Communist doctrines but are typically less concerned with ideology than the rebels. They rely primarily on material incentives and desires for revenge against the guerrillas to attract recruits. Interviews with former rebels who have been captured by the army or have deserted reveal that few teenagers express firm Marxist ideological convictions and that many speak of changing sides—either signing up with the paramilitaries or a criminal gang—once they are released from custody. In short, for many displaced youths the decision to join the guerrillas or the militias is a "rational economic choice" dictated by which group dominates in a particular area or region rather than an ideological commitment.

The lack of adequate governmental programs and resources to deal with the displaced masses literally leaves many with no realistic economic alternative. If and when Colombia's internal conflicts finally give way to formal peace, crime rates will almost certainly continue to soar among the uneducated, unemployed, and maladapted youths and young adults who have been forcibly uprooted from their homes and families and irreparably traumatized by the violence that have endured (Johnson January 23, 2000; Sanjuán 1998).

Colombia's Internal Conflicts and Regional Security

President Pastrana's peace initiative was also hindered by the growing spillover from the nation's internal conflicts into surrounding countries. Colombian guerrillas, paramilitaries, and drug traffickers routinely cross over into the neighboring territories of Panama, Venezuela, Brazil, Peru, and Ecuador for safe haven, supplies, arms trafficking, and drug smuggling. Incidents of cross-border kidnappings and assassinations have also risen dramatically in recent years, and thousands of Colombia's displaced peasants have sought refuge across the borders in Venezuela and Panama.[8]

During 1999, Brazil, Peru, and Ecuador sent substantial military reinforcements to their borders with Colombia to strengthen their defenses against cross-border incursions. As the primary route for gunrunning and drug smuggling in and out of Colombia and a key zone of conflict between the FARC and the AUC paramilitaries, however, the Panama–Colombian border was by far the most contentious of Colombia's bilateral relations in 1999. The departure of U.S. troops from the Canal Zone at the end of the year and the limited military capacity of Panama's National Police raised serious questions about the future security of the canal itself (Bagley 1999).

From the U.S. perspective, the Colombia's inability to secure its own borders or to curb cross-border drug trafficking and guerrilla incursions effectively converted the country into a serious threat to regional security in northern South America. Over 1999 the Clinton administration worked to "contain" the Colombian "threat" by pressing Colombia's neighbors to form a "Group of Friends" to intervene diplomatically (and perhaps even militarily) in the Colombian crisis. The reluctance of the neighboring country governments to commit to this U.S. initiative became apparent from the outset and Washington's diplomatic efforts produced no meaningful collective response vis-à-vis Colombia. This failure, along with growing U.S. concern over Colombia's internal stability, ultimately prompted Washington in late 1999 to propose major unilateral increases in U.S. assistance to Colombia designed to bolster the Pastrana administration's capacity to deal with the country's mounting problems.[9]

Drug Trafficking, Guerrilla Warfare, and U.S.–Colombian Relations

Already deeply troubled by skyrocketing drug production and trafficking; escalating guerrilla and paramilitary violence; and deteriorating political and economic conditions in Colombia, as early as March 1, 1998, Washington opted once again to "certify" Colombia as "fully cooperating" with the

U.S.-led war on drugs for the first time since 1994. In 1996 and 1997, the Samper government was decertified outright and the flow of U.S. aid was severely curtailed (except to the National Police). Although Clinton did not ultimately impose trade sanctions on Colombia as the U.S. legislation authorizes in cases of decertification, Washington's use of "coercive" diplomacy during this period did exert a profoundly chilling effect on overall business activity and foreign investment inflows from 1996 onward (Bagley 1998).

Combined with the global economic slowdown, and Samper's own populist and clientelistic economic mismanagement during his term, U.S. decertification helped to send the Colombian economy into a tailspin in 1997–1998. Indeed, in 1999 Colombia experienced its worst economic recession in 70 years as the economy contracted by almost 6 percent while unemployment levels topped 18 percent (Orrego August 7, 1999; *Revista Semana* March 8 and November 1, 1999b). The severity of Colombia's economic crisis and the widespread popular discontent caused by it greatly compounded the problems of common criminality and governability faced by President Pastrana during the first year and a half in office while simultaneously fueling and emboldening the country's guerrillas. The guerrillas' actions in turn exacerbated and prolonged the country's current economic downturn (*Revista Semana* January 17, 2000a and March 6, 2000).

By early 1998 the deteriorating situation in Colombia had become so worrisome to U.S. authorities that, despite the fact that President Samper's tarnished four-year term was not scheduled to end until August 1998, Washington proceeded to recertify Colombia on March 1 anyway. This decision cleared the way for the Clinton administration to provide US$289 million in counternarcotics aid to Colombia in the Fiscal Year (FY) 1999, a sum which immediately catapulted Colombia into the position of the third-ranking recipient of U.S. foreign aid worldwide, behind only Israel and Egypt. Because the U.S. fiscal year does not begin until October 1 of each calendar year, the new U.S. aid funds began to flow into Colombia only in late 1998 (well after President Pastrana took office on August 7). This timing assured that the tainted Samper government received no direct benefits from the FY 1999 increase in U.S. assistance.[10]

Once Pastrana took office, U.S.–Colombian bilateral relations warmed rapidly. In October 1998, President Clinton hosted President Pastrana in a state visit to Washington, clearly underscoring the contrast with former President Samper who had been officially denied a visa to travel to the United States in 1996. Although skeptical, the Clinton administration publicly endorsed President Pastrana's peace overtures toward the FARC guerrillas in late 1998. In fact, at the request of President Pastrana, the

Clinton administration even agreed to send emissaries to meet secretly with representatives of the FARC in Costa Rica in December 1998 to discuss the FARC's willingness to undertake drug eradication programs as part of the peace process. Once publicly revealed to the Republican majority in the U.S. Congress, however, these secret talks proved so controversial in Washington that the Clinton administration was forced to disavow them and pledge to refrain from any future discussions with FARC "terrorists" (*El Nuevo Herald* January 4, 1999).

The Clinton administration continued to back Pastrana's peace initiative throughout 1999 in its public diplomacy. Yet, as the negotiation process bogged down month after month, key U.S. policy-makers clearly reached the conclusion that the FARC would never negotiate seriously unless compelled to do so by defeat on the battlefield. Indicating an important shift, in March 1999 Washington agreed to begin sharing U.S. intelligence on drug trafficking and guerrilla activity with Pastrana government and the Colombian military, including data obtained from satellite observation of the *zona de despeje* (Albright August 10, 1999; Reuters August 11, 1999).[11]

By mid-1999 more than 300 American personnel were stationed in Colombia: 200 U.S. military trainers and advisors and more than 100 Drug Enforcement Administration (DEA) and Central Intelligence Agency (CIA) operatives. Drug control remained the stated U.S. policy priority in Colombia. The primary U.S. mission was to train and equip a new 950-man mobile anti-narcotics battalion within the Colombian army (*Revista Semana* January 17, 2000a).

But stalemate in the peace process and setbacks suffered by the military in combat against the FARC over 1998–1999, combined with mounting evidence of FARC's deepening involvement in the drug trade, forced Washington to accept that the war on drugs could no longer be neatly distinguished from the guerrilla war. At the urging of Washington, in September 1999 the Pastrana government released a document entitled "Plan Colombia" in which it set out its general strategy for dealing with the multiple ills besetting the country from drug trafficking and political violence through humanitarian crisis and economic stagnation to institutional corruption. The price tag attached to the plan was US$7.5 billion over a three-year period of which Colombia promised to foot US$4 billion. It was hoped that Washington would provide US$1.5–2 billion and that the reminder would come from the multilateral financial institutions (e.g. IMF, World Bank, and IDB) and the European Union (Colombia. Presidencia de la República 1999).[12]

After failing to push an earlier request through the U.S. Congress in late 1999, on January 11, 2000, the Clinton administration submitted a new bill to the U.S. Congress for a US$1.28 billion emergency aid program for Colombia. Intended to help Bogota fight the country's mushrooming narcotics trade and to prop up its democracy over the next two years, about half of the money was included as a supplemental budget request for FY 2000. The other half was incorporated in Clinton's budget proposal to Congress for FY 2001 presented on February 7, 2000 (Albright January 11, 2000; U.S. White House January 11, 2000).

In effect, with this new aid proposal the Clinton administration unveiled a dramatic shift in U.S. strategy toward Colombia. In 1999, as in previous years, virtually all of Washington's anti-narcotics aid had been channeled through the National Police rather than the military. The new package, in contrast, assigned the bulk of future U.S. assistance to the Colombian armed forces (Army, Air Force, and Navy). Of the total US$1.573 billion to be provided over the next two years, almost two-thirds—US$940 million—were destined to the military, versus US$96 million for the police. To underwrite training, equipment, and the purchase of 30 Black Hawk and 33 Huey helicopters for two new anti-narcotics battalions, the army was slated to receive US$599 million (US$512 million in FY 2000 and US$88 million in 2001). For interdiction activities, the Air Force and the Navy would receive US$341 million (US$238 in FY 2000 and US$103 million in 2001) (Gómez Maseri January 12, 2000).

While the White House National Security Advisor for Latin America Arturo Valenzuela claimed that the new U.S. aid had "nothing to do" with the anti-guerrilla struggle, U.S. Drug Czar Barry McCaffrey more forthrightly admitted that the money would make an "important" contribution to the Colombian army's fight against the guerrillas. In practice, Washington's rhetorical efforts to maintain a strict division between U.S. anti-narcotics aid and the Colombian military's anti-guerrilla operations were both disingenuous and futile. Colombian reality simply does not lend itself to such facile distinctions. Indeed, during his late January 2000 trip to Washington to shore up U.S. congressional support for President Clinton's aid package for Colombia, President Pastrana openly recognized that to the extent that the FARC are "in the business," U.S. anti-narcotics funds and equipment would be used against the guerrillas (Torres de la Llosa January 27, 2000).

Implications of the Shift in U.S. Policy Priorities toward Colombia

At bottom, the Clinton administration became progressively more concerned about the stability of Colombian democracy and the regional security implications of a potential state collapse in Colombia than it was about drug control *per se*, although the two obviously remained closely intertwined.

Indeed, in mid-January 2000, Secretary of State Madeleine Albright explicitly singled out Colombia, along with three other countries (Nigeria, Indonesia, and Ukraine) for special attention, because "[e]ach can be a major force for stability and progress in its region, and each is at a critical point along the democratic path" (Dudley January 15, 2000; Reuters January 25, 2000).

While such heightened attention from Washington is often accompanied by sorely needed resources, past experience indicated that it also typically implies greater U.S. "conditionality" and increased U.S. involvement in the domestic affairs of the country in question. The Colombian case is no exception. In the first place, Washington has stipulated that the greatest part of U.S. assistance be used for drug control operations in the south of the country where two-thirds of the coca crop is grown and where the FARC is most active in protecting fields, processing laboratories and landing strips. Intensification of government conflict with FARC forces were becoming an inevitable outcome of the U.S. mandate given to Bogota.

Second, the Clinton administration was keenly aware of past Colombian military involvement in human rights abuses and tied increased U.S. aid directly to permanent monitoring of the activities of the new anti-narcotics battalions and to U.S. certification that no police or military involvement with paramilitary groups occurs. In fact, US$93 million are explicitly earmarked in the new budget proposal for strengthening human rights, the administration of justice and democracy in Colombia (US$45 million in FY 2000 and US$48 million in 2001). Conscious of the likelihood of heightened scrutiny of the human rights record of his embattled armed forces, during a trip to Washington in late January 2000, Pastrana explicitly asked that American aid not be tied to human rights. Despite Pastrana's preferences, however, Congressional Democrats like Senator Patrick J. Leahy (D-Vt) appeared determined to press for such conditions.

Third, Washington, somewhat contradictorily, stipulated that all operations of Colombia's new U.S.-financed anti-narcotics units must relate directly to drug control missions rather than general anti-guerrilla actions. This distinction was unquestionably hard to make in the field. Yet noncompliance would almost certainly provoke intense political debate within the U.S. Congress and could potentially lead to denial of future U.S. assistance. The quantum leap in total U.S. aid in 2000 and the accompanying conditionality, in effect, convert Colombian military performance into a high-profile "intermestic" (both international and domestic) issue within the

American political system to an even greater extent than it has been in the past (*Revista Semana* February 28, 2000b; Radu n.d.).

Finally, U.S. officials also urged that Colombia step up its coca and opium poppy eradication efforts. In compliance, on January 21, 2000, the Colombian National Police pledged to expand their aerial herbicidal spraying campaign from the 40,000 hectares targeted in 1999 to 80,000 in 2000. A total of US$145 million was earmarked in the aid package for alternative development projects between 2000 and 2001 (US$92 million in FY 2000 and US$53 million in 2001). Although the intent of this policy was clearly to weaken the FARC by reducing its income from coca cultivation, the unintended outcome could well be to strengthen the guerrilla movement by driving thousands of embittered and poverty-stricken peasants into its ranks.[13]

The numbers of U.S. military trainers and advisors, DEA agents, CIA operatives, and Agency for International Development (AID) personnel in Colombia could also rise substantially along with the upsurge in U.S. aid flows over the next few years. In light of past bitter experiences in Vietnam, there is virtually zero probability that Washington will send American combat troops to fight in Colombia anytime in the foreseeable future. Nonetheless, the shift in U.S. strategy currently underway signals unmistakably that Washington is no longer targeting Colombia's drug cartels so much as it is the country's surging "narcoguerrilla" (Sweeny 1999; Marcella and Schultz 2000; Tokatlian 2000b).

Underscoring this possibility, in late February 2000 a senior FARC commander, Raúl Reyes, stated that his organization viewed the U.S. aid package as nothing more than a thinly disguised declaration of war by Washington on the FARC. He, in turn, declared "war" on the United States and vowed that the FARC would fight against foreign intervention in Colombia (Associated Press February 29, 2000; Reuters February 29, 2000). To avoid exposing U.S. military personnel and risking the U.S. domestic outcry that would inevitably ensue, Washington may opt instead for the well-established private business practice known as "outsourcing." This strategy would involve hiring civilian contractors (many of whom are highly qualified former U.S. service members) to support its aid program rather than sharply increasing levels of U.S. military staffing. While perhaps expedient from Washington's viewpoint, human rights organizations such as Amnesty International warn that such a strategy raises serious questions of accountability. According to a recent poll sponsored by the *El Tiempo* news organization in Bogota, the more likely scenario was one of escalating conflict between the FARC and the Colombian military, at least for the foreseeable future. This assertion was proven right when the peace negotiations broke down in 2002.

Conclusions

The implicit logic of the U.S. strategy was to force the FARC to negotiate seriously with the Pastrana government by demonstrating to them on the battlefield that they have more to gain from a peace settlement than from a continuation of the war. Whether this strategy will work at all is very much open to doubt. What should not be doubted is that the U.S. aid package sets the stage for an even more violent and bloody phase in Colombia's ongoing internal conflicts over the next few years. If the strategy has any chance of working at all, Washington will have to sustain its heightened levels of funding for Bogota for the better part of the 2000s and additional donors will have to be found (most likely in Europe) to supplement U.S. commitments.

Even assuming sustained inflows of U.S. and European assistance many critics remain skeptical about the prospects for ending political violence and drug trafficking in Colombia with the strategy currently embraced by Bogota and Washington. In broad strokes, the critics can be divided into two basic camps.[14] On the one hand, there is a "hard-line" that claims that the FARC is now so deeply involved in (and well financed by) the drug trade and other illegal activities that it would never agree to a peace settlement that would oblige it to lay down its arms and give up its illicit sources of income. The logic of this camp leads to the conclusion that the FARC will first have to be defeated militarily in a protracted counterinsurgency war before peace may be reestablished or drug cultivation curbed in Colombia. Washington should recognize this reality, the hard-liners claim, "[. . .] first, by declaring the absolute primacy of the war against the communists, rather than the war on drugs" (Radu n.d.).

From this perspective, Washington's insistence on distinguishing between anti-drug and anti-guerrilla operations (and funding only the former) was considered artificial and self-defeating. Moreover, tying U.S. aid to respect for human rights and the elimination of military and police links to paramilitary groups only hamstrings Colombia's security forces while leaving the guerrillas free to operate unfettered by such constraints. In the final analysis, the hard-liners' skepticism stems from their belief that the Colombian Armed Forces will not be able to defeat the guerrillas, even with U.S. aid, if Washington insists on micromanaging the war effort (Radu n.d., 2–3).

Among the hard-liners there are important differences in emphasis that should not be overlooked. Some doubt that even with U.S.-backing that the

Colombian elite actually possess the will to fight. "Why should a single U.S. dollar, to say nothing of a U.S. soldier, be sent to prop up a military in which no Colombian with a high school diploma is required to serve?" "Does the Colombian government—feckless, corrupt and inconstant—deserve our help to survive?" (Peters March 5, 2000). The basic point of this line of argument is that—as Vietnam revealed—no amount of U.S. aid will save a regime unable to save itself. It may serve only to prolong the "gruesome" *status quo*. Such doubts do not necessarily lead hard-liners to reject the need for the Clinton aid package. Indeed, even the most wary believed that the aid should have been sent to provide the Pastrana government a "last" chance to demonstrate its will and capacity to "rescue" Colombia from terrorists and narcoguerrillas of all stripes. If Bogota responded effectively, well and good. However, if it did not, most cautioned that the United States should not deploy American combat troops to fight Colombia's battles. In such a scenario, the better alternative, some—although certainly not all—believed, would have been to allow the current corrupt, oligarchical, and morally bankrupt regime to collapse rather than to postpone its death throes indefinitely at the cost of American lives. In the wake of such a collapse, they admitted, the United States might end up having to fight in Colombia to protect its strategic interests anyway. But, they claimed, Washington could have done so as part of a regional consensus on the need for intervention and as a member of a coalition fighting in support of a "worthy" new regime rather than artificially propping up "unworthy" incumbents (Peters March 5, 2000).

On the other hand, there was a "reformist-line" that contended that the country's ongoing internal conflicts would never be permanently resolved unless Bogota first undertook major socioeconomic and political reforms designed to address the glaring inequities in Colombian society and to democratize its corrupt, elitist, and exclusionary political system. From this perspective, current U.S. strategy during the Clinton administration reflected neither a realistic plan to fight drugs nor a viable long-term program for the restoration of peace and stability. "Washington should have learned long ago that partnership with an abusive and ineffective Latin American military rarely produces positive results and often undermines democracy in the region" (*New York Times* February 13, 2000).

U.S. rhetoric aside, the reformers continue to believe that Washington's aid package was far too heavily skewed toward military solutions and devoted far too few resources to institution building and structural economic reform. Reform advocates did not ignore the need to reorganize and strengthen the Colombian armed forces. Indeed, they viewed this task as an essential component of institution building. But they underscored the crucial importance of strict observance of human rights by the military and of severing ties between government forces and the paramilitaries, rather than equipping them to fight a protracted counterinsurgency war. They also emphasized the fundamental need to end military impunity by subordinating military personnel to civilian judicial scrutiny and sanctions. This, in turn, would have required Washington and Bogota to assign higher priority and more funds to the reform of the debilitated Colombian judicial system.

The priority given to the Colombian military left little or nothing for desperately needed crop substitution and alternative development programs or infrastructural investments in roads, bridges, schools, and public health facilities. Rather than weaning the Colombian peasantry from coca cultivation, the strategy was much more likely to "balloon" coca production farther out onto the vast agricultural frontier of Colombia's eastern plains, into its Amazon region and deeper into Brazil and other neighboring countries.

While generally embracing a more "development-oriented" U.S. policy approach toward Colombia, some reformers also placed heavy emphasis on the need for Washington to spend more money on reducing U.S. demand. Such critics maintained that the U.S. had consistently underfunded prevention, education, treatment, and rehabilitation programs at home.

> Just compare the US$1.6 billion request for Colombia during an 18-month period with the US$2 billion for all prevention and treatment in the proposed 2001 budget [. . .] Frankly, it will be much more valuable to America's health over the long haul to spend money domestically than on Blackhawk helicopters [. . .]" (Seattle Post-Intelligence Editorial Board 2000).

Clearly, Clinton's strategy toward Colombia fully satisfied neither the hard-liners nor the reformers. In effect, it sought to straddle the line between them. The drug war remained the formal priority and human rights monitoring a condition of U.S. aid. Yet the bulk of U.S. assistance was to be channeled into the Colombian military rather than into socioeconomic and institutional reforms. This "two track" strategy may well prove capable of propping up the Colombian political regime at least for the next few years, but it is unlikely to foster either lasting peace or enduring political stability in the coming decade.

Notes

* Professor of International Studies, School of International Studies, University of Miami, Coral Gables, Florida.

1. For information on the impact of the drug industry in the Colombian economy see Berry in this volume.

2. For analyses of the problems of institutional corruption in Colombia see Cepeda Ulloa (1997, 1996a,b, 1994) and Roll (1997).

3. Accurate information on FARC's drug-related earnings is exceedingly difficult to obtain, hence estimates vary widely from a low of US$100 million to a high of US$600 million annually. The figures presented here are based on interviews with knowledgeable informants conducted by the author in Colombia in November 1999. For discussions of FARC's income sources see *Revista Semana* (March 8, 1999a), Farah (November 4, 1999), and EFE (May 12, 1999).

4. For his original statement of intentions in regards to the peace process see Pastrana (1998, 17). For an overview of peace initiatives in Colombia since the 1980s see Tokatlian (1999).

5. In an early March 2000 visit to Washington to lobby U.S. lawmakers on the Clinton aid package, Colombian Vice President Gustavo Bell declared that seven top military commanders had recently been dismissed by the Pastrana administration for collaborating with rightist paramilitary groups. He also announced that seven paramilitary members had been killed and 42 captured by government forces in the first two months of the year 2000 (Gedda March 8, 2000).

6. Until May 1999 the ELN controlled roughly 30,000 hectares of coca in Catatumbo, Norte de Santander, but then lost control of this area to AUC. Because of the ELN's official position not to finance its activities from drug trafficking and its comparatively smaller size, it is of less concern to Washington than the FARC (Lozada March 26, 2000).

7. On March 7, 2000, a recently released EPL kidnap victim announced to the press that the EPL had decided to enter into peace talks with the Pastrana government (*El Tiempo* March 7, 2000).

8. See the Venezuelan case in Sanjuán in this volume.

9. Although top U.S. officials fueled Colombian expectations of a major new U.S. aid package throughout the second half of 1999, partisan bickering and intense disputes over budgetary priorities between congressional Republicans and Democrats led to the tabling of Clinton's initial aid request in the U.S. Congress in late 1999 (Shifter 2000, 51).

10. The US$289 million was three times the amount of aid that Colombia had received from the United States in FY 1998 during the last full year of the Samper government. Under Samper, virtually all of the reduced flow of U.S. counternarcotics aid to Colombia was channeled through the National Police headed by General Jose Rosso Serrano rather than the military, which was viewed by U.S. authorities to be corrupt and deeply involved in human rights abuses (GAO February 12, 1998; 1999b).

11. Personal interviews conducted by the author with U.S. government officials during 1999.

12. Clearly indicating that it was intended primarily to convince the United States to support the Pastrana government, Plan Colombia was initially written in

English and first circulated in Washington before it was made available in Spanish to the Colombian Congress in Bogota.

13. On the counterproductive effects of coca eradication programs in Colombia see Youngers (June 2, 1997), Tokatlian (2000a).

14. Although this section refers to the debate during the Clinton administration, it could be argued that both the hard-line and the reformist arguments stressed by these two groups are still valid under the Bush administration.

References

Agence France Presse. January 2, 2000. Ataques recuerdan que la guerra continúa en Colombia. *El Nuevo Herald.*

———. January 15, 2000. Guerra total a paramilitares. *El Nuevo Herald.*

Albright, Madeleine K. January 11, 2000. *Statement on U.S. Assistance to Colombia.* Washington, D.C.: Office of the Spokesman U.S. Department of State.

———. August 10, 1999. Colombia's Struggles and How We Can Help. *The New York Times.*

Ambrus, Steven and Joe Contreras. November 29, 1999. Fighting the Enemy Within: The "FARC Republic": A new Outlaw State in the Heart of South America. *Newsweek.*

Asociación Nacional de Institutos Financieros (ANIF). 2000. *La economía de la cocaína: a clave para entender Colombia.* Bogotá: ANIF.

Associated Press. January 10, 2000. Colombian Militias Tax Drug trade. *The New York Times.*

———. January 28, 2000. Colombia Breaks Kidnap World Record. *The New York Times.*

———. February 11, 2000. Jamaican Fishermen's Tainted Boom: Rising Trade in Cocaine. *The New York Times.*

———. February 29, 2000. Colombia Rebels Rips Pastrana Plan. *The Washington Post.*

Bagley, Bruce Michael. 1989–1990. Dateline Drug Wars: Colombia: The Wrong Strategy. *Foreign Policy 77* (Winter): 154–71.

———. 1998. Hablando duro: La política internacional antinarcóticos de los Estados Unidos en los años noventa. In *Colombia y Estados Unidos: problemas y perspectivas,* edited by Juan Gabriel Tokatlian, 103–18. Bogotá: Tercer Mundo Editores.

———. 1999. Panama-Colombia border conflicts could threaten the Canal. Special to CNN Interactive. December http://cnn/SPECIALS/1999/panama.canal/border

Cabrera Lémuz, Adalid. December 19, 1999. Bolivia erradica una cifra record de coca. *El Nuevo Herald.*

Cepeda Ulloa, Fernando, Coord. 1994. *La corrupción administrativa en Colombia. diagnóstico y recomendaciones para combatirla.* Bogotá: Tercer Mundo Editores, Contraloría General de la República y Fedesarrollo.

————. 1996a. El Congreso colombiano ante la crisis. In *Tras las huellas de la crisis política*, edited by Francisco Leal Buitrago. Bogotá: Tercer Mundo Editores, FESCOL, IEPRI (U.N.).

————. 1996b. Virtudes y vicios del proceso descentralizador. In *El reto de la descentralización*, edited by Jaime Jaramillo Vallejo. Bogotá: Pontificia Universidad Javeriana, CEJA y Fundación Konrad Adenauer.

————. 1997. Seguimiento y evolución de la lucha contra la corrupción. In *La corrupción y la lucha contra la corrupción*, edited by Beatriz Franco-Cuervo, 99–116. Bogotá: Funcación Konrad Adenauer y el Goethe-Institut.

Clawson, Patrick L. and Reenselaer W. Lee III. 1998. *The Andean Cocaine Industry.* New York: St. Martin's Griffin.

Colombia. Presidencia de la República. 1997. *La lucha contra las drogas ilícitas. 1996, un año de grandes progresos.* Bogotá: Presidencia de la República.

————. 1999. *Plan Colombia.* September, Bogotá: Presidencia de la República.

Consultoría para los Derechos Humanos y el Desplazamiento (CODHES). 1999. *Crisis humanitaria y catástrofe social.* Bogotá: CODHES.

Dillon, Sam. August 22, 1997. Trial of a Drug Czar Tests Mexico's New Democracy. *The New York Times.*

Dudley, Steven. January 15, 2000. Albright Discusses Anti-Drug aid in Colombia. *The Washington Post.*

EFE. May 12, 1999. La guerrilla obtuvo $3.121 millones en ocho años. *El Nuevo Herald.*

El Espectador. February 8, 2000. Coca, nudo para el despeje.

El Nuevo Herald. January 4, 1999. Estados Unidos y guerrilla de Colombia hablan de paz.

————. August 17 1999. Chávez no tratará directamente con la guerrilla colombiana.

El Tiempo (Colombia). January 8, 2000. Eln sí pide despeje en el sur de Bolívar.

————. March 7, 2000. Sucesos del día.

————. March 8, 2000. El "boom" de las invasiones.

Farah, Douglas. November 4, 1999. Drug Sales Change Colombia's Power Balance. *The Washington Post.*

General Accounting Office (GAO). 1996. *Customs Service: Drug Interdiction Efforts.* Washington, D.C.: U.S. General Accounting Office, September, GAO/GGD-96-189BR.

————. February 12, 1998. *Drug control: U.S. Counternarcotics Efforts in Colombia Face Continuing Challenges.* Washington, D.C.: U.S. General Accounting Office, GAO/NSIAD-98-60.

————. June 22, 1999a. *Drug Control: Narcotics Threat from Colombia Continues to Grow.* Washington, D.C.: U.S. General Accounting Office, GAO/NSIAD-99-136.

————. 1999b. *Drug Control: Assets DOD Contributes to Reducing the Illegal Drug Supply Have Declined.* Washington, D.C.: U.S. General Accounting Office, December, GAO/NSIAD-00-9.

Gedda, George. March 8, 2000. Colombia breaking paramilitary ties. *The Washington Post.*

Golden, Tim. January 9, 2000. Mexican Tale of Absolute Corruption. *The New York Times.*

Golden, Tim. July 11, 1997. Mexico and Drugs: Was U.S. Napping? *The New York Times.*

Gómez Maseri, Sergio. January 12, 2000. Clinton le apuesta a Colombia. *El Tiempo.*

Human Rights Watch. 1996. *Colombia's Killer Networks: The Military-Paramilitary partnership and the United States.* November, Washington, D.C.: Human Rights Watch Publications.

Johnson, Tim. January 23, 2000. Colombia's Child Soldiers. *The Miami Herald.*

———. February 5, 2000. Radar Gap Helps Colombian Drug Smugglers. *The Miami Herald.*

———. February 11, 2000. Colombia's War on Drugs Goes Airborne. *The Miami Herald.*

Kidwell, David. February 13, 2000. Haiti Now a Major Route for Cocaine Entering U.S. *The Miami Herald.*

Kovaleski, Sergio F. August 11, 1999. Thousands Roam Colombia to Escape Brutal Rural War. *The Washington Post.*

Krauss, Clifford. August 19, 1999. Peru's Drug Success Erodes as Traffickers Adapt. *The New York Times.*

Lozada, Diana. March 26, 2000. Unidad de paz, "diez obstáculos comel ELN." *El Tiempo.*

Lupsha, Peter. 1995. Transnational Narco-corruption and Narco-investment: A Focus on Mexico. *Transnational Organized Crime Journal* (Spring), 84–101.

Marcella, Gabriel and Donald Schultz. 2000. Colombia's Three Wars: U.S. strategy at the Crossroads. *Strategic Review* 28 (Winter): 3–22.

Martínez, Margarita. December 20, 1999. Colombia Sergeants Convicted. *The Washington Post.*

New York Times. February 13, 2000. Dangerous Plans for Colombia.

Office of National Drug Control Policy. 1997. *The National Drug Control Strategy, 1997.* February, Washington, D.C.: The White House.

———. 1998. *The National Drug Control Strategy, 1998: A Ten Year Plan.* Washington, D.C.: The White House.

Orrego, Henry. August 7, 1999. Saldo en rojo muestra la economía de Colombia. *El Nuevo Herald.*

Pastrana, Andrés. 1998. Una política de paz para el cambio. Unpublished document. Bogotá, June 8.

Peters, Ralph. March 5, 2000. The U.S. is Setting a Trap for Itself in Colombia. *The Washington Post.*

Radu, Michael. n.d. *Aid to Colombia: A Study in Muddled Arguments.* Distributed by e-mail by the Foreign Policy Research Institute, Philadelphia, PA.

Revista Cambio. November 29–December 6, 1999. Carlos Castaño, jefe de las autodefensas.

Revista Semana. March 8, 1999a. Informe especial: los negocios de las FARC. Edición 879.

———. March 8, 1999b. Economía y negocios: en tierra de ciegos . . . Edición 879.

———. April 26, 1999. ¿Narco-Castaño? Edición 886.

———. June 14, 1999. El ELN y los alemanes. Edición 893.

———. June 21, 1999. La bofetada. Edición 894.

———. October 25, 1999. Narcotráfico: el Imperio de "Juvenal." Edición 912.

———. November 1, 1999a. Narcotráfico: cuentas pendientes. Edición 913.

———. November 1, 1999b. Economía y Negocios: El Chorro. Edición 913.

———. December 20, 1999. Sí estamos cobrando. Edición 918.

———. January 17, 2000a. Luz al final del túnel. Edición 924.

———. February 28, 2000b. La suerte de ERP. Edición 930.

———. March 27, 2000a. Los acuerdos de paz. Edición 932.

———. March 27, 2000b. Violencia joven. Edición 932.

Reuters. April 9, 1999. Pastrana destituye a generales acusados de nexos paramilitares. *El Nuevo Herald*.

———. July 29, 1999. Colombia's Pastrana Plays Down FARC's Drug Links. *The Miami Herald*.

———. August 11, 1999. High-level Visit Signal U.S. Alarm over Colombia. *The Washington Post*.

———. November 25, 1999. Se han desplazado un millón 700 mil colombianos por la guerra. *La Jornada*.

———. January 25, 2000. Albright Declares "New Relationship" with Colombia. *The New York Times*.

———. January 29, 2000. Cae en combate el líder del tercer grupo guerrillero colombiano. *El Nuevo Herald*.

———. February 10, 2000. Traffickers Moving Back to Caribbean—U.S. Drug Czar. *The New York Times*.

———. February 29, 2000. Colombia Rebels "Declare War" on United States. *The New York Times*.

———. March 4, 2000. Former Cycling Champ Kidnapped in Colombia. *The New York Times*.

Reyes, Alejandro. October 17, 1999. Investigación sobre geografía de la violencia. *El Tiempo*.

Riley, Michael. January 26, 2000. Mexico Claims Greater Success in War on Drugs. *Houston Chronicle*.

Robinson, Linda. 1999–2000. Where Angels Fear to Tread: Colombia and Latin America's tier of turmoil. *World Policy Journal* (Winter).

Rohter, Larry. October 27, 1998. Haiti paralysis Brings a Boom in Drug Trade. *The New York Times*.

———. October 21, 1999. Crisis in Colombia as Civil Strife Uproots Peasants. *The New York Times*.

Rohter, Larry. March 5, 2000. Driven by Fear, Colombians Leave in Droves. *The New York Times*.

52 • Bruce Michael Bagley

Roll, David. 1997. La corrupción política en Colombia, de subrealismo a la realidad virtual. In *La corrupción y la lucha contra la corrupción*, edited by Franco-Cuervo, B., 117–34. Bogotá: Fundación Konrad Adenauer y el Goethe Institut.

Sandoval, Ricardo. January 17, 2000. Albright Hails Mexican Role on Drugs. *The Miami Herald.*

Sanjuán, Prieto Rafael. 1998. Conflicto armado en Colombia y deplazamiento forzado: ¿qué protección? *Revista IIDH* 28 (July–December): 39–68.

Seattle Post-Intelligencer Editorial Board. *Spraying Coca Crop is a Misplaced Priority.* March 9, 2000, Seattle Post-Intelligencer.

Semple, Kirk. October 14, 1999. Major Arrests Sabotage Colombian Drug Network. *The Washington Post.*

Shifter, Michael. 2000. The United States and Colombia: Partners in Ambiguity. *Current History* (February).

Sweeny, John P. March 25, 1999. *Tread Cautiously in Colombia's Civil War.* Backgrounder No. 1264. Washington, D.C.: The Heritage Foundation.

The Economist. March 4, 2000. Andean Coca Wars. Special: A Crop that Refuses to Die.

Thompson. Alan. November 29, 1999. Colombia: "Mafia links" Boost Cocaine Exports. *The Financial Times.*

Tokatlian, Juan Gabriel. 1999. Colombia en guerra: las diplomacias por la paz. *Desarrollo Económico—Revista de Ciencias Sociales* (Buenos Aires) 39 (October–December): 339–60.

———. 2000a. Estados Unidos y la fumigación de cultivos ilícitos en Colombia: la funesta rutinización de una estrategia desacertada. Unpublished document. Buenos Aires, Argentina, February.

———. 2000b. Colombian Catastrophe. *The World Today* 56 (January): 13–15.

Torres de la Llosa, Luis. January 27, 2000. La ayuda de Estados Unidos irá contra las FARC si trafican droga. *El Nuevo Herald.*

U.S. Department of State. 1999. *International Narcotics Control Strategy Report.* Washington, D.C.: U.S. Government Printing Office.

U.S. White House. January 11, 2000. *Fact Sheet: Colombia Assistance Package.* Grand Canyon, Arizona: Office of the Press Spokesman, The White House.

Waller, J. Michael. 1999. The Narcostate Next Door. *Insight Magazine* www.insightmag.com/news/1999/12/27/world/Mexican.standoff.The.Narcostate.Next.Door-208352.shtml

Youngers, Coletta. June 2, 1997. Coca Eradication Efforts in Colombia. In *WOLA Briefing Series: Issues in International Drug Policy*, edited by WOLA. Washington, D.C.: WOLA.

CHAPTER 3

Colombia: Internal War, Regional Insecurity, and Foreign Intervention

Juan Gabriel Tokatlian[*]

Introduction

The Andean Region is presently engulfed in a profound crisis of unpredictable consequences. Colombia is just the tip of the iceberg within an enormous ice floe of problems, the manifestations of which have been accumulating for some time and for which solutions have been postponed. In fact, since the 1990s and now at the beginning of the twenty-first century, the Andean region has become the major focus of instability and continental concern. On the human rights front, and in comparison with any other region of the Americas, the Andean area is where rights are most systematically violated—Colombia is the most dramatic case in point. As far as drugs are concerned, the Andes is the major area of cultivation, processing and trafficking of coca on the continent, and the five countries (together with Mexico) are the key actors in the illicit narcotics trade. In terms of corruption, some of the countries with the highest levels in the world are to be found in this area; the cases of Bolivia, Ecuador, and Venezuela underline the point.

Looking at environmental concerns, Andean countries exhibit severe and worrisome degrees of degradation, especially in the Amazon basin shared with Brazil. In socioeconomic terms, all of the Andean nations display alarming rates of unemployment, marginalization, poverty, and insecurity, combined with low quality-of-life indicators, scant and volatile growth, severe concentration of income, and meager investment. And in each of the five countries, although to different degrees, the partial crumbling of the state has been exacerbated during the last decade.

Additionally, during the post–Cold War era, it is in the Andean region—particularly Ecuador, Peru, and Venezuela—where the military has maintained considerable political influence and corporativist responsibility. At the same time, the Andean Community of Nations has persistently lost influence. Finally, the Andean world is continually more dependent on Washington in material and political terms and more distant from the Southern Cone, culturally and diplomatically. The United States sphere of influence[1] is being displaced from its traditional *mare nostrum*—the broad Caribbean Basin—and moving with increasing strength toward the Andean apex of the Southern Cone.

Summing up, then, the entire Andean region is simultaneously enduring a diverse range of severe problems. Demonstrations of social conflict in the area tend to expand, while the incapacity of democratic regimes to process age-old unsatisfied citizens' demands remains intact. In this context, the case of Colombia is undoubtedly the most catastrophic. Colombia stands out for the enormous dimensions of its crisis, although it is by no means an isolated and solitary example: the Andes are experiencing conditions of ungovernability, and dangerous institutional cataclysms are predictable.

Responses to the Colombian crisis will, therefore, serve as potential models for foreign intervention in the domestic affairs of the hemisphere. At the same time, what will be played out here is how, and how much, our own area (Latin America), region (South America), and zone (Southern Cone) will be able to support the resolution of this situation? The most difficult case—Colombia—should be confronted rather than avoided: this is the only way to determine whether South American countries' diplomatic capacity has matured sufficiently to face with greater autonomy the challenges of the new century.

The Nature of the War

The armed conflict in Colombia can be analyzed from different perspectives, and with this in mind I would like to underline two points of view: one regarding the state, and the other, regarding the war itself. For an increasing number of national and international analysts, this Andean country is suffering from a collapse of the state, similar to that which precipitated the experience known as *La Violence*;[2] only this time more peculiar and complex. According to the expression coined by Oquist (1978) regarding the "partial collapse of the state" in Colombia in the 1940s and 1950s, the "specific articulations"—internal and nonexogenous—that characterized violence were: (1) the "break down of established political institutions"; (2) the "loss of state legitimacy"; (3) "internal contradictions within the state's armed apparatus"; and (4) the "physical absence of the state." Except for the third factor, and despite the reforms introduced in the 1991 Constitution, the other indicators have emerged forcefully since the mid-1970s and have consolidated in the twenty-first century.

Adopting recent definitions, a collapsed state is characterized by the implosion of the structures of authority and legitimacy (Zartman 1995; Reno 2000). The result is a phenomenon of ungovernability, resulting from the articulation between internal forces and external pressure. Simultaneous manifestations of war and criminality on the domestic front, combined with Plan Colombia and the Andean Regional Initiative competing in the external arena, constitute a lethal combination. From my understanding, Colombia—which is not an unusual or exceptional case—is headed in this direction of collapse.

Sooner or later the situation may become one in which the country is witness to a failed state—that is, a state incapable of protecting its citizens and communities from the forces that threaten the security of its very existence.[3] Within such a framework, it cannot be said Colombia has an anarchic state—complete absence of central government, but it does reflect the mixture of a phantom state—authority is exercised in certain limited areas and is nonexistent in others—and of an anemic state—whereby energies are consumed in confronting the multipronged offensive by armed groups.

In this context, it is worth remembering that according to one of the main reports from the extremely significant *United States Commission on National Security/21st Century*—cochaired by Gary Hart and Warren Rudman—the United States must establish priorities in the event of an expansion of the failed state phenomena. It asserts,

> Not every such problem must be primarily a U.S. responsibility, particularly in a world where other powers are amassing significant wealth and human resources. There are countries whose domestic stability is, for differing reasons, of major importance to U.S. interests (such as Mexico, Colombia, Russia, and Saudi Arabia). Without prejudging the likelihood of domestic upheaval, these countries should be a priority focus of U.S. planning in a manner appropriate to the respective cases. For cases of lesser priority, the United States should help the international community develop innovative mechanisms to manage the problems of failed states. (U.S. Commission on National Security/21st Century 2001, 13)

Colombia confronts violent and diffuse upheaval driven equally by guerrilla movements, organized crime, and reactionary groups, which appear to have sufficient force to corner the state but without the capacity to build a new kind of authority. A traditional enlightened ruling elite does not exist; neither is there a closely knit, vigorous, and civilizing opposition. Rather what we see are debased illegitimacies, applicable both to the existing state of affairs as well as to opposing factions. On the horizon is the frightening failure of the rule of law and no immediate alternative in the foreseeable future with the capacity to bring order, peace, and social well-being. In the end, a mixture of political warfare, criminal violence, and humanitarian violations predominates.

This conflict is increasingly complex. Some of its defining tendencies include: (1) an irregular war, predominant for decades in Colombia, is revealing the increasing number of ways it is being transformed into a civil war involving heavily armed groups with articulated polarized ideological projects and backed by their own bases of social support; (2) a political war that is increasingly looking more like a criminal war, where armed actors constantly debase their political profile, abandon practices based on principles, and take on delinquent behavior. In addition, the Colombian conflict is more than the sum of differences and contradictory local wars; the country is experiencing a national war, which is to say, disputes are not circumscribed by regional logic alone, but rather acquire the logic of an extended confrontation throughout the entire nation. In this context, as rural confrontation continues and worsens in an increasing number of areas in the country, new urban conflict scenarios are becoming visible.

At a parallel level, the war in Colombia is no longer simply domestic. The gradual, precise, and persistent involvement of the United States in the internal conflict has turned the country into an epicenter of a low-intensity warfare that is increasingly international in scope. And finally, the Colombian war is no longer limited in terms of victims, armed participants, and reach. The data could not be more eloquent.[4]

This mutating complicated and critical level of conflict has been fostering U.S. interference in the affairs of the country. Neither a unanimous opinion in the United States, nor definitive consensus between it and Latin America, exists about the best way out of the Colombian armed conflict. However, there is relative agreement about the potential negative consequences at the continental level, particularly among neighboring countries.

Washington, with tacit Latin American consent evident in the midst of notorious regional silence, has assumed an unusual modality of indirect intervention in the Colombian situation. On the one hand, former models of intervention, typical of the Cold War era, can be observed: just as in El Salvador, the United States is supporting militarily (e.g. giving assistance, arms, training, information) a country in a internal war that is becoming increasingly bloodier. However, the greater geopolitical importance of Colombia; its territorial, demographic, and economic dimensions; and the combination of different types of threats (drug trafficking, organized crime, guerrillas, terrorism, and paramilitaries) have contributed to increasing U.S. assistance.

On the other hand, a new kind of post–Cold War interventionism is forecast. Pressure on, and support (according to each case) to, neighboring countries in order to create a diplomatic and military "sanitary cordon" around Colombia is one modality; while the development of contingency plans for the potential greater use of force with the eventual participation of countries friendly to Washington is another.

This two-pronged model, increasingly perfected during the last few years, has several components: among them, an increase in security assistance to Colombia; the framing of Colombia as a "problem-country" in the hemispheric and international arenas; growth of regional diplomacy to mobilize countries in the area, using strategies to contain the Colombian phenomena; and an increase in official rhetoric linked to the presence of the inexorable "narcoguerrilla" threat in Colombia.

Potentially, this new interventionism in Colombia could take three forms. First, "intervention by imposition"—Washington consolidates an *ad hoc* coalition that decides to become militarily involved in this Andean country to establish a new "order" against the will of Colombians and despite efforts at internal negotiations; second, "intervention by desertion"—the Colombian state cannot contain the internal armed conflict nor guarantee national sovereignty, and serves as an excuse for Washington to head up a temporary interventionist coalition until the established power in Bogota is strengthened; and third, "intervention by invitation"—an elected government requests external support given the impossibility of autonomously preserving internal order, national unity, and democratic institutionality. In this case, the Colombian military, together with foreign forces led by the United States, joined by various countries in the hemisphere, act jointly with the hope of avoiding national implosion. Although such scenarios produce justifiable rejection today, the political probability of one of them being taken seriously cannot be rejected, the last being the least improbable.

In short, the debased nature of the Colombian war combined with U.S. interventionism in Colombia has evolved to the point of constituting a serious problem of regional security. This, despite the fact, that generally, Latin

American countries remain impassive vis-à-vis this explosive combination of phenomena.

The U.S. Plan Colombia

The U.S. multimillion dollar security assistance plan to Colombia is well underway: in 2000, the Congress in Washington authorized US$1.319 billion as a response to a complex and debased internal war. Component B of the so-called "Plan Colombia"—a plan designed in 1999 in the Presidential Palace at the suggestion of the White House—will go ahead after intense debate in Washington, insignificant discussions in Bogota, and a worrying silence in the hemisphere.[5]

The U.S. Plan Colombia, which involved US$7.5 billion from the Andrés Pastrana administration, included three parts. Component A was domestic and was the largest. It proposed reducing the negative effects of the crisis experienced in the country by applying measures to bring the state in closer contact with areas most affected by the violence. This part of Plan Colombia was designed to strengthen institutional presence throughout the country. The idea of "offering a carrot" is implicit in its design—pacification through state contact with the community and a negotiated settlement.

Plan B refers to U.S. assistance. Washington is offering more of the same, but within a shorter time frame and for a different beneficiary. In reality, Colombia received US$1.38 billion in antinarcotics and security assistance between 1989 and 1999.[6] Now, the country will receive a similar amount, reduced to two years, and the principal beneficiary will be the army rather than the police, as was the case throughout the decade of the 1990s. This is the "stick"—complement to the "carrot." The underlying logic is that only with increased firepower and greater geographic armed forces coverage can the increasing territorial power of the guerrillas and the enormous regional influence of drug trafficking be counterbalanced. If during the 1990s—with all the U.S. security resources provided to Colombia—violence, human rights violations, and the escalation of the war increased as never before, nothing indicates that these same problems will not get worse.[7]

U.S. Plan Colombia contains several precise components. The specific package for Colombia totals US$860.3 million; of this, military assistance makes up US$519.2 million while support for the police amounts to US$123.1 million. Clearly the idea is to strengthen the armed forces to ensure a more offensive perspective on the war. The goal is also to improve the capacity of the police to fight the drug war (e.g. 2 Blackhawk and 12 UH-1H Huey helicopters and training for fumigation activities). Other categories include: alternative development (US$68.5 million), assistance to the displaced (US$37.5 million), human rights (US$51 million), judicial reform (US$13 million), rule of law (US$45 million), and peace (US$3 million). The remainder of the US$1.319 billion package—US$458.8 million—is divided into two major categories: support to other countries bordering Colombia (US$180 million) and resources for direct use by U.S. authorities (US$278.8 million). With respect to this last category, US$276.8 million are for the Department of Defense (improvements to bases in Ecuador, Aruba, and Curacao; routine and classified intelligence programs; and radar equipment, among others). If the overall total package is broken down into its diverse components, beneficiaries, and objectives, approximately 75 percent is directed toward combat readiness for the already eternal and inefficient "war against drugs"—a war that increasingly takes on the characteristics of an "anti-narcoguerrilla struggle," to use Washington's nomenclature.

Plan C embodies European support for peace. This portion of "Plan Colombia" represents the part of the contribution to be used for improving social conditions in regions where the state has the least presence. Europe does not tend to resolve anything, but rather to compensate for erroneous policies, particularly those induced by the United States. This component is not new: Europe has always promised "other" assistance—it has done the same since 1990 with its announced System of Andean Preferential Treatment; "another" perspective—that of coresponsibility on the drugs issues; and "another" spirit—favoring human rights and dialogue for peace. And, as on previous occasions, not much can be hoped for from the promises—they are consistently overtaken by actions. State contributions from Europe have been more symbolic than practical. The Donors' Meeting in Madrid in July 2002 proves the point: only Spain (US$100 million) and Norway (US$20 million) committed resources to Plan Colombia. Months later, the European Union decided to contribute 105 million euros for the 2000–2006 period as a way of providing institutional support to the peace process and with the goal of promoting the defense of human rights, environmental protection, and illicit crop substitution. European diplomatic, material, and economic support has been and will be much less than that of Washington.

As Walters (2002) argues, the failure of the negotiated solutions is explained by the absence of a third party, external to the adversaries, equipped with the will and capacity to satisfy both the necessary guarantees for the demobilization and disarmament of the combatants, as well as the requirements for securing the stipulated agreements of cogovernance. The crux of a peaceful end to an internal war lies in real guarantees of survival for the armed actors, and in the safe execution of the agreement by the state and its opponents in regard to shared power. The third party must satisfy three conditions: First, that the intervening party (a state or a group of states) has tangible interests in the case affected by a war; second, the third party must be willing to use force to guarantee the fulfillment of the agreement; and third, it must demonstrate constant resolve. In this sense, it is clear that a role of the United States in the resolution of the Colombian conflict is inescapable. The question is whether or not South America understands that it has interests at play in the Colombian case, and whether or not it is capable of formulating a pacific solution to the war in this Andean country.

To that end, in my view, Colombia should not be the object of a military intervention, but rather of a political interference. Colombia needs some sort of new Contadora,[8] similar to that in Central America driven by Mercosur. This would imply the following:

- The new Contadora must be useful for offering a realistic diagnostic of the Colombian situation, avoid faulty premises, and specify the real nature of the existing threats.
- If during the 1980s, the Contadora in Central America was intended to open political and diplomatic spaces so that Nicaragua and El Salvador were not "lost" by the West, today the Contadora for Colombia should prevent the country from being "lost" to the continent in terms of democracy.
- Although balanced in its approach, the Contadora for Central America was perceived by the White House and part of the legislature in Washington as anti-American; the Contadora for Colombia should be, without a doubt, understood as an valid and valuable alternative to committing the United States to a long-term solution to the Colombian conflict.
- The Contadora for Central America was able to disaggregate the components of the regional crisis and to define procedures, processes, and specific and general policies; the Contadora for the Colombian case needs to develop a similar capacity for understanding the simultaneous juxtaposition and autonomy of distinct violent phenomena in the country.
- In Central America the Contadora was confined to dealing only with the political armed conflict; in Colombia, a new Contadora should bring a different understanding of the internal war and of situations such as the illicit drug business—a crucial question in the Colombian case which was not present in that of Central America. This would involve assuring that the eventual resolution of the Colombian case would not precipitate a

displacement of the lucrative illicit empire of the drug traffickers to the neighboring countries.

- In the 1980s Contadora brought a diplomatic voice to a crisis that was basically political in Central America; in Colombia, a Contadora should go beyond this and present itself as a force prepared to push for a global solution to the Colombian conflict with a variety of instruments.

- In Central America, Contadora avoided the propagation of a low-intensity conflict throughout the area, but it did not contribute to shaping a new democratic pact in the states with high levels of violence; in Colombia, a Contadora should make it clear that it is not advisable to resolve only the armed confrontations without modifying the current political structure.

With this scenario, Colombia would appear to urgently require a Plan D: one capable of seriously resolving the present war, rather than containing it in the short term. This Plan D should be articulated by Colombians and draw on support from Latin Americans. Such an alliance could repoliticize the Colombian crisis—return to the politicization of the conduct of the state and the behavior of the guerrilla. Although such an option has not been genuinely attempted, it might potentially facilitate the resolution of this devastating war.

Clinton and Colombia

Unquestionably, the armed conflict in Colombia has a significant international dimension. External factors condition the possibilities for peace and war (e.g. increasing drug consumption in the most industrialized countries; massive and clandestine arms provision; U.S. foreign policy, the upsurge in transnational organized crime; institutional uncertainty in the entire Andean region; recurring squabbles among neighboring countries), while the internal human drama increasingly impacts regionally and resounds internationally. However, emphasizing the magnitude of the Colombian tragedy in no way justifies military interference; instead, measured political intervention should be encouraged.

The urgency of a Contadora for Colombia needs to be evaluated within the parameters of a new strategic configuration in the area. For this reason, the presence of Bill Clinton in Cartagena at the end of August 2000, as part of a ten-hour visit to Colombia, symbolized the crossing of a fine line—the United States wanted to ensure its sphere of influence beyond the Caribbean Basin. This visit was immensely significant. The meeting between Clinton and Pastrana sealed a strategic pact—more than an individual relationship—inaugurating a new moment in inter-American relationships. Against a common backdrop, this short summit, in reality, included multiple messages for different audiences: the Colombian case became definitively politicized, and from that moment on, a complex struggle for power spilling over the country's borders was settled.

Regarding internal policy, Clinton put the Colombian conflict and its effects on U.S. security on a highly visible public plane; he demonstrated he was capable of applying the heavy hand in the "war against drugs;" he attempted to articulate a state policy vis-à-vis the case of Colombia (bipartisan, integrated, and long term); and he went out of his way to calm the fears of those who were seeing a new Vietnam in the treatment of Colombia. In terms of the relationship between Washington and Bogota, the visit strengthened Pastrana domestically but restricted his margin of external maneuver in the medium term; it implied a significant political strike against the guerrilla; and legitimated increasing U.S. interference in the affairs of Colombia.

Taking regional implications into account, the visit reaffirmed U.S. preference for unilateralism in hemispheric affairs; it obstructed the summit of South American presidents organized by Brazil at the time; contributed to sealing the fate of Colombia as the major security problem in the area; and strengthened increasing Andean and Amazon militarization in order to contain the consequences of the Colombian crisis.

Clearly, the fundamental point to be made is that Washington already dominates its Caribbean *mare nostrum* and is now anxious for effective control in the Andes, in its South American "backyard."[9] The defining of regional alliances and balance therefore becomes paramount. The United States is enforcing a security cordon around Colombia with the half-hearted agreement of Panama and Ecuador and the ambivalent support of Peru. Panama, a close ally of the United States, has armed its borders. Ecuador, going through a delicate internal period and having chosen to "dollarize" its economy, *de facto* accepted Washington's Plan Colombia since it would obtain US$81.3 million—US$20 million for antinarcotics activities and US$61.3 for improving the radar system in the Eloy Alfaro airport.

Among Colombia's small neighboring countries, the United States can rely on either their implicit or explicit support. For example, Nicaragua, one of Colombia's maritime neighbors, is taking advantage of the situation to push for control over the San Andrés and Providencia Archipelago, an area belonging to Colombia but where marginal secessionist revolts occur. Jamaica, Honduras, Haiti, Costa Rica, and the Dominican Republic, also maritime neighbors of Colombia—increasingly affected by drug trafficking—do not question Plan Colombia or the militarization of the

Caribbean Basin encouraged by Washington and thereby, support the argument of the "war on drugs." To the north of Colombia, in areas of less immediate concern, the prospect is equally disheartening. Some of the Caribbean islands have aligned with the United States: Washington will provide US$10.3 million and US$43.9 million from Plan Colombia for improvements to radar systems in the airports of Queen Beatrix in Aruba and International Hato in Curacao, respectively. Cuba, on the other hand, is trying to play a discreet and constructive role: Castro has facilitated dialogue within the Ejército de Liberación Nacional (ELN) and tries to use his diminished influence over the Fuerzas Armadas Revolucionarias de Colombia (FARC) to prevent Colombia from becoming a disaster. Mexico, for its part, oscillates between support and distance—in recent years, Mexican diplomacy has attempted to differentiate itself from Colombia, and with eyes on Washington, emphasizes the difference between both countries in the area of drugs and insurgency.

Moving to the south of Colombia, Bolivia silently accompanies the United States (it will receive US$110 million dollars from Plan Colombia and Clinton requested total pardon of its US$4.500 million dollar foreign debt). Chile waits on the sidelines, without categorically condemning Washington; in reality, it supports Plan Colombia. Argentinean diplomacy fluctuates between asepsis and skepticism—formally supporting peace but neither doing much for Colombia nor censuring the United States. The southern part of the Southern Cone is geographically distant from the Colombian situation and politically less inclined to vehemently criticize Washington. Its immediate traditional interests do not appear to be at stake—a major strategic error. The enormous instability being precipitated in the Andean world will affect the whole of the region, sooner or later.

Similarly, the positions of Brazil and Venezuela in South America are increasingly convergent, even though motives are not exactly identical. Venezuela has fortified its borders with Colombia. Complex friction and recurring incidents augment a delicate situation: a historic lawsuit in the Gulf of Venezuela, recent separatist manifestations in the Colombian departments of Northern Santander and Vichada, and the convergence around the "Bolivarian spirit" between Venezuelan President Hugo Chávez and the FARC. In the case of Caracas, multifaceted border disputes weigh as heavily as the danger of the domino effect in the midst of Venezuelan upheaval and the desire for distance from Washington on several fronts.

Brazil has significantly increased the presence of military forces on its borders. A porous border is equally useful to both guerrillas and drug traffickers, while an increasing presence of U.S. advisors in Colombia places the former in a state of serious alert. Metaphorically speaking, "narcos" and "green berets" are perceived as equal threats in a country that has historically been able to define its borders without problems and imminent danger. At the same time, the enormous expansion of drug trafficking in Brazil cannot be minimized—there are clear manifestations of higher levels of consumption and additional transportation routes, as well as new discoveries of illicit crops and more urban violence linked to organized crime.

It is worthwhile emphasizing, however, that Colombia is neither Vietnam nor El Salvador. Direct U.S. military intervention is not on the immediate horizon, although it is true that indirect U.S. military intervention, accompanied by a gradual implementation of a diplomatic-military cordon around Colombia, is evolving and becoming more complex. However, unarmed Colombian men and women have no need for the Vietnam or El Salvador paradigm; what Colombia requires is a new Contadora to politically settle its internal war.

Bush and Bogota

The appointment, by U.S. President George W. Bush (2000–2004), of individuals responsible for significant aspects of international and hemispheric policy development, placed Colombia on alert and Latin America in a situation requiring reflection. The profile of several of these functionaries, who have significant influence in the conduct of Washington's foreign affairs, provokes concern and generates uncertainty. Their personalities, background, and opinions suggest retrenchment in matters of peace and ambiguity on issues of drug trafficking. Contradiction and obstinacy intermingle in each of them and will confusedly influence official bilateral relationships and complicate a solution to Colombia's vital problems. All of this may also negatively exacerbate inter-American relations and obstruct hemispheric advances in commercial negotiations.

The spectrum of prominent decision-makers can be divided into six categories. On the one hand, we find crusaders like John Ashcroft (Attorney General, Department of Justice), Asa Hutchison (Director of the DEA[10]), and John Walters (Anti-Drug Czar) who constitute a group of moral extremists pushing Colombia to undertake a "war against drugs" until the last Colombian drops. On the other, there are the recalcitrant, like John Negroponte (U.S. Representative at the UN), Otto Reich (Assistant Secretary of State for Western Hemispheric Affairs[11]) and Roger Noriega (U.S. Permanent Representative at the Organization of American States, OAS).[12] The background of the first two is colored by their fervent and clandestine promotion of the Nicaraguan contras and their recognized disregard for human rights. Noriega's only merit is having been the right-hand man of the ultraconservative Republican Congressman from North Carolina, Jesse Helms, who led the powerful Senate Foreign Affairs Commission until May 2001.

Similarly, dysfunctional people like Paul O'Neill (former Secretary of Treasury[13]) and Richard Armitage (Deputy Secretary of State) stand out— their behavior has the potential to affect the seriousness of the international fight against drugs. True to form, O'Neill left U.S. main partners, associated with the Organization for Economic Development Cooperation (OEDC), flabbergasted at the beginning of 2001 when he affirmed that Washington would no longer support the efforts of OEDC members to combat "fiscal paradises," which is well known, are major centers for narcotics money laundering. According to several sources, Armitage, who was associated with the Central Intelligence Agency (CIA) in the 1970s, previously proposed the use of heroin to weaken the combat capacity of communists in Indochina and Afghanistan.

At another level, one finds orthodox thinkers like Condoleezza Rice (National Security Advisor) and Paula Dobriansky (Under Secretary for Global Affairs at the Department of State), women who preserve a Cold War mentality centered on Russia and China. For them, Colombia will be increasingly perceived as geopolitically key and representing a dual threat to the power of the United States—ideological (Marxist) and criminal (corrupt). Then there are the hawks like Donald Rumsfeld (Secretary of Defense) and Paul Wolfowitz (Deputy Secretary of Defense) who propose the insurance of the U.S. unipolar power status at whatever cost, and who appear to conceive of regionalizing the treatment of the Colombian situation with a military rather than diplomatic sheen. Finally, the warriors like Richard Cheney (vice-president) stand out. As a Congressman, he was a staunch supporter of Oliver North in the Iran–Contras affair and later, as Secretary of Defense under George Bush senior, the architect of the "sea blockade" around Colombia in January 1990. Within this scenario, the Secretary of State, Colin Powell, appears, at the outset of the George W. Bush administration to be the least warlike and the most moderate. However confusion should be avoided for they are all quite similar; they have similar mind-sets and reference codes more appropriate to the Cold War era than to an era of globalization, and they are, at the end of the day, more ideological than pragmatic. They are to be located much closer to the right than the center and they appear to be more susceptible to heavyhandedness than to deliberation; they project the ominous threat of force rather than prudent diplomacy; and they wish to ensure the economic primacy, the military self-sufficiency, and the unilateral political position of the United States to the detriment of a balanced multipolar, multilateral, and stable scheme of affairs. The future of Colombian–U.S. ties will be conditioned by the balance of power and the action strategies that these actors and their respective bureaucracies put in place. From this perspective, the future does not look promising. The combined effects of Washington's policies toward Bogota, and the Colombian and Andean situation on the inter-American system, is notorious. A future of intensified war and abundant drugs will only cause more human rights violations, more displacement, more militarization, more environmental degradation, more corruption and more drug trafficking, as well as less investment, less stability, less governability, less security, and less economic growth for South America.

Therefore, systematic monitoring of Washington's policies toward Bogota is paramount. President Bush's administration team presented the Andean Initiative for Congressional consideration in 2001. As a result of changes introduced in the House of Representatives and the Senate, this US$882.3 million initiative for the fight against drugs was reduced to US$731 million at the beginning of 2002. It combines something of the "carrot" (US$291 million in social and economic assistance) and a lot of "stick" (US$440 million in antinarcotics and security assistance), and reflects continuity between present government policy and that of Bill Clinton in terms of indirect but conclusive involvement in the Colombian crisis.[14]

The new Republican strategy has three fundamental goals: consolidate the offensive war-preparedness dimension of the Washington version of Plan Colombia; "Americanize" the war against drugs in the northern part of South America; and consolidate a diplomatic-military security cordon around Colombia. On the one hand, the strategy indicates persistent U.S. concern for, and clear interest in, strengthening the military capacity of the Colombian state; while on the other, it is an attempt to significantly concentrate a common punitive antidrug policy based on militant prohibition in the area around Colombia. The complete prohibitionist package tends—as has already been the case in Colombia and Mexico—to include demands for criminalization, militarization, fumigation, interdiction, and extradition to be taken seriously. Finally, it attempts to co-opt Washington's allies (Panama, Ecuador, and Bolivia), convince the Plan Colombia vacillators (Peru), and pressure opponents (Brazil and Venezuela) to accept the U.S. strategy for drug trafficking and counterinsurgency.[15] The goal is to build a circle of contention and coercion around Colombia.

The Andean Initiative, therefore, reinforces Plan Colombia; secures a vision that reinforces repression against the lucrative drug trade in areas of cultivation, processing, and trafficking; and strengthens a ring of potential control around Colombia in the eventuality of uncontrollable internal implosion.

In this context, U.S. policy toward Colombia could include two phases or components that are not necessarily mutually exclusive. The Bush government could further politicize the Colombia situation, assuming, for example, that the real threat in the country emanates not only from drug trafficking and organized crime, but from an insurgency that is economically, territorially, and militarily strong. At the end of the day, all would intertwine and blur together—guerrillas, terrorism, and organized drug-crime would become, relatively speaking, the same thing. The United States could promise additional military, technical, and intelligence assistance with the breakdown of the political dialogue with the FARC, and in order not to appear to be sabotaging peace in Colombia, Washington could agree to the initiation of talks with a weakened ELN. In short, this first phase is cheap—the Colombians shoot on one side and promote dialogue on the other, while the United States intervenes indirectly with more war assistance, avoiding its own military casualties.

Should this strategy fail, the design of a second broader phase would commence. In this scenario, interventionist strategies increase and begin with the more sophisticated use of military and interdiction technology: experimentation with new arms (as in the case of Iraq, Bosnia, and Kosovo); massive fumigation of illicit crops; capture of guerrillas, drug traffickers, and paramilitary in third countries, at sea, or on the country's porous borders (Panama and Ecuador preferentially); increased presence of mercenaries disguised as private security companies (already contemplated in the U.S. version of Plan Colombia); and higher numbers of advisors on the ground. Gradually, more extensive militarized intervention in Colombian affairs would become legitimate. And for this to happen, Washington would need to build an *ad hoc* Latin American coalition to accompany its strategy.

After September 11, 2001

The infamous terrorist attacks of September 11, 2001 against the twin towers of the World Trade Center in New York and against the Pentagon in Washington mark the end of one era in world politics and ushers in a new stage in international relations. In a tragic and symbolic manner, the post–Cold War era came to an end. This hiatus of only one decade between the prolonged Cold War and a vaguely distinguishable future scheme, terminated in a way that causes concern.

Immediately, George W. Bush announced the initiation of a "new war," characterized by its nonconventional nature, nearly unlimited prolongation, planetary scope, and annihilating tendencies. In his presentation—put into practice with the counterattack against Afghanistan—two elements should be pointed out. First, the prospect of a future "day after the war" when the conquerors declare victory and agree to build a new world order disappears. The fact that Washington and not the UN Security Council announced the commencement of the "war against terrorism" implies that the United States reserves the right to inform the world when the objective of armed confrontation has been met. In this sense, it is worth noting that countries operating with a utilitarian rationale, looking for supposed favors for supporting the United States, are mistaken: conviction rather than opportunism is what eventually will be rewarded when the elusive end to terrorism is achieved.

Second, with his arguments, Bush wiped out the distinction between war and peace. If the confrontation against terrorism is unlimited in time and geographic scope, peace becomes diluted in the constant of war, and a period of "Hot Peace" begins. The Cold War between two superpowers—the United States and the Soviet Union—had game rules and only a slight possibility of becoming a direct and massive conflict. Hot Peace among several states, illegal transnational groups, and rebel forces using indiscriminate violence lacks game rules and has a high probability of producing a countless number of victims.

The call to the international "war against terrorism" begs the question of how to wage a nontraditional battle given that the terrorist phenomenon embodies an asymmetrical conflict in which, paradoxically, the greatest advantages are on the side of the weaker actor who chooses the instrument, place, moment, and objective of its acts of force. The United States, like many other countries, has coexisted within this asymmetrical situation, and in fact, the strategy practiced since the 1980s by Washington against international terrorism was embedded in this complex dynamic of asymmetry. The architect of the strategy was the father of the actual President of the United States, George Bush, who, in his position as vice-president in the Ronald Reagan government, directed the 1985 Task Force on Combating Terrorism. The conclusions of his report guided U.S. public policy from 1986 until 2000 and his four fundamental principles were: terrorism constituted a "potential threat against U.S. national security"; states that provided refuge to terrorism should have to suffer the "consequences" of their decisions; Washington will make "no concessions" to terrorism; and the government of the United States will combat terrorism "without sacrificing basic freedoms nor endangering democratic principles."

After the September 11 attacks, confronting asymmetrical conflict has moved to the center of international debate. Two alternatives are being proposed. The model that the Bush administration appears to prefer is one that attempts to reach a state of symmetry with the opponent. The fundamental principle is to make international terrorism—redefined today as a lethal threat against national security—impractical. This aspiration implies that the most powerful actor becomes as treacherous as the weakest. Improving the capacity of good intelligence gathering, increasing universal cooperation in the antiterrorism struggle, applying additional sanctions against states that harbor international terrorism, and fomenting ostracism against those that stimulate terrorist groups are not the only elements involved. The strategy also involves reducing civil liberties with the objective of eventually improving security, legitimizing clandestine assassinations, moving ahead with the annihilation of suspected terrorists, ignoring norms of international human rights law, and privatizing the fight against terrorist groups. The foreseeable outcome is a weakening of democracy within and beyond the United States. It will be the Huntington of the "waves of Democracy" (Huntington 1991) rather than the one of the "clash of civilizations" (Huntington 1996), the one that was right: democratic advances can be slowed down and even reversed. The "third wave of democracy" mentioned by Huntington will dissipate in the sands of the "war against terrorism."

A second model contemplated by European specialists, for example, would be directed to overcoming asymmetry in a longer time frame, and with other than repressive measures. In this case, an attempt would be made to render terrorism improbable, unnecessary, and illegitimate. To accomplish this, dissuasion, development, and dialogue are required. Military and political dissuasion obviously corresponds to the role of the state and implies additional prevention, intelligence, and sophistication. The effect of dissuasion is to make terrorist behavior improbable.

Political, social, and economic development involves the state as well as the private sector. If terrorism is to become unnecessary, improvements in the concrete living conditions of millions of people must be realized, both in the Arab world and in the periphery. Finally, dialogue lies within the purview of the nonstate sector—nongovernmental organizations, political parties, the churches, and youth, among many others. Closer proximity and communication among cultures, religions, and civilizations are urgently required if resorting to terrorism is to be illegitimated. The potential result of this alternative could be the gradual and effective reduction of terrorism within the parameters of a moderate process of democratization with greater international impact.

However, whichever model predominates for dealing with asymmetric conflicts, the strategic scenario in Colombia changed drastically after September 11. Colombia became the main reference point for hemispheric insecurity. And with each passing day, Colombians will have less time to define their armed conflict in political terms and will endure increasing pressure to define it in criminal terms. There are two choices: preserve some essential spaces for reinitiating a notably different type of negotiation with a guerrilla force of Marxist origins that preserves its characterization as a political interlocutor, or consolidate conditions leading to an essentially military confrontation against the terrorist enemy of whatever ideological stripe.

Externally, the limits and range of one or the other options for Colombia will be determined by three phenomena. First, the final results of U.S. military action in the Middle East need to be observed. It is likely that, in addition to a massive attack involving enormous technological display, a new modality of armed confrontation combining elements of conventional with guerrilla warfare within a long-term framework will emerge. If this exercise in the use of force is successful in terms of the objective being met (the disarticulation of terrorist enclaves) and in relation to the legitimacy gained (its proportionality and precision receive broad worldwide support), experimentation in other countries identified as fertile territory for terrorism will be very possible.

Second, the debates in Washington around Plan Colombia, after the first phase of the counterattack initiated by the United States against international terrorism, will have to be carefully analyzed. In this sense, it is not surprising that Plan Colombia shifted its fundamental goal as an antidrug plan, in compliance with what the U.S. executive requested and with what the legislature approved in 2000, and became an antiterrorist plan, aimed at combating the FARC and ELN, and even the ultra–right-wing paramilitary, Autodefensas Unidas de Colombia (AUC).

Third, the use of the Inter-American Treaty of Reciprocal Assistance (ITRA), revived by an OAS resolution on September 21, 2001 in support of the United States, needs to be evaluated. Considerable analysis of the unexpected rebirth of this 1947 treaty is required, especially regarding articles 3 and 6 dealing with what the Consultative Organism considers an attack against members of the inter-American defense system and aggressions against a state that are not armed aggressions. They could eventually be invoked in the case of an uncontrollable worsening of the Colombian crisis.

In this sense, two questions arise. On the one hand, if Colombia does not advance toward a resolution of its armed conflict, the country will be left definitively subject to external forces and factors outside its control. On the other, if South America maintains its present contempt for the Colombian situation, the implacable logic that follows is a "war against terrorism" in the heart of the Southern Cone.

A Role for Mercosur in the Uribe Administration?

The greatest dilemma confronting the Colombian president, the Liberal dissident Álvaro Uribe, is the recovery of the authority of the state, or the fall into authoritarianism. The election in which he triumphed had as its central theme "authority," with a focus on the recovery of the state's monopoly of force. With a convincing victory, Uribe (53 percent) obtained 22 percent more votes than his closest contender, the ruling Liberal Horacio Serpa (31 percent)—but not massive—Uribe obtained this total in a vote with only 47 percent electoral participation—it does not seem sensible to interpret the success of Álvaro Uribe as a "blank check" of the grand majority of the citizens in favor of an inflexible policy of "mano dura."[16]

After the first year of administration, the momentous dilemma remains. In essence, Uribe must prevent Colombia from devolving into a failed state, incapable of protecting individuals from the violent forces that threaten them, and guarantee the indispensable legitimacy in order to avoid an institutional collapse.

Resolving this dilemma requires strengthening democratic governability, a principle intersection of the interests of Colombia and South America. If the South Americans—in particular, the Mercosur countries—want to play a positive role in the Colombian situation they must establish basic parameters within which to orient their support. For this, it is indispensable to closely analyze the concrete policies implemented by the Uribe government. The guiding criteria for this inquiry could be what I call the "democratic test." This is a simple test which establishes that all decisions taken by the executive must be evaluated according to their effective contribution to a democratic state. If a governmental decision reaffirms the rule of law, assures the legitimate use of force, protects the human rights of the unarmed or betters the material conditions of society, then the administration passes the test. If, on the contrary, a decision undermines democracy, weakens institutions, destroys achievements reached in the plan of fundamental rights, or favors the interests of a few, the government fails the exam.

This test is consistent with the request by President Uribe to the international community to not put both the government and the guerilla in equal conditions, of curbing the capacity of the insurgents to deploy its "parallel diplomacy," and of criticizing its resort to terror. The states of South America do not endorse the organizations that resort to terrorist practices in Colombia. At the same time, the South American governments want to get to know better the Colombian government, which seeks greater support and assistance.

In this sense, the results of the passing or failing of the democratic test should be categorized. If there are advances that favor the democratic strengthening of the state, then support and external cooperation should increase. If there are excessive retreats in democracy, criticism and the limitation of external support should equally be made known.

The parameters of evaluation of the democratic test should not be dogmatic, nor ideological, but rather rigorous and precise. For example, Uribe's decision to modernize the state could contribute to democracy; nevertheless, various components of the approved Anti-Terrorist Statute undermine it.[17] The Ministry of Defense has presented a transcendental *White Book on Defense and Democratic Security* that contains some principles and plans that could reinforce democracy. However, parallel to this, the Ministry of the Interior and Justice adopted positions and measures that stigmatize the unarmed opposition and antagonize public powers; phenomena that weaken democracy.

A Final Brief Reflection

In short, to prevent Colombia from becoming a laboratory for different types of military intervention, Latin American countries—especially those of South America—should assume a protagonist role in the resolution of the Colombian crisis through diplomatic measures. The country deserves and requires the kind of political solidarity that was prevalent toward Central America in Contadora rather than the military arrogance displayed by the North Atlantic Treaty Organization (NATO) in Kosovo, the lucubration that invokes putting in place the ITRA, and even less the probability that the most backward sectors in Washington instigate an additional scenario of "war against terrorism" in South America. This would only predict more human insecurity for Colombia and less regional security in the continent.

Notes

* Director of Political Science and International Relations of the Humanities, Department of the University of San Andrés (Victoria, Argentina).

1. On the notion of sphere of influence in international politics, see Keal (1983).
2. On the period of *La Violencia* see Thoumi and Rojas in this volume.
3. Regarding the phenomena of failed states, see Dorff (1996), Gros (1996), Norton and Miskel (1997), Woodward (1999), and Thürer (1999).
4. See Appendix in this volume.
5. More about the initiatives part of Plan Colombia and the allotment of budget for the different programs can be found in the chapter 2 by Bagley and Camacho in this volume.
6. The statistics on U.S. assistance to Colombia can be analyzed in the Appendix of this volume.
7. The George W. Bush designed the US$ 882 million Andean Regional Initiative as a continuation of Plan Colombia. The U.S. Congress, at the same time, is discussing the prolongation of the Andean Trade Preference Act, while the national and international antidrug budget for 2002 included just 31% of the US$19.2 billion for demand reduction. In addition, the Drug Czar John Walters, who was Bennett's right-hand man, has emerged with a renewed "war on drugs" crusade. Colombia reinstated extradition measures after a constitutional reform was passed.
8. The Contadora Group was formed by Colombia, Mexico, Panama, and Venezuela to foster peace negotiations in Central America.
9. It is worthwhile noting that during the twentieth century, of the 39 countries where the United States employed its armed forces in our continent, 38 times the Caribbean Basin served as the theater of operations, and only once in South America (in Bolivia in 1986 with Operation Blast Furnace). For further information, see Grimmett (May 17, 1999).
10. Asa Hutchinson left the Direction of the Drug Enforcement Administration (DEA) and became the Under Secretary for Border and Transportation Security, within the Department of Homeland Security on January 29, 2003.
11. He was named Special Envoy to the Western Hemisphere in November 25, 2002, but has submitted his resignation to the president in May 2004, probably to incorporate himself in the reelection campaign of George W. Bush of 2004.
12. Roger Noriega was appointed Assistant Secretary of State for Western Hemisphere Affairs on March 24, 2003.
13. Paul O'Neill was fired by President George W. Bush in 2003. The current Secretary of Treasure is John Snow.
14. For more on the Andean Regional Initiative see chapter 4 by Camacho and the Appendix by CIP in this volume.
15. Brazil and Venezuela would receive US$12 and US$8 million, respectively, in anti-narcotic and security assistance from the Andean Regional Initiative.
16. While at the beginning of 1998 Colombians demonstrated their saturation with the armed conflict, in the 2002 elections the rejection was against a model of negotiation—between the government of President Pastrana and the FARC— seen and lived by the citizens as a costly and dramatic farce. Even though the triumph of Uribe was the expression of weariness in the face of the insurgency, it also demonstrated fatigue of the violence in general.

17. The Anti-Terrorist Statute was passed by the Colombian Congress in December 2003 and contains measures to fight against terrorism.

References

Center for International Policy. Colombia Project. *http://ciponline.org.*

Dorff, Robert H. 1996. Democratization and Failed States: The Challenge of Ungovernability. *Parameters* (Summer): 17–31.

Grimmett, Richard. May 17, 1999. Instances of Use of United States Armed Forces Abroad, 1798–1999. *CRS Report for Congress.*

Gros, Jean-Germain. 1996. Toward a Taxonomy of Failed States in the New World Order: Decaying Somalia, Liberia, Rwanda, and Haiti. *Third World Quarterly* 17: 455–71.

Huntington, Samuel P. 1991. *The Third Wave: Democratization in the Late Twentieth Century.* Norman: University of Oklahoma Press.

———. 1996. *The Clash of Civilizations and the Remaking of World Order.* New York: Simon & Schuster.

Keal, Paul E. 1983. Contemporary Understanding about Spheres of Influence. *Review of International Studies* 9.

Norton, R.J. and J.F. Miskel. 1997. Spotting Trouble: Identifying Faltering & Failing States". *Naval War College Review* (Spring): 79–91.

Oquist, Paul. 1978. *Violencia, conflicto y política en Colombia.* Bogotá: Banco Popular Library.

Reno, William. 2000. Economic Motivations of Warfare in Collapsed States. *National Strategy Forum Review* 10 (Winter).

Serafino, Nina M. June 13, 2001. Colombia: U.S. Assistance and Current Legislation. *CRS Report to Congress.*

Thürer, Daniel. 1999. The Failed State and International Law. *International Review of the Red Cross* 836 (December): 731–61.

U.S. Commission on National Security/21st Century. 2001. *Road Map for National Security: Addendum on Structure and Process Analyses. Seeking a National Strategy. A Concert for Preserving and Promoting Freedom. The Phase II Report on a U.S. National Security Strategy for the 21st Century.* Washington: U.S. Commission on National Security. *http://www.nssg.gov* (consulted on October 7, 2003).

Walters, Barbara F. 2002. *Committing to Peace: The Successful Settlement of Civil Wars.* Princeton: Princeton University Press.

Woodward, Susan L. 1999. Failed States: Warlordism and Tribal Warfare. *Naval War College Review* (Spring).

Zartman, I. William, ed. 1995. *Collapsed States: The Disintegration and Restoration of Legitimate Authority.* Boulder, Colorado: Lynne Rienner Publisher.

PART 2

Ripples Through the Region

CHAPTER 4

Plan Colombia and the Andean Regional Initiative: The Ups and Downs of a Policy

Álvaro Camacho Guizado[*]

Introduction

Undoubtedly, one of the issues that have contributed most significantly to defining Colombian political perspectives and its international relations, especially with the United States and the countries of the Andean Region, is the so-called Plan Colombia. The most ambitious plan ever of U.S. government cooperation with Colombia, through which an enormous military, financial, and political effort has been put into place to eradicate the production of illicit crops—cocaine and heroin—will have resounding consequences for the configuration of Colombian policy vis-à-vis these crops. In a very significant way, it will also affect "irregular" organizations that challenge the country's institutional stability through armed struggle.

It becomes clear that a plan of this magnitude will also affect Colombian perspectives at the international level regarding both aspects of the conflict. Within the realm of possibilities is the expansion of illicit crops to neighboring countries, to varying degrees of course, as is the possibility of the relative failure of the Plan in Colombia. This will result in new orientations in U.S. policy toward the country.

To substantiate my arguments, I would like to touch on several topics, the first referring to the significant changes that have taken place in the structure of narcotrafficking. I begin with the first half of the 1990s, a period characterized principally by the dismantling of the so-called Cali and Medellin "cartels"—the major axis for the production and export of illicit drugs. The second describes how changes in narcotrafficking organizations have, at the same time, been accompanied by modifications in the overall thrust of political action—illegal business managers have established alliances with numerous landowners and other powerful social sectors in order to finance armed paramilitary organizations of the extreme right. On a parallel track, a third process is related to the changes in the demand structure for illicit drugs. This change is identified by the role such drugs play in the financing of irregular organizations and the war in Colombia. The fourth is a brief description of the nature of Plan Colombia and its relationship to President Andrés Pastrana's original proposal. The fifth refers to President George W. Bush's response to similar demands presented by the Andean countries, articulated in the Andean Regional Initiative. And finally, I speculate about several possible perspectives these new initiatives may generate, especially in reference to their organizational dynamic and their effects in the region, above all in Colombia.

Changes in Narcotrafficking Structures in Colombia

The decline of the large Colombian organizations, consequence of the death of Pablo Escobar, the capture of the Rodríguez Orejuela brothers, and the relatively erratic survival of the so-called "Cartel" of the Norte del Valle, has resulted fundamentally in a profound change in the composition of these organizations.[1] Instead of a monopolistic structure, one encounters fragmented organizations whose size fluctuates between 15 and 25 members, to the point that the National Police calculate that there may be between 200 and 300 groups of Colombian traffickers.

Another important change is related to the physiognomy of the organizations; they involve young drug traffickers, better educated than their predecessors, relatively inconspicuous, who have diversified routes and export techniques that are difficult to detect. For this reason, their dismantling and capture is much more problematic.

Parallel to this fragmentation, there has been a notable increase in the area under cultivation, and consequentially, in the supply of cocaine and heroin. Since 1998 an area of 35,000 hectares sown with coca in Colombia has expanded to 160,000 hectares and 6,200 hectares of poppy. This recent increase has coincided *grosso modo* with the number of hectares fumigated under Plan Colombia, so that for each hectare fumigated, another comes into production.

The new traffickers have strengthened former as well as new links with international organizations, especially in Mexico and Europe. Regarding Mexico, it is interesting to note that the Colombians, given the magnitude and size of their organizations, lack the operational capacity to control the entire marketing cycle. As a result of lessons learned from the failures of their predecessors, they do not try, at least directly, to influence national policy. In this sense, they are not political enemies of the Colombian state. The new organizations are, above all, forms of highly organized economic delinquency; however, by defending their business, they do not represent a direct political threat to the national government, as did the former powerful entrepreneurs of the business who, either through narcoterrorism or through penetration of state structures, confronted and accelerated the dismantling of the state itself.

Narcotrafficking and Violence

What is not implied in this analysis is that drug traffickers are totally absent from national politics. Rather, involvement in this terrain is realized through their activities as financiers of extreme right-wing armed paramilitary organizations. Contrary to their predecessors, the most noteworthy form of political action of present-day drug dealers consists of establishing relations with the wealthy and powerful of society who respond to guerrilla threats by organizing and financing the right-wing paramilitary. This kind of alliance is useful not only for protecting their fortunes as landowners and property-owners, but also to seek legitimacy as defenders of the interests of the dominant classes in Colombia. There are many legal business people who consider an alliance with drug traffickers as the preferred option for confronting threats directed at them by insurgent organizations.

In this sense, the political role of narcotrafficking has been displaced: no longer is it the action of the narcoterrorists who plants a bomb, or kills state employees, journalists, or political leaders opposed to them; nor is it the person who tries to penetrate the state in order to influence political decisions in his favor. Although such activity is still visible, it happens with much less force than previously. Today's threat is of another kind, involving, basically but not exclusively, the creation of a third armed force in the conflict, a force designed to confront insurgent groups and whose preferred method consists of massacring peasants and social leaders whom the paramilitary suspect of being auxiliaries of the guerrilla.

Paradoxically, these organizations, while pretending to support state institutionality and the existing political regime, have moved over to the side of terrorism with their criminal activity. The result is increasing threats to the very institutionality and order they propose to defend. Both the Colombian and U.S. governments have recognized this fact:

> A wealth of evidence exists to demonstrate that the self-defense groups contribute to the degradation of the Colombian situation by attacking the civilian population, especially peasants and the poorest. Although not well known, the self-defense groups also attack functionaries of the state and political leaders [. . .] The assassination of civilians and so-called massacres, combined with other forms of terror and attack against the civilian population, are recognized war strategies of the self-defense groups and constitute violations of international humanitarian law [. . .] They resort on many occasions to the horrific practice of massacre; they assassinate and provoke the disappearance and displacement of thousands of defenseless civilians, especially unarmed peasants, workers, and other people living in rural areas. The self-defense groups and the guerrillas justify the killing of civilians by defining them as adversaries and consequently, as military objects. (Observatory for Human Rights and International Humanitarian Law 2000, 3–4)

New Forms of Demand

Such processes have been simultaneously accompanied by a phenomenon involving changes in the international demand structure for cocaine and heroin. Here, the most important change to be observed is the intensification and diversification of markets—demand in the United States has tended to decrease, as declared by the U.S. Department of State:

> We have seen positive results from our collective efforts. According to present calculations, existing levels of consumption (that is to say, use of an illicit drug during the previous month) among people 12 years old and over stands at nearly 13.9 millions US citizens, or 6.4 percent of the population. This figure represents a decrease of more than 50 percent since 1979 when 14.1 percent of U.S. citizens were defined as drug users. [n.d., 1]

At the same time, European demand is on the rise and Colombian exporters are increasingly privileging export to these markets.

In Colombia, on the other hand, demand has diversified. What in previous years was mainly the purchase of production by narcotraffickers for export, as an economic activity, has been radically transformed. Today in

Colombia a three-pronged demand model has, in effect, been consolidated. First, there is the traditional type developed directly by drug traffickers in their role as business people. Second, the relatively marginal activity of the Fuerzas Armadas Revolucionarias de Colombia (FARC) who impose taxes on direct producers and first-rung intermediaries in the commercial chain has been transformed today into pressure which, united to the third, that of paramilitary groups presently organized under the banner of the so-called Autodefensas Unidas de Colombia (AUC), increasingly drives the dynamic of cocaine and heroin production (Aranguren 2001). From income received in this fashion, the irregular organizations finance their troops, and more significantly, they acquire arms for their struggle. As a result, Colombian drug trafficking is now linked not only with consumer markets, but also has well-established relations with international organizations involved in the illegal arms trade. In this way, two of the most powerful worldwide mafias are linked. In recent years, therefore, illicit drugs have become fundamental for fuelling the internal Colombian conflict and have put the country on the radar screen of the justice systems of other countries and of international justice organizations.

Plan Colombia

These fundamental modifications in the structure, dynamics, and significance of the drug trade in Colombia are at the root of changes witnessed in U.S. policy toward Colombia. After the decade of the 1970s, due to crop development and the export of marijuana to the United States, and later with the increased production and export of cocaine, the central policy of the United States toward Colombia has been to exert constant pressure for the eradication of these crops and suspension of their shipment (Camacho 1988; Tokatlian 1997, 2000). Nevertheless, pressure for change in internal political configurations did not constitute a fundamental part of this policy. Only after accusations indicating that the election of President Ernesto Samper appeared to have been favored by financing from the Cali "Cartel," did the Clinton administration opt for toughening its policy. As such, it proceeded to decertify Colombia on two occasions, revoked President Samper's visa, and radicalized its criticisms of the Colombian government. As part of the policy for the direct fight against drugs, given the changes described in the nature of the narcotrafficking organizations, the Clinton administration proceeded to strengthen the Colombian National Police Force and to build up its capacity for the task of eradicating the production of coca and heroin by means of aerial fumigation.

With the arrival of Andrés Pastrana in the Presidency in 1998, U.S. policy underwent another modification. Pastrana publicly presented its Development Plan, *Change in order to Build Peace, 1998–2002*, which in essence constituted the principle axis of presidential policy. The heart of the Plan was based on recognition of the need for economic development as the basis for achieving peace; for institutional strengthening; for human capital development through education; for the strengthening of social capital through the promotion of associative enterprises; for defense of the environment; and the substitution of illicit crops.

My purpose is not to go into details concerning the process that led to Pastrana's Development Plan being subjected to fundamental changes during negotiations between the Colombian and U.S. governments.[2] Suffice it to say that there were significant differences between the original versions and the final result known today as Plan Colombia. The first version, included in the Development Plan as Plan Colombia pointed out

that the policy for peace involved political reform, negotiation with armed groups, and investments and actions for peace, among which "the putting in place" of a special plan for economic, social and environmental reconstruction in areas most affected by the conflict was included— Plan Colombia. (García 2001, 200)

Regarding illicit crop policy, the Plan contemplated that:

The government has structured Plan Colombia to push forward action on three fronts: substitution of illicit crops by means of alternative development programs, attention to the problem of the displaced, and priority and focalized attention in areas where violence has become critical. (García 2001, 200)

Later on, based on its presentation to the U.S. Department of State and on suggestions from functionaries, the Plan underwent substantial modifications. In reality, the version submitted to the U.S. Senate is the *Plan for Peace, Prosperity and Strengthening of the State* (Oficina del Presidente de la República de Colombia 1999),[3] which in synthesis includes the following ten strategies:

- Development of policies to deal with employment, to strengthen the state's tax-collection capacity, and to expand international trade, accompanied by improved access to external markets, a crucial factor in the modernization of Colombia's economic base.

- Application of an austerity plan combined with fiscal and financial adjustments in order to promote economic activity and to recover Colombia's prestige in international financial markets.
- Initiation of peace negotiations with insurgent groups based on territorial integrity, democracy, and human rights, in such a way that it becomes possible to develop the rule of law and the struggle against narcotrafficking.
- Implementation of a program for restructuring and modernizing the Armed Forces and Police in order to guarantee the rule of law and to provide security throughout the nation, all the while ensuring strict adherence to human rights and international humanitarian law.
- Development of a plan for strengthening the justice system and human rights, with the objective of reaffirming the rule of law and of assuring equal and impartial justice for all.
- Implementation of an antinarcotics strategy, together with other countries affected by the problem, in order to combat all links in the illicit drug cycle and to prevent the product of this illicit trade from fueling the violence of the insurgent and other armed organizations.
- Support for alternative development by implementing agricultural proposals and viable economic ventures that include protection of the environment in areas of tropical forest, and the fight against the expansion of illicit crops in the Amazon Basin and in vast areas of natural parks. The strategy includes sustainable, integral, and participatory production projects, and provides special attention to regions that combine a high incidence of conflict with low levels of state presence, fragile levels of social capital, and serious degradation of the environment, such as the Magdalena Medio, the Colombian Macizo, and the southwestern part of Colombia.
- Encouragement of increased social participation in programs developed by local governments, committing communities to anticorruption initiatives and constant pressure on armed actors, so that kidnapping, violence, and internal displacement of individuals and communities can be overcome. This strategy includes collaboration with local business people and labor groups with the goal of promoting innovative production models and the strengthening of formal and nonformal institutions that encourage change in cultural norms fomenting violence. It also contemplates the promotion of pedagogical mechanisms and programs in order to increase tolerance, essential values of peaceful coexistence, and participation in public affairs.
- Implementation of a program of human development that guarantees appropriate health and educational services for all vulnerable groups of the Colombian population.

- Emphasis on international coresponsibility regarding the drug problem, integrated actions, and balanced treatment of all the links in the chain. This strategy considers that the role of the international community is extremely important in the peace process, in accordance with the terms of international law, and with the consent of the Colombian government.

In order to put the Plan into practice, the Colombian government designed a financial strategy, the total cost of which was US$7.5 million, with the Colombian government providing US$4.0 million, the United States US$1.58 billion, multilateral agencies US$1.0 billion, and Europe and other countries US$1.0 billion.

Later on, and due especially to pressures from the Republican lobby in the U.S. Congress and from the Clinton administration, the Plan underwent substantial changes. In essence, what had been a development plan was transformed primarily into an antinarcotics strategy. The eradication of illicit crops, which had been the exclusive purview of the National Police, was reinforced by the conformation of three antinarcotics battalions for the Armed Forces with the corresponding military equipment—helicopters, planes, arms, munitions, and other complementary resources—charged with confronting irregular armed groups protecting illicit crops.

The Plan's antinarcotics strategy can be summed up under the following objectives:

Strengthen the Fight Against Narcotrafficking and Dismantle its Organizations Through Integrated Efforts Directed by the Armed Forces. (1) combat illicit crop production through continuous and systematic action by the Army and Police especially in Putumayo and the south of the country, fortifying the capacity of the Police to eradicate such crops; (2) establish military control over the south of the country for the purpose of eradication [. . .]; (3) reestablish government control over key drug-producing areas.

Strengthen the Justice System and Fight Corruption. (1) strengthen the institutions of the Attorney General's Office, the courts, the Ombudsman's Office, especially human rights units; (2) reinforce and train technical investigation units; (3) support anticorruption groups [. . .]; (4) reform the incarceration system; (5) apply extradition laws; and (6) implement a proposal to use verbal testimony in criminal cases [. . .] and elaborate rules for criminal procedures [. . .].

Neutralize the Narcotraffickers' Financial System and Confiscate their Resources. (1) strengthen anticontraband efforts; (2) undertake an aggressive program for the confiscation of assets; (3) freeze and confiscate bank accounts and assets in Colombia and abroad.

Neutralize and Combat Perpetrators of Violence Allied with Narcotraffickers. (1) increase security against kidnapping, extortion, and terrorism; (2) prevent the acquisition of arms by those groups benefiting from the drug trade, through coordinated international efforts.

Integrate National Initiatives with Regional and International Efforts. (1) share information and intelligence with other security agencies in the country; (2) support and coordinate with regional and international operations and efforts.

Strengthen and Extend Alternative Development Plans in Areas Affected by Narcotrafficking. (1) offer opportunities for alternative employment and social services to the population living in areas of cultivation; (2) promote mass information campaigns concerning the danger of illicit drugs (Oficina del Presidente de la República de Colombia 1999).

Transformations in the Plan

An examination of these objectives and the priority assigned to them in the Plan, reveals that the first modification suffered by the Colombian government initiative was the transformation of a development plan into a primarily antinarcotics plan.[4] In 2000, the U.S. Congress approved US$1.3 billion for the Andean Region, of which US$862.3 million were designated to Colombia (the remainder going to Peru, Ecuador, and Bolivia). The remainder, US$218 million, is reserved for alternative development, support of the displaced population, judicial reform, the strengthening of justice, and the promotion of human rights.

Objective four of the antinarcotics strategy is key to understanding how the transition from a policy of crop substitution and alternative development to a military strategy to fight insurgent groups took place. By signaling the functions, responsibilities, and resources assigned to different government departments, it becomes clear that the Armed Forces were primarily assigned the task of combating insurgents, paramilitary groups, and criminal organizations as top priority. Recalling that the U.S. government had been insisting on the characterization of the insurgency as "narcoguerrillas" (Camacho 1988), the significance of this militarization of the antinarcotics struggle is well understood.

In synthesis, the new strategy has two dimensions: on the one hand, it is a question of preventing the FARC from protecting illicit crops or from supposedly defending their own crops; and on the other, it is an attempt to reduce this organization's sources of funding. Later on, due to the growth of the paramilitary organizations, and to their own recognition that they also generate profits from narcotrafficking and control production areas, the U.S. and Colombian authorities proposed that the radius of the Plan be broadened in order to direct it against such organizations. Until now, however, aerial fumigation has been concentrated in the area of Putumayo, a stronghold of the FARC.

Since the end of 2001, and given the worsening of the armed conflict, President Pastrana insisted that the destination of assistance contemplated in the Plan was not to be limited exclusively to combating narcotrafficking. In practice this means that the Plan's entire military, logistical, and financial apparatus could be reoriented to the counterinsurgency struggle. Pastrana's arguments are designed to prove to the United States that the Colombian guerrillas' terrorist activities affect the export of Colombian oil to the United States (Colombia occupies the tenth place in the orders of suppliers of crude to the United States). Therefore, Pastrana requested that U.S. military personnel trained Colombians in the protection of oil installations, several of which are owned by American companies (World Associated Press January 23, 2002). One could speculate whether an appeal to concrete business interests instead of the traditional rhetoric about the war on drugs, political stability, and peace in Colombia will bear fruit. In any case, this new twist in reasoning is noteworthy.

Given that this modification implies a change in the original legal provisions of the U.S. Congress, debates within this body intensified in 2002 and the Colombian Ambassador in Washington, Luis Alberto Moreno (1998 to date) has been taking forceful initiatives in this regard (*El Espectador* January 20, 2002).

Although it is early to make a concrete prognosis, two historical facts indicate that this tendency may be the route to be followed. On the one hand, the existence of a waiver, by which the President of the United States can bypass, with justification, the ban on providing funds to units of the Armed Forces accused of involvement in human rights violations, may be one path for introducing new exceptions to the original limits of the Plan. And a worsening of the conflict in Colombia could very well justify such a measure.

Second, two significant studies point in the same direction. One of them from the Rand Corporation (Rabasa and Chalk 2001), an influential think-tank of U.S. researchers, suggests that the United States ought to reconsider whether the distinction between antinarcotics policies and counterinsurgency policies is sustainable, and if Colombia and its allies will be successful in the war against drugs if the Colombian government cannot exert territorial control. As a consequence, according to the authors of the study, the main effort of the Colombian government should be directed toward overcoming a focus on criminality related to drugs and should substitute it for a political–military strategy (Rabasa and Chalk 2001). The other study, authored at the Hoover Organization, another influential think-tank shaping U.S. policy, puts forward a similar point of view. According to them, the principle weakness of U.S. policy toward Colombia is the separation between the antinarcotics and the counterinsurgency struggle. They maintain that the only way to be successful is to cut existing links between organized crime and political subversion (Buscaglia and Ratliff 2001).

In addition, a sector of the Republican caucus in the U.S. Congress has exerted pressure in the same direction. All of which is to say that there is a series of influential forces that may strongly influence this change in the overall thrust of Plan Colombia. This third modification is undoubtedly as relevant as the former and greatly contributes to further complicating the already complex panorama of the Colombian armed conflict.

A First Evaluation of the Plan

In August 2001, the Office of the Comptroller General of the Republic (CGR), the state organism charged with control over the use of the financial resources of the Nation, published a first evaluation report of Plan Colombia. It is worth quoting *in extenso*:

From this first effort of the CGR, the following conclusions are briefly outlined:

- New resources, available in July 2001, only amount to US$2.051 billion dollars, which is to say, about 27 percent of the total amount envisioned in the Plan. This means that success in the short term, of the initially defined goal of US$7.5 billion dollars, will be difficult to reach.
- Nearly 58 percent of the resources obtained for the Plan is the result of internal and external debt, an unadvisable strategy given the critical situation of the national public debt.
- In general, the goals of the socioeconomic programs are modest vis-à-vis current needs, meaning that objectives end up being rhetorical. The majority of foreseeable activities are of an assistentialist nature, which means low probability for self-sustainability—they respond to a sense of emergency rather than the self-directed generation of resources.
- Up until now, forced eradication has not been a disincentive for the expansion of illicit crops. It would seem that the incentive to produce responds more to the powerful stimulus of a wealthy market rather than to losses provoked by eradication. Consequently, the study of other methods for the eradication of illicit crops becomes highly recommendable.

• Huge differences exist among diverse information sources regarding calculations about direct investment by the Colombian state in the antidrugs struggle. According to the National Narcotics Body, such activity has signified an expenditure of approximately US$2.5 billion during the past six years (1995–2001), while other entities estimate much greater sums. As a result, combined efforts among diverse actors are required to determine the reality of the situation. From whatever angle, the sums removed from the provision of goods and services for citizens' well-being are huge.

• The environmental component has not received adequate consideration, to the point that aerial fumigation for illicit crop eradication does not include, as is required by law, a management plan minimizing or mitigating environmental damage. It would seem that the crop substitution programs have not taken environmentally sustainable agriculture alternatives into consideration.

• It is conceivable that 50 percent of what is forecast in the Plan will not be completed during the tenure of the Pastrana administration. For this reason, effective continuity and implementation will require the explicit commitment of the next government and more vigorous collaboration from the international community, especially from European countries. (Oficina de la Contraloría General de la República, 2001, 4–5)

The panorama, to say the least, is dramatic, not only because the level of implementation has been low, but also because a substantial portion of the resources emanate from public debt, and as a result, further burden the depressed Colombian economy. It is also rather alarming that the Colombian government has assigned significant resources to eradication to the detriment of the satisfaction of other needs of the Colombian population, and that it has done so without meaningful consideration of the environmental effects of aerial fumigation. This report is truly a contrast with the Plan's rhetoric.

The Andean Regional Initiative[5]

It is logical to expect that a plan, like the one described, should affect neighboring countries. On the one hand, it can be assumed that the eradication of Colombian crops means that, if international prices for cocaine and heroin do not fall—the most likely scenario—these crops will be displaced within Colombia's borders, and likewise, to neighboring countries (U.S. Embassy in Colombia 2002, 10). In Peru, in particular, it is feared that producers will recover abandoned plantations and attempt to substitute the supply from

Colombia. And Ecuadorian and Venezuelan authorities fear that resistance to the Plan by the Colombian guerrilla will lead them to cross their borders.

As a response to concerns and pressures from the Andean countries, the Bush administration designed the Regional Andean Initiative, the principal goals of which are: to promote and support democracy and democratic institutions; to foster sustainable economic development and trade liberalization; and to significantly reduce, at source, the supply of illicit drugs in the United States, while at the same time, reducing U.S. demand. The conceptual framework for these goals is derived from the following diagnosis:

> The Andean Region represents a challenge as well as an important opportunity for United States foreign policy during the next few years—significant U.S. national interests are at stake. Democracy is under pressure in all of the Andean countries and doubts increase concerning the capacity of democratic governments to offer basic services and greater prosperity. Economic development is slow and progress towards trade liberalization is inconsistent. The Andes continue to produce virtually all of the world's cocaine and an increasing amount of the heroin, thereby representing a direct threat to our public health and national security. All of these on-going, persistent problems are inter-related. Weak economies produce political malaise that in turn threatens democracy, as well as ensuring a labor force for the production and trafficking of narcotics and for the illegal armed groups. Weak democratic institutions, corruption, and political instability discourage investment, contributing to slow economic growth and providing fertile terrain for the appearance of illicit drug traffickers and other groups operating outside the law. Trade in illicit drugs also has the effect of distorting the economy and discouraging legitimate investment. None of the Region's problems can be resolved on its own. Instead, they must be attacked in a coordinated manner, together with appropriate public diplomatic initiatives, in order to make progress on our goals for the Region. For this reason, the Department of State proposes to designate nearly US$880 million dollars worth of funds from fiscal year 2002 for the Administration's Regional Andean Initiative. (U.S. Embassy in Colombia 2002, 2)

Clearly the central axis of the Initiative is to fight drug trafficking, since it supposedly constitutes a double threat to the United States. On the one hand, exports to the U.S. threaten the public health of citizens; while on the other, such criminal activity destabilizes the Region and creates a problem for national security. As a result, the National Drug Control Strategy constitutes the central part of the Initiative, and by implementing this strategy, the United States hopes to

> reduce the illicit production of coca by 20 percent by the end of 2002 (base year: 1999) and 40 percent by the end of 2007. This includes a reduction by 30 percent in the Colombian production of coca and the elimination of the illegal production of coca in Bolivia by the end of 2002. (U.S. Embassy in Colombia 2002, 8)

In order to meet the proposed goals, US$731 million were assigned to the Initiative, US$399 million (54.48 percent) of which corresponded to Colombia. The military component is designated basically to maintaining the thrust created by Plan Colombia, in other words, to ensuring equipment maintenance, munitions, fuel, training of military and police troops, and the expansion of aerial fumigation of illicit crops (Desde Abajo 2001).

Regarding the military component, the Initiative presumes:

> That the capacity of the Andean Armed Forces to successfully carry out essential missions in support of democratic institutions, to control international borders, and to back up anti-drug efforts, has declined significantly during the [1990s]. In general, the Andean Armed Forces have demonstrated limited capacity to undertake the endeavors required of them. In addition, they are still influenced, to a certain degree, by historic regional rivalries, which do not represent, however, real present-day threats to national security. The majority has to deal with the pressure of deteriorated and obsolete equipment that is continually more difficult and costly to maintain and operate. They would benefit enormously from a modest injection of support for security measures in the form of Foreign Military Financing (FMF) and International Military Education and Training (IMET), and from increased contact with the U.S. military in general. The impact in terms of professionalism, respect for human rights, and combat-readiness, would be appreciable. We need to continue working with the Armed Forces of host countries, the Organization of American States, and the Inter-American Defense Board in order to ensure subordination to legitimate civilian authority, adherence to constitutional norms, and respect for human rights [. . .] (U.S. Embassy in Colombia 2002, 12)

It is still very early to define the course of events that will evolve from the Initiative. Nevertheless, with it, President Bush was trying to show not only his interest in contributing to a reduction in the supply of cocaine and heroin in his country, but also in reaffirming the hegemonic role of the United States in relation to political stability in the region. In reality, by limiting the effort to Colombia, not only does it not satisfy the interests of the other countries, but also leaves the door open for unilateral actions by one of them and the possibility to upset the regional balance of power and stability. It would not be surprising that, in the absence of a financial and political initiative by the United States, one of the Andean countries opted, for example, to reach out to international markets in the search for arms to defend itself against eventual threats emanating from the activities of Plan Colombia.

Finally, the Andean Regional Initiative coincided with the events of September 11, 2001 and their consequences worldwide. Even if the region as such, and the war on drugs, in particular, have lost political space in the list of U.S. government priorities, terrorist activity has produced a relatively strong reaction on the part of the U.S. government as far as the irregular armed groups in Colombia are concerned. Guerrillas and paramilitaries have moved to the front of the list of organizations denominated as terrorist, and fighting them is linked with the U.S. military policy to confront terrorism on a worldwide scale. The relative loss of interest regarding the war against drugs, on the one hand, and the drugs–terrorism link, on the other—operate to produce a precarious balance of interests and efforts. As is to be expected, all of this will have particular repercussions in Colombia and the Andean region, and one of them could be, as indicated above, the reorientation of Plan Colombian financing to the counterinsurgency military struggle. As such, the impact of a decision of this nature in the Andean Regional Initiative and the reactions among countries in the region, are still to be seen.

The International Drug Complex

In this final section, I would like to explore a few ideas of a methodological nature in order to arrive at an approximation of what may be the future of Plan Colombia and the Andean Regional Initiative. I suggest that their conversion could result in a new configuration, different from that referred to as the Industrial Military Complex during the Cold War in the United States (Galbraith 1985).

The Industrial Military Complex is a system whose dynamic is based fundamentally on its own reproduction. Its internal mechanics are geared toward political–military decisions being sustained by the demand for goods, equipment, and personnel, which in turn stimulates industrial production and employment of ex-military personnel and experts. It also represents the reason for the existence of certain state bureaucracies. In this sense, the reproductive needs of the industrial apparatus and of state bureaucracies become important *stimuli* for the development of military war policies. In these conditions, policies tend to reproduce themselves and to have a broader focus, moving beyond even the initial needs.

Referring to the case at hand, the implementation of a model of this type leads one to think that policies associated with the war on drugs, and in particular, with Plan Colombia and the Andean Regional Initiative, could become as addictive as the illicit drugs they attempt to combat (Baum 1997). Consequently, one of my hypotheses is that a step might be taken to complement the International Drug Complex with the Military Industrial Complex.

The notion of an International Drug Complex has been developed by Hans T. Van der Veen (1999), based on the consideration that:

> Just as individuals can become addicted to drug use, so the societies in which we live can become addicts of the profits generated by the drug business. And this would appear to be equally true of the agencies designed to control drugs [. . .] within and between social forces at both extremes of the law, the dynamic is not one of reciprocal control, but rather of mutual reinforcement, either through concerted actions or through more systematic interactions. In this scheme, a "community of interests" develops—a coalition of groups with created psychological, moral, and material interests—between drug managers and state security agencies or the power elites that control them. Such mutual support takes on different forms and is expressed at multiple levels that change with time and space. Nevertheless, the consequence of this collusion is something that advances the interests of both groups to the detriment of the societies in which they appear. According to this focus, the drug industry and the state agencies that pursue it are not necessarily in opposition. Rather they develop a dynamic that is more or less inter-related and interdependent—a kind of "coalition" in which they contradict and support each other and in which the interests of both are served, independent of the democratic control exercised by citizens and sometimes by the government itself.

One of the most visible foundations of the institutionalization of the International Drug Complex, and related to the Industrial Military Complex, is the construction of an ideology, according to which political complementarities between drug traffickers and the Colombian guerrilla go beyond economics. This is expressed by the notion of narcoguerrilla outlined above. Given this relationship, the war on drugs, then, should be centered on the struggle against the insurgent groups. Tasks of supply reduction, traditionally assigned to civilian and police institutions take on new priorities, resulting in the organization of a system of resource, arms, and military personnel provision.

Upon examining the components and tendencies described in Plan Colombia, the stated hypothesis can be sustained if one takes into consideration the prevalence of the military aspects of Plan Colombia over other parts and the allotment of resources for the acquisition of military equipment. This necessarily provokes considerable pressure from the manufacturing industries whose managers rely on their political representatives in the government and the U.S. Congress to obtain prerogatives in the production of the equipment. The same can be said about the numerous organizations of ex-military and ex-members of security bodies, who survive, precisely, on military expenditures. (*Revista Cambio* October 2, 2000; Castro Caycedo 2001)

A Final Reflection

The purpose of the preceding comments is to provide a panorama both of the transformations experienced in Colombian drug trafficking as well as recent policies designed ultimately to confront it. The first point stresses the transformational dynamic adopted by the illegal drug barons whose new organizational structures make them more difficult to detect and combat. As a result, the war against drugs needs to deal with new strategic demands.

And second, the result of the aerial fumigation policy has led to an expansion of illicit crops in other regions of the country, a fact registered by the government of the United States:

Even though we stress our point of view to the region that the corrosive effects of production and trafficking have been spilling over Colombia's borders for years, we do not believe that Plan Colombia results either in the flight of a significant number of refugees, or in a significant increase in trans-border operations by the FARC, ELN or the AUC. We do believe, however, that the result will be an important dislocation of the cocaine industry. Traffickers will undoubtedly try to relocate as their operations in the south of Colombia are disrupted. We believe they will attempt, at first, to relocate in other attractive areas within Colombia, and then try to return to their traditional areas of cultivation in Peru and Bolivia. However, if their operations are contained, they could well attempt to move more crops, processing and/or trafficking routes to other countries like Ecuador, Brazil or Venezuela. (U.S. Embassy in Colombia 2001, 10)

It is nothing more than the implicit recognition that the war against drugs, as presently implemented, is producing a "hydra effect"—the process by which the elimination of one head sprouts many more (Bertram, Sharp, and Andreas 1996). The play between increased repression and higher prices permits such a premonition. And it would appear that a perverse sort of community of interests between militarization of the war on drugs and the interests of narcotraffickers is being created.

As is clearly recognized by both the Colombian and U.S. governments, an inextricable relationship exists between the production of illicit drugs and the poverty of Colombian peasants, and between this production and the expansion of irregular armed groups of the extreme left and right, both of which feed off drug profits. This means that strategies need to be varied and integrated. Even if the initial phase of Plan Colombia stressed poverty eradication and support for alternative development in production areas, the dynamic of U.S. policies accelerated the transformation of the Plan from a socioeconomic to an antinarcotics strategy, with the later introduction of a counterinsurgency component. It is exactly for this reason that the very dynamic of the Industrial Military Complex can be expected to accelerate and combine with that of the International Drug Complex. And the consequences will be an expansion of illicit crops and exacerbation of the Colombian conflict.

It would be preferable, on all accounts, for U.S. policy to concentrate on one of its more useful perspectives, trying to address the problems of the region not separately but in a more comprehensive manner and deploying initiatives of public diplomacy to advance their goals in the region.

Notes

* Álvaro Camacho is Director of the Center for Socio-cultural and International Studies (CESO). Los Andes University, Bogota, Colombia.
1. In this section, I am using the work of López Restrepo and Camacho Guizado, and Pécaut (2001).
2. See details in García (2001), and Ramírez (2001).
3. During the first days of 2000, Andrés Pastrana presented the Plan to the European Union and the government of Japan. In this version, emphasis on military aspects was blurred, the order of priorities was modified and economic and social development took precedence over the antinarotics struggle.
4. Details on designated amounts and component parts are to be found in Desde Abajo (2001).

5. For more information relating to the Andean Regional Initiative, see Tokatlian, Chapter 3 in this volume.

References

Aranguren Molina, M. 2001. *Mi confesión. Carlos Castaño revela sus secretos.* Bogotá: Editores Oveja Negra.

Bertram, Eva, Kenneth Sharpe, and Peter Andreas. 1996. *Drug War Politics: The Price of Denial.* Berkeley: The University of California Press.

Baum, Dan. 1997. *Smoke and Mirrors. The War on Drugs and the Politics of Failure.* Boston, New York, and London: Little Brown and Company.

Buscaglia, Edgardo, and William Ratliff. 2001. *New Hoover Essay in Public Policy. War and Lack of Governance in Colombia: Narcos, Guerrillas, and U.S. Policy.* Essays in Public Policy, No. 107. Stanford, CA: Hoover Institute http://www.news.excite. com/printstory/news/bw/010718/ca-hoover-institution.html

Camacho Guizado, Álvaro. 1988. *Droga y sociedad en Colombia: el poder y el estigma.* Cali/Bogotá: Cidse/Cerec.

Castro Caycedo, G. 2001. *Con los brazos en alto.* Bogotá: Planeta.

Desde Abajo. 2001. *Del Plan Colombia a la Iniciativa Andina.* Bogotá: Desde Abajo.

El Espectador. January 20, 2002. "Plan B" of Plan Colombia.

Galbraith, John K. 1985. *La anatomía del poder.* Barcelona: Plaza y Janés.

García, Andelfo. 2001. Plan Colombia y ayuda estadounidense: una fusión traumática. In *El Plan Colombia y la internacionalización del conflicto,* edited by L.A. Restrepo, 115–75. Bogotá: Planeta/Institute of Political Studies and International Relations of the National University.

Observatory for Human Rights and International Humanitarian Law. 2000. *Panorama de los grupos de autodefensa.* Bogotá: Oficina del Vicepresidente de la República.

Oficina de la Contraloría General de la República. 2001. *Plan Colombia. Primer Informe de Evaluación.* Bogotá: Oficina de la Contraloría General de la República.

Rabasa, Ángel and Peter Chalk. 2001. *Colombian Labyrinth. The Synergy of Drugs and Insurgency and Its Implications for Regional Stability.* Prepared for the United States Air Force, Project Air Force, Santa Monica, Rand Corporation.

Revista Cambio. October 2, 2000. El despegue.

Tokatlian, Juan Gabriel. 1997. *En el límite. La (torpe) norteamericanización de la guerra contra las drogas.* Bogotá: Norma Publishing Group.

———. 2000. *Globalización, narcotráfico y violencia. Siete ensayos sobre Colombia.* Bogotá: Norma Publishing Group.

U.S. Department of State. n.d. *Drugs, Data and Statistics.* http://www.whitehouse-drug policy.gov/drugabuse/toc.html

U.S. Embassy in Colombia. 2002. *The Andean Regional Initiative.* Bogotá: U.S. Embassy in Colombia.

Van der Veen, Hans. T. 1999. *The International drug complex.* Amsterdam: Centre for Drug Research, Universiteit van Amsterdam. http://www.frw.uva.nl/cedroli-brary/complex.html

CHAPTER 5

Venezuela and the Colombian Conflict: Tensions, Problems, and Uncertainties

*Ana María Sanjuán**

Introduction

For reasons of historic, geographic, and cultural nature, and due to an intense and complex relationship, Venezuela finds itself deeply involved in the domestic Colombian conflict. Currently, both countries find themselves going through a period of critical circumstances of a different nature; in the case of Colombia, related to the upsurge in armed confrontation and the fight against narcotrafficking, and in the case of Venezuela, to the collapse of governance, product of an incomplete political–institutional transition and a redefinition of civilian–military relationships. These crises were aggravated throughout 2000 by the rupture of the peace process in Colombia and by extreme political polarization in Venezuela. In analyzing the implications of the worsening Colombian conflict for Venezuela, at least three issues need to be taken into consideration: (1) new tensions created both in the field of foreign as well as domestic policy; (2) the worsening of prior security problems between Colombia and Venezuela with their respective corollary implications for the National Armed Forces and for narcotrafficking, environmental equilibrium, and forced migrations; and (3) uncertainties created around future management by the current Venezuelan leadership elite of the bilateral relationship and the Colombian conflict, taking into account the international post–September 11 context, the domestic governability crisis and the increasing political–institutional instability. In the following text, necessarily of a preliminary nature, given the magnitude and the speed of political change in Venezuela, these aspects are discussed after a brief review of some of the fundamental factors in the relationship between Venezuela and Colombia.

Background

As a consequence of the September 11 terrorist attacks on the United States, and in the midst of an incomplete transition, in which concepts such as balance of power, international and domestic security, as well as the role of the Armed Forces are the object of daily revision, the United States initiated a series of military actions within the framework of a mega political, military, legal, financial, and policing strategy against world terrorism. In the Andean region, the regional juncture was affected even before September 11, due to the worsening of the Colombian conflict, in response to the vulnerable situation of the peace negotiations and the redefinition of U.S. hemispheric security scheme in a post–Cold War scenario (Bonilla 2001; OSAL 2001).

Beyond the theme of drug trafficking, a primary point on the U.S. security agenda, a new issue emerges for Colombia. Beginning with the extended use of the term "global terrorism" by the United States and the international community, Colombia is singled out as being a threat for having the largest number of terrorist organizations in the Western Hemisphere, measured by the concept of "Terrorist Groups with an International Reach." Colombia now typifies the two most sensitive and controversial situations in the new global context: drug trafficking and terrorism (Bonilla 2001; Trinkunas 2001).

The new international context and the shift in concepts of security seriously affect the Andean region, already framed as a source of regional insecurity, because of its human rights crisis, its protagonist role in the drug problem, high levels of corruption in some countries of the region, environmental problems, vulnerability related to civilian control over the Armed Forces, increasing social and political conflict, recurring governance crises, and major dependence on the United States (Tokatlian 2001).

In this complex context, as well as in previous less-critical moments, relations between Venezuela and Colombia have oscillated between periods of stability and moments of great tension, even though understanding has always predominated and confrontation has been avoided. During the 1990s, several mechanisms for agreement and understanding were created that allowed for a nonviolent response to the most serious conflicts that have risen between the two countries. Unfortunately, many of these mechanisms were deactivated between 1991 and 2002, placing relations between both countries on a critical edge. The worsening of the Colombian domestic conflict and the implementation of Plan Colombia have taken place within a context of crisis in Colombian–Venezuelan relations, which has impeded these countries' ability to pay attention to complex bilateral security problems (Ramírez and Cadenas 1999).

Within Latin America, Colombia and Venezuela share one of the most significant borders, extending for something more than 2,200 kilometers. This historically problematic space for both countries is the point from which the Venezuelan position regarding the Colombian conflict has been developed—a conflict classified by Venezuelan military institutions as "a threat to regional security."

Following the Latin American tradition, the political elite in these countries has delegated authority to the Armed Forces for the handling of security matters in the bilateral relation. This gives the relationship several distinguishing characteristics. A first element is that, although Colombia and Venezuela were among the few countries in the region that did not undergo military dictatorships, their Armed Forces, for reasons associated with the domestic situation of both societies (violence and the insurgency conflict in Colombia, and the stability of democracy in Venezuela), enjoy a series of institutional prerogatives. This allows them to function with a high degree of autonomy and to fulfill a political role of singular importance in the handling of matters inherent to them (Manrique 1996; Müller Rojas 1997).

Despite multiple cooperation mechanisms established between the Colombian and Venezuelan Armed Forces since the 1990s, another characteristic of the bilateral relationship is the existence of an unresolved legal dispute between both countries—the delimitation of marine and submarine waters in the Gulf of Venezuela. This means that established security relations between the two countries are guided by structural elements of profound mistrust—more pronounced in the Venezuelan case—which affect the level of collaboration required in dissimilar conflicts, and that have even led them to engage in an arms race during the most critical moments. Moreover, the initiation of the so-called war on drugs on the continent in the mid-1980s affected these relationships, since it was treated as a theme of national security by the United States and the Armed Forces of Colombia and Venezuela. The counterinsurgency struggle has been associated with the war against drugs, which in the Venezuelan case means that, in matters of security, concepts such as "narcoguerrilla" and the "common enemy" prevail. The Venezuelan Armed Forces has perceived Colombia's domestic conflict based on these concepts (Müller and Vivas 1992; Battaglini 2000).

Venezuela is one of the countries most affected by the Colombian conflict. Since 1985 the Colombian guerrillas—both the Ejercito de Liberación Nacional (ELN) and the Fuerzas Armadas Revolucionarias de Colombia (FARC), as well as the paramilitary forces like the AUC—have carried out a series of incursions on Venezuelan territory. One of the consequences is a growing insecurity on the border, implying an increase in the number of abductions of individuals and airplanes and payment of "war taxes." This has resulted in a series of high and differentiated costs for Venezuela, including political costs, since nationals in the area demand government provision of greater security, on the threat that should the state continue to be incapable of providing security in the area, they would form private defense groups. In addition to the insecurity and violence prevailing in border areas, resulting in high rates of criminal activity, contraband in arms, automobiles, gasoline and precursors, other problems affecting the fluidity of the bilateral relationship also exist such as forced displacement and migration, ecological vulnerability, and narcotrafficking (Sanjuán 1999).

As the Colombian conflict has worsened since the mid-1990s, incursions in Venezuelan territory by the different armed actors as well as direct attacks on the Venezuelan Army border posts and on the National Guard have increased. As a result, the government of Rafael Caldera (1994–1999) decided to create two zones of battle operations in three states bordering on Colombia. The purpose of these zones was to ensure direct attention to the area's security problems through combined Armed Forces operations, since Venezuela considers the Colombian state to have continuously exhibited severe limitations in containing the problem. Nearly half of the military troops of the country were assigned to these zones, and this continues to be the case.

With the implementation of this new security strategy on the border, the Venezuelan Armed Forces' purpose was to have recourse to the use of "hot pursuit," a procedure allowing them to combat the Colombian insurgency even beyond the borderlines in the case of an attack on a border post. This proposal was loudly rejected by Colombia and by several sectors in Venezuela because, according to what was described, it would mean becoming involved in a conflict that had nothing to do with the country. However, in order to attend to specific problems in the area, diverse official and nonofficial mechanisms of cooperation have existed between both Armed Forces. As is to be expected, the above-mentioned circumstances have implied increasing involvement by Venezuelan armed institutions in areas bordering on Colombia, especially in policing responsibilities. This has resulted in grave repercussions in the area of human rights violations: between 1995 and

1998, the zones of battle operations functioned along with the suspension of certain constitutional guarantees in border municipalities. And even if some of the illicit activities diminished, such as guerrilla attacks, the security strategies implicit in the maintenance of these zones continue to have negative impacts, not only in the border area but also within the Armed Forces themselves (Torres Velasco 1998).

When Hugo Chávez (1999–2004) took office in Venezuela, the already complicated bilateral relationship suffered new perturbations, motivated fundamentally by Chávez's strong antineoliberal rhetoric and his positions regarding the need for greater popular protagonist action vindicating social policy in the region. The international community and a good part of the Venezuelan establishment worriedly observed his meteoric rise to the presidency in Venezuela during 1998 and discovered parallels between his inflammatory discourse and the revolutionary proposals of the most radical groups in Latin America. His military past and coup experience, his neopopulist tendencies, and his improvisation and clumsiness regarding several foreign policy issues converted President Chávez into a factor of concern in the handling of the Colombian conflict. He took office just as a complex peace process was beginning and the fundamental strategies of Plan Colombian were being delineated. It is in this context that a series of diplomatic and border conflicts have taken place with Colombia, which have greatly influenced the crises in the bilateral relationship. Paramilitary incursions, an increase in the number of displaced people, detention of Venezuelans in Colombia, hijacking of planes and kidnapping of Venezuelan businessmen, the discovery in Venezuela of the American indigenous assassinated by the FARC, detention in Venezuela and subsequent extradition of José María Ballestas, denouncements by the Colombian military high command concerning the presence of guerrilla training camps on the Venezuelan border are some of the events that have marked the rhythm of the relationship since 2000.

Venezuela not only has rocky diplomatic relations with Colombia, but also with the United States. In this regard, and with respect to the Colombian conflict, the U.S. behavior requires mention—particularly its attempts to stir up support in the region to contain any "overflows" that might evolve from the Colombian violence. Reactions to the diverse U.S. proposals have been negative in Venezuela, especially within the government, and are considered to constitute a dangerous precedent, possibly leading toward much more direct U.S. intervention in the Andean region. Washington's support to strengthen the Colombian Armed Forces and the development of U.S. military activities in neighboring countries in the name of fighting drugs have constituted another point of tension. Despite enormous internal contradictions at the heart of the military institution, the Venezuelan government placed limits on the proposal to establish an "operational triangle over Colombia," formulated by the United States—a precedent to Plan Colombia—by refusing to grant permission to U.S. airships to use Venezuelan national air space and by protesting the development of military facilities in Aruba and Curazao. However, in response to domestic military pressures and for the sake of stability in the relationship with the United States, a radar installation for antinarcotics operations was authorized in the border region of San Fernando de Atabapo (Sanjuán 1999).

In summary, a series of tensions exists between Venezuela and Colombia that can be characterized by their nature and origin as both historic and current. Those of a historic nature originate with traditional border problems, and are inscribed within the realist logic of varying threats to binational security. Current tensions derive from the impacts of Hugo Chávez's leadership, the new peace process in Colombia, and the formulation and development of Plan Colombia. These present-day tensions have introduced the greatest elements of crisis and confrontation in the Venezuela–Colombian bilateral relationship between 1999 and 2002.

New Tensions between Colombia and Venezuela: Changes in Foreign Policies and Crises on the Domestic Front

Changes in Foreign Policies and in the Bilateral Relationship

In order to overcome some of the problems of the bilateral relationship after 1990 and starting with their respective processes of economic restructuring and liberalization, Venezuela and Colombia viewed their bilateral relation through the frame of globalization. As such, military protagonism was displaced, giving way to new actors and political mechanisms for reaching agreements in the relationship. Institutional mechanisms for dialogue and communication were created through presidential commissions to handle fundamental problems, while political mediation and consultative mechanisms responded to specific junctures. Not without criticisms due to the indefinite subordination of the maritime dispute, these mechanisms allowed for significant fluidity in the relationship, increasing levels of confidence, and bilateral integration, especially in the economic sphere: in five years of their existence, bilateral commerce increased tenfold, and both countries respectively became each other's most important trading partners after the United States (Ramírez and Cadenas 1999).

Within Venezuela and Colombia, some of the most important foundations of these mutually agreed to integration policies have been threatened by several concurrent crises: at the most general level, due to the global consequences of September 11; at the regional level, because of the increasing involvement of all the countries in the region in the U.S. security logic with respect to drug trafficking; in the binational sphere, because of the deepening of the Colombian armed conflict since 1999, the peace process, and the implicit strategies in the design and development of Plan Colombia in Colombia; and on the part of Venezuela, due to the strategic direction of the new political regime signaled by institutional changes and the development of a new foreign policy agenda designed to promote a kind of "Bolivarian" integration fed by the search for less international asymmetry, in opposition to U.S. hegemony (Tokatlian 2001). All of this has promoted numerous tensions and misunderstandings in which the coordinated binational policies in specific areas and additional mechanisms for regional integration have suffered an important setback. Bilateral relationships have gone through significant imbalances since 1999 while levels of mutual distrust have increased. Despite the fact that all the presidential commissions affected by the crises have been reinstated, spaces for collaboration remain severely compromised.

For Colombia, the most recent causes of friction have centered on the controversial positions of President Chávez regarding the Colombian conflict in particular, and regarding several Latin American political themes in general—liberation of peoples, integration of the oppressed, staunch criticisms of neoliberalism—as well as his stated interest in promoting some of the fundamental principles of the "Bolivarian revolution" at the continental level. This project, proposing to constitute an alternative to the region's political and economic establishment, suggests the formation of an alternative regime, distinct from neoliberalism, through the creation of strategic alliances with emerging political and social actors or those antagonistic to the establishment.

Even if this proposal would have likely entered into a crisis mode after the events of September 11, the positions of the Venezuelan government regarding the Colombian situation have proven to be quite vague, displaying a more favorable disposition toward the guerrilla's agenda. Venezuela's questioned perspective of "neutrality" vis-à-vis the domestic conflict in Colombia has been viewed nationally and internationally as an attempt to confer belligerent status on the guerrilla, which would in fact modify both the nature of this conflict as well as the development of the peace process that took place in Colombia between 1999 and the beginning of 2002. Although Venezuela has held the position for several years, even before Hugo Chávez took office, that a direct relation with the guerrilla enabled Venezuela to reduce increasing border problems (hence, diminishing serious bilateral crises), this behavior has profoundly irritated certain sectors of the Colombian society, which consider the Venezuelan government to be an exacerbating factor in the Colombian conflict, affecting some of its internal dynamics. From the Venezuelan side, visible tensions in the bilateral relationship with Colombia emanate from several sources. The first is related, obviously, to the serious repercussions that the Colombian conflict has on the social, economic, political, and institutional life of Venezuela. For the Venezuelan government, another source of perturbation and cause of mistrust in the bilateral relationship has to do with the strengthening of relations between Colombia and the United States. The nexus between the policy for peace and the U.S. policy to eradicate illicit crops and their traffic from the Andean region established by the Colombian and U.S. governments is observed with concern due to implicit threats for Venezuela's security. The degree of U.S. involvement in Colombia is considered a threat to the country's sovereignty and interests, and, although for different motives, is a sensitive point for the new political elite and the national Armed Forces. Some authorities have pointed out that reliance on Plan Colombia as the point of intervention over one of the factors in the Colombian crisis, namely drug trafficking, generates a series of negative external factors both in the region as well as in Venezuela. For this reason, Venezuela widely rejected it when it was formulated, approved, and its first phases were implemented; even now its implementation continues to be regarded as a serious obstacle to the peaceful resolution of the armed conflict. Additionally, the strengthening of the Colombian military complex, both in terms of armament as well as strategies and training, is seen as negatively affecting the military equilibrium in the Andean region (Castillo 2001).

Environmental damages, a regional arms race, population movements and refugee flows, the changing routes of drug trafficking, and upswings in violence within the country are some of the most serious external factors identified by both the Venezuelan military as well as the political leadership. Another cause of malaise has been the lack of bilateral and regional consultation by Colombia in the formulation of Plan Colombia, as well as fears that the antidrug strategy adopted could become a much more overt counterinsurgency plan, with risks of extending the conflict toward Venezuela. In addition, there is concern that in the event that Plan Colombia meets its proposed objectives, the narcotrafficking problem could be exported to Venezuela.

From 2001 on, for economic and political reasons of both external and domestic nature, a moderate change in the focus and behavior of Venezuela toward the Colombian conflict has been observed, even to the point of subduing some of the criticisms of the Plan, although vindicating the peace process as the only route to resolving the conflict. At the same time, the Venezuelan government continues to expresses concern about the possibility of unilateral foreign intervention. For this reason, it has increased its own military response capacity along the entire border with Colombia.

Crisis on the Venezuelan Domestic Front

As far as the Venezuelan domestic front is concerned, the worsening of the Colombian conflict has had an important sociopolitical impact, due to the huge breach in political attitudes and behavior among the different groups battling it outside and inside the country. Conflicting discourses among Venezuelan elites concerning the handling of the conflict through foreign, domestic, and military policy illustrate very distinct conceptions about the kind of relationship that should be maintained with Colombia. In fact, an enormous polarization of opinions exist regarding what is understood to be the official position on the guerrilla, reflecting a rupture in political consensus about what ought to be the priorities of a bilateral and regional integration process. This is currently evidenced by the clear separation between the perceptions of the military and civilian forces about what should be the behavior of the Venezuelan state vis-à-vis increasing incursion by the different Colombian armed actors in Venezuela and the significance of the U.S. presence in Colombia.

The Colombian conflict has been, and continues to be, a key player in the political chess game of Venezuela. For Venezuelan society in general, and for the border population in particular, exacerbation of violence in Colombia constitutes an increasingly worrisome threat for the country's security, given Colombia's character as an "internal neighbor" and its longstanding presence in all social strata of the country. Among the political opposition to the government of President Chávez, there are concerns about the inevitable "Colombianization" of Venezuela due to the high incidence of insecurity, especially on the border. These sectors also call for firmer condemnation of the insurgency as well as for unrestricted support for Plan Colombia, conceived to be the only mechanism to resolve Colombia's domestic conflict notwithstanding its undesirable effects. On the other hand, the official sector, significantly divided between moderates and radicals, views this highly charged defense of U.S. intervention in Colombia with enormous suspicion. It considers that one of the central but hidden objectives of Plan Colombia is to confront the expansion of the popular leadership of President Chávez, through the use of force, in order to bring to an end his revolutionary response to American hegemony.

Worsening of Recurring Binational and Subregional Security Problems

Potential Conflicts in the Area of Security and National Defense

The escalation of the Colombian conflict has had a negative impact in the area of Venezuelan defense and security. What is currently perceived as the Colombian threat helps to justify the need for National Armed Forces with exceptional powers and extraordinary resources in order to reaffirm sovereignty and national self-determination, given the existence of a security scheme that motivates unilateral behavior. In addition, this factor contributes to an imbalance in civilian–military relations in Venezuela. The renewed role for military forces in political life after the 1999 constitutional reform must be considered. They were granted wide-ranging mandates in the country's development, as well as the extension of faculties and competences greatly exceeding those agreed to by the convergent two-party political system, in force between 1958 and 1998 (Manrique 1996; Müller 1997).

In Venezuela, traditionally, the military has enjoyed enormous prerogatives in terms of political influence and independence of action in the management of issues central to the bilateral relation with Colombia; issues such as those dealing with borders, the hypothesis of a conflict over sovereignty, the acquisition of arms, and defense policy design. From mid-2001 onward, the worsening of the armed conflict and the development of Plan Colombia have affected areas under the military is mandate. At the same time, the Plan's undesired collateral effects—for example, increased coca and poppy plantations in Venezuelan territory; the setting up of laboratories and the expansion in drug trafficking and exit routes; the use of the country as an area of relief and refuge by the guerrilla; and the contamination of rivers, plants, and people with chemicals or biological substances, or as a result of the destruction of the Colombian petroleum infrastructure—all grant (if possible) increased preeminence to the military in the management of security issues and Venezuelan border spaces.

The security crisis on the Colombian–Venezuelan border is not new. Since the 1990s, regular operations by state coercive forces have proved insufficient for maintaining security in the area, resulting in a serious loss of legitimacy for the Venezuelan state. In an attempt to compensate for limitations in its ability to provide stability and security on the western Venezuelan border, Venezuela has militarized the management of public security. State interventions, for the purpose of managing border area stability, have affected border communities, and since they have been developed from the perspective of former security paradigms they come into relative conflict with Venezuela's doctrinal revolution and the management of "new missions" in the postglobalization era (Müller and Vivas 1992; Montenegro 2001).

Besides the permanent challenge on its western border, two other tensions affecting Venezuelan military institutions are evident. One of them is the perceived military disadvantage vis-à-vis Colombia, and the second is the "neutral" position proposed by the Venezuelan government regarding the guerrilla. With respect to the imbalance of forces, growing concern within the Venezuelan military has developed regarding the military component of Plan Colombia, which increases Colombia's neighbor's capacity principally in air equipment and helicopters. As the perception of Colombia as a threat intensifies, former conflicts derived from unresolved issues are given new force and the realist paradigm persists. This situation also justifies the strengthening of military power in a local context where there is an almost critical redefinition of civilian–military relations and total renovation of the framework for the country's legal operations. The pressure to compensate for the perceived imbalance, real or not, implies not only practical effects in terms of an increased defense budget, but also augments the autonomy of the National Armed Forces in the management of this and other collateral problems, strengthening them as fundamental actors in bilateral affairs and in the handling of their relationships with civilians in Venezuelan domestic politics.

Venezuelan "neutrality" vis-à-vis the guerrilla, as well as to a crisis in the "common enemy" doctrine that guided Venezuelan military behavior regarding the Colombian conflict up until 1999, is a point of intense domestic controversy. The position of the Venezuelan Armed Forces on terrorism, and the redefinition of the new global and regional security regime, reveal that there is more continuity than change in the paradigm that has guided Venezuelan military policy vis-à-vis the guerrilla and other geostrategic issues, especially that regarding the alliance with the United States in the area of hemispheric security. For an important sector of the armed forces, with or without the development of Plan Colombia, the principal and most imminent security threat is the transposing of Colombian violence to Venezuela. Although the Venezuelan military supports a negotiated solution to the Colombian conflict—and on prior occasions has accepted some attempts at bilateral negotiations by civilian authorities with armed groups—it is difficult for them to accept more explicit and solid pacts with what continues to be called the narcoguerrilla in detriment of their natural relationship with the Colombian Armed Forces. They sustain that despite the change of attitude on the part of the Venezuelan government regarding the Colombian conflict and the opposition to the methodology of "hot pursuit" by Colombia (and by Venezuelan authorities as well), irregular activities in border areas have not noticeably diminished, as not even the guerrilla have control over the number of criminal groups operating in the zone. Furthermore, the activities of these groups on the border area are vital for their financial stability, even more so now that the development of Plan Colombia implies a severe threat to their access to their traditional sources of revenue.

The context described above became even more complex once the security measures after September 11 were imposed and the Colombian peace process was suspended at the beginning of 2002. From that moment on, the Venezuelan military has been subjected to several pressures regarding their behavior toward the Colombian conflict: from the United States, that through its bilateral cooperation programs presses for full support for Plan Colombia and its war against drugs and terrorism; from their Colombian counterparts, for the reestablishment of military collaboration schemes in effect prior to 1999 to fight the insurgency and drug trafficking; and lastly, from the Venezuelan political opposition, which is exerting strong pressure to extract critical statements from the Venezuelan armed forces concerning the handling of the guerrilla problem in the country (which, within political circles, is supposed to cause broad discontent among high military commands).

Viewed from the military perspective, further consequences of the intensification of the Colombian conflict include: the challenge of maintaining nearly 30,000 Venezuelan soldiers in two operational zones, which also affect the human rights of inhabitants living in the zones; the fluidity of economic integration for security reasons; and the handling of relationships among neighbors. Problems of ecological and environmental degradation and those caused by frequent population displacement are similarly considered to be part of the nation's security problems (Ministry of Defense 2000).

Narcotrafficking

A crucial issue with repercussions for Venezuela as a result of the intensification of the Colombian domestic conflict and the development of Plan Colombia is the problem of narcotrafficking. Although, until now, the country's specific participation in the transnational drug trafficking business has been related particularly to money laundering, transport of arms, and exit routes, this situation could change: the displacement of illicit crops to several Venezuelan border-states is now a proven fact as a consequence of the eradication efforts in Colombia. In a context in which a probable increase in narcotrafficking operations in Venezuela is expected, the lack of preparation and the incapacity of the Venezuelan state to adequately handle the issue—due to vulnerabilities such as corruption, institutional weakness, legal deficiencies, inadequate policing capacity, and the partial collapse of the penal justice system—are visible. Augmented militarization of the fight against drug trafficking, an increase in the crisis of citizen security, and the affirmation of several doctrinal dilemmas at the heart of the Armed Forces are only some of the problems that will become more serious.

Although Venezuelan policies to cope with the traffic of illicit drugs have always followed the main strategies proposed by the United States in the hemisphere, new crises could appear, based on the rejection of air interdiction and the development of radar systems in Venezuelan territory. Even if the military authorities share the view that drug trafficking is a national security problem, the current proposal to handle the problem, as a result of the dynamics of plan Colombia, puts into question traditional security schemes that had prevailed within Venezuelan armed forces.

Migrations—Displaced People[1]

It is believed that contemporary migratory phenomena are increasingly associated with themes of poverty, lack of governance, civil wars, and other problems of a domestic nature, but at the same time, are a source of international tension (Rojas Aravena 1999). The deepening of the Colombian conflict during the last few years has caused great internal displacement and the exodus of people to neighboring countries. Since the 1950s there has been an important transborder movement between Colombia and Venezuela, a product of open borders and border areas with long-time historic, cultural, and commercial exchanges. As a result, many Colombian migrants have been settling in Venezuela for decades, becoming fully integrated into the life of the country. The majority has never legalized their situation despite their being completely incorporated into the communities in which they have settled.

However, recent migration, a product of the worsening domestic conflict in Colombia, has assumed other characteristics, among which two are distinguishable: transitory migration and regular migration. Transitory migration is that formed by numerous groups who in a moment of extreme danger or declared conflict cross the border with the idea of temporarily settling in Venezuela and return to Colombia as soon as the situation of danger has passed.[2] This phenomenon is registered more commonly in border communities where there is fluid communication on a daily basis, resulting from commercial exchanges and family relationships. While regular migration is also the result of the conflict, it takes place within family groups or on an individual basis. Frequently they maintain family, work, or commercial relationships with individuals or families who live on the other side of the border. Their inclusion in the labor market is extremely precarious, and their opportunities in Venezuela are limited to working exchange plots on farms or large estates, and during certain established periods, in frankly unfavorable conditions. This group of migrants tends to remain in the new communities and not to register with national authorities for reasons of security or fear. Of the migrant groups mentioned above, although the first is the most evident, it is the regular migration among family groups that brings the greatest number of people to Venezuela and its frequency has accelerated as the conflict intensifies. Although this type of migration involves the most people, it is at the same time the least visible, difficult to estimate its true magnitude, as well as the profile and needs of the people involved. This gradual and constant entry of people and families to Venezuela generates problems such as: increased demand for the provision of social services such as education and health; increase in the rate of citizen insecurity; as well as a worsening of poverty indicators in areas traditionally underprivileged and mainly marginalized from development processes. Unfortunately, conditions of extreme competition for survival among the members of the poorest communities as well as difficult living conditions contribute on occasion to the appearance of xenophobic sentiments among the inhabitants of these border areas. This situation favors an increase in violence, conflict, and the desire of migrants to remain invisible as a form of protection.

It is in these border areas where the absence of authorities and institutions of both states is notable, and where the presence of armed groups is concentrated. At the same time, the irregular geography allows for the concentration of illicit crops, the trafficking of arms and chemical precursors, in addition to the activities of diverse criminal groups. This means that the humanitarian impact on victims displaced because of the conflict worsens. Notwithstanding the seriousness of this problem for Venezuela, no concerted effort by the public agencies responsible exists yet. All of this reinforces the fact that attention continues to be provided principally by the Ministry of Defense, with the limitations that this entails.

Environment

The worsening of the domestic confrontation in Colombia also increases environmental degradation and ecological vulnerability in Venezuela. The ecological impact of the conflict in the country has two fundamental causes: the chemical eradication of illicit crops and damages to Colombia's petroleum infrastructure. Venezuela is a country where water levels are lower than those of Colombia because the majority of the waters in the western zone originate in Colombia. This means that both countries share extremely important hydroresources. Close to protective areas of hydrographic watersheds, powerful chemical agents are being used in fumigation (*glifosato*, *imazapyr*, *tebuthiuron*, and *hongo fusarium*), contaminating Venezuelan waterways and seriously compromising the country's ecological security. Regarding the blowing up of oil pipelines, Venezuela has been particularly affected by those that have occurred along the Caño Limón-Coveñas line where 28 oil spills have been registered since 1979, and from which nearly 87,000 barrels have ended up in Venezuela by way of the Catatumbo, Tara, and Socuavo Rivers. According to the authorities, this has caused increasing ecological deterioration in the ecosystem of the rivers that flow into Lake Maracaibo (Castillo 2001). In order to estimate the magnitude of environmental damage in Venezuela, it must be remembered that the Catatumbo River, one of the principal tributaries of Lake Maracaibo, supplies nearly 60 percent of the potable water consumed in the state of Zulia (Castillo 2001).

This complex problem needs to be addressed by the Ministry of the Environment, the Institute for the Conservation of Lake Maracaibo (ICLAM), and the National Guard.

Uncertainties in the Short and Medium Term: Preliminary Conclusions

The eventual decline of regimes plus political disenchantment provide opportunities in which governing bodies and elites tend to mobilize for reasons of national security in order to justify specific political practices. In this case, there are at least three risks for Venezuela with regard to the Colombian conflict, all of them feasible in the current circumstances: a rapid race forward by the regime that deepens political radicalization and compromises the country vis-à-vis new global geopolitical restructuring; greater political–institutional instability due to the economic crisis motivated by the decline in oil profits; and a crisis in governance, including one propelled by the Armed Forces, as a result of probable political instability in the short term. At the same time, all of these circumstances would have some repercussion—positive or negative—for the Colombian conflict.

The traditional disagreements between Colombia and Venezuela need to be overcome through the structuring of alternative bilateral agendas that go beyond those of traditional security. For Venezuela and Colombia, the main challenge is that of promoting a framework of trust and general cooperation and the design of stable mechanisms for conflict prevention. Overcoming isolationism and unilateralism in the handling of hemispheric, national, and regional problems is required.

To respond to the complexity of new missions and to the emerging concept of sovereignty, it is imperative to promote cooperative, jointly shared initiatives in the search for a regional, or at least a bilateral security project. Current handling of the binational conflict and the prevalence of images, ideas, and perceptions by political actors in Colombia and Venezuela (whose particular agendas do not necessarily include integration and cooperation as a strategic concern) about the bilateral relationship have led the relationship to a point of near collapse.

Considering the complexity of the Colombian–Venezuelan bilateral relationship what is recommended is a wide-ranging discussion among the most representative sectors committed to the integration of both countries. Among others, there are several topics of bilateral interest: the creation of effective early-warning mechanisms; promotion of spaces for dialogue among nontraditional actors; increase in measures of mutual trust and security in nonconflictive areas; promotion of a dialogue regarding alternative solutions to traditional problems within the framework of new security schemes; and the introduction of control mechanisms, arms limitation, and even disarmament. All of these can contribute to the design of a new, binational, regional, and hemispheric security regime.

Post Script: Internal Crises Contribute to the Increase in Tension between Colombian and Venezuelan

Many events have occurred in the Colombian–Venezuelan relationship that have contributed to the cyclical worsening of tensions between the two countries. The Colombian conflict played a significant role in the already polarized political situation of Venezuela, which became increasingly evident in the coup of April 2001 and persists at critical levels.

Similarly, there have been numerous grave security problems along the Colombian–Venezuelan border, which derive, in part, from the internal intensification of the Colombian conflict, characterized by the illegal traffic of drugs, gasoline, arms, livestock, stolen vehicles, and petrochemical products; the extension of drug cultivation and the invasion of farms; as well as the kidnapping and extortion of civilians. These problems have been dealt with in an ambiguous, and at times, contradictory manner by the Venezuelan authorities. According to local residents, groups such as the guerrilla (FARC and ELN), the Colombia self-defense groups (Autodefensas Unidas de Colombia, AUC), and Venezuelan guerilla groups (Frente Bolivariano de Liberación, FBL) and self-defense groups (Autodefensas Unidas de Venezuela, AUV) operate and move around this area quite easily (*El Universal* March 2003; Weffer and Velandia March 2003).

The elevated levels of violence and insecurity caused by confrontations between the guerrillas, the paramilitaries, and the Colombian and

Venezuelan armed forces have resulted in entire populations being displaced into Venezuelan territory, provoking humanitarian and refugee crises. As a result, both national and international human rights organizations, as well as UN bodies such as the UNCR and the UNDP, have called upon the Venezuelan government to develop state policies to deal with the humanitarian repercussions.

Among the many regional impacts of the Colombian conflict, three recent trends and issues are of particular relevance to Venezuela. The first is a consequence of President Álvaro Uribe's emphasis on a military force against armed actors through a policy of "democratic security," and the inability of the Colombian state to contain this conflict within its borders. As was mentioned, the main consequence of this for Venezuela is an increased presence of armed actors, and with this an increase in rates of crime within the border populations. In addition, this has led to an increase in the number of Colombians residing in Venezuela as a result of the conflict. There are approximately 180,000 Colombians currently living in Venezuela, although only 2,000 have requested refugee status and are still awaiting approval from the Venezuelan government.

The second issue, which has generated controversy between Colombia and Venezuela as well as for Venezuelan domestic politics, was President Chavez's declaration of Venezuela's neutrality vis-à-vis the conflict. Accordingly, in spite of requests from Colombia, the U.S., and the European Union, Venezuela has not officially labeled Colombian guerrilla groups as terrorists, stating that this enables Venezuela to collaborate with the Colombian peace process. Nevertheless, it is interpreted by certain political sectors in Colombia and the United States, and by the Venezuelan opposition, as tacit government support for the guerrilla. Critics also point to the failure of the Venezuelan state to control the movement and operation of the guerrilla into its territory.

The third issue deals with the military support that Colombia receives from the United States through Plan Colombia. According to the Venezuelan armed forces, this situation has resulted in an important imbalance between both countries, significant given that the two countries face contentious border issues that are yet to be resolved.

Within Venezuela, several other factors have had an impact on the bilateral relationship between the two countries. Venezuela's relations with Colombia enters into the dynamic of political polarization in Venezuela, reflecting the logic of "my enemy's enemy is my friend," with the opposition and government respectively leveraging different views on the management of bilateral relations with Colombia for political ends. This represents a setback as it impedes the design of state policies to improve the situation, and contributes not only to internal fragmentation but influences both countries' alignment with the international community. Also, due to the participation of large numbers of military and ex-military in Venezuelan politics, this situation tends to be analyzed through a military lens, including the logic of "friend–enemy" and confrontation. Finally, Venezuela's relations with Colombia are intrinsically linked to Colombia's relationship with the United States, resulting in a "triangular" frame of analysis of any occurrence, which, given the persistent tensions between Venezuela and the United States, has contributed to the increased friction in Colombian–Venezuelan relations.

There are further points of contention between the governments of both countries, which contribute to the climate of mistrust, and which threaten to destabilize the bilateral and regional mechanisms of security cooperation, necessary for resolving the recurring crises in the relationship. These controversial issues include: divergent positions toward the Free Trade Area of the Americas and subregional commercial integration, terrorism, democracy, and relations with the United States. In light of these differences, it is likely that bilateral relations will stagnate in the short term; with negative repercussions for the potential for regional and hemispheric mechanisms to effectively deal with the Colombian conflict.

Nevertheless, it is essential to encourage peaceful, democratic solutions to the many differences that exist in the bilateral relationship. The creation of new mechanisms for cooperation and the promotion measures to increase mutual trust must be based on two premises: In Venezuela's case, it must be understood that in the short, and possibly the medium term, the policy of democratic security and Plan Colombia/Andean Regional Initiative, with what they entail, will continue in Colombia. For Colombia, it is important that it accepts that political instability in Venezuela might also persist, and that these contradictions will continue to permeate their relationship.

The search for a minimum basis of agreement is contingent upon resisting certain perceptions, such as the view that Plan Colombia is a mechanism to facilitate the North American invasion of Venezuela, or that Colombian guerrillas maintain a strategic sanctuary in Venezuela. These perceptions must be viewed with great caution, as they are used to influence respective domestic politics rather than to improve bilateral relations. Finally, there is a need to broaden the spaces in which difficult issues can be debated freely in order to lessen tensions and to create new mechanisms of cooperation between the two countries.

Notes

* Director Centre for Peace and Human Rights, Central University of Venezuela. Ana María Sanjuan is Professor of the Graduate Seminar in Human Rights at The Central University of Venezuela.
1. This information is based on a diagnostic profile of the refugee population in border areas, elaborated by ACNUR (2001).
2. The most recent case in Venezuela of this type of migration was that registered in June 1999, in the community of Casigua El Cubo, State of Zulia, where between 10,000 and 15,000 people were displaced from La Gabarra, Colombia. They were fleeing from an attack of the AUC. The Ministry of Defense, the Ministry of the Interior and Justice, and the Ministry of Foreign Affairs attended to this crisis. After a few days in Venezuela, nearly the entire population returned to their place of origin.

References

Alto Comisionado de las Naciones Unidas para los Refugiados (ACNUR). 2001. *Informe 2001*. Caracas: ACNUR.

Asamblea Nacional. 2001. *Informe de la Comisión Especial para el seguimiento de las consecuencias del Plan Colombia en Venezuela*. Unpublished manuscript, Caracas.

Battaglini, Ó. 2000. *La seguridad y defensa del Estado venezolano durante el período de la Post-Guerra Fría 1989–2000 (antecedentes y perspectivas)*. Thesis presented to the Institute of Superior Studies of National Defense, Caracas.

Bonilla, A. 2001. *National Security in the Andes: Regional Effects of the Washington and Bogota Agenda*. Paper prepared for the 2001 meeting of the Latin American Studies Association, September 5–8, Washington.

Castillo, H. 2001. *Plan Colombia and Venezuelan Civilian and Military Relations*. Paper presented at the Panel of civil–military relations of REDES, of the Center for Hemispheric Defense Studies, Washington.

El Universal. March 2003. Entrevista con Roberto Guisti.

Manrique, M. 1996. *La seguridad en las Fuerzas Armadas venezolanas*. Caracas: Tropykos Editorial Fund/Faculty of Legal and Political Sciences, UCV.

Ministerio de Defensa de la República Bolivariana de Venezuela. 2000. *El componente militar latinoamericano y la seguridad hemisférica*. Presentation made to the IV Ministerial Conference on Defense in the Americas, October, Manaus, Brazil.

Montenegro, E.G. 2001. *New Threats in Latin America: Considerations Concerning Employment of the Armed Forces*. Paper prepared for the 2001 meeting of the Latin American Studies Association, September 5–8, Washington.

Müller Rojas, A. 1997. *Un nuevo rol para los militares latino-americanos: el tutelaje político*. Presentation made to the IV National Symposium of Strategic Studies, Caracas.

Müller Rojas, A. and Vivas Gallardo, F. 1992. *Política de seguridad y defensa de la soberanía*. Caracas: Comisión Presidencial para Asuntos Fronterizos entre Colombia y Venezuela.

Observatory on Security and Defense in Latin America, University Institute Ortega y Gasset [OSAL]. 2001. *La seguridad en América Latina después de los atentados de Nueva York y Washington.* Unpublished manuscript, Madrid.

Ramírez, S. and Cadenas, J.M. 1999. *Colombia-Venezuela: agenda común para el siglo XXI.* Colombia: Tercer Mundo Editores.

Rojas Aravena, F. 1999. *Cooperación y Seguridad Internacional en las Américas.* Caracas: Nueva Sociedad.

Sanjuán, A.M. 1999. Las complejas relaciones militares entre Colombia y Venezuela. *Ideele* 176.

Tokatlian, J.G. 2001. La desconcertación sudamericana. *Nueva Sociedad* 176 (November–December): 125–32.

Torres Velasco, J. 1998. *Venezuela y Colombia: seguridad nacional ¿y ciudadana?, una visión binacional.* Unpublished manuscript, Bogotá.

Trinkunas, H. 2001. *A crisis in civil-military relations in the Andes?* Paper prepared for the 2001 meeting of the Latin American Studies Association, September 5–8, Washington.

Weffer, Laura and Karenina Velandia. March 2003. *El Nacional.*

PART 3

New Perspectives on Drugs

CHAPTER 6

Winners and Losers from the Illicit Drug Industry in Colombia

Albert Berry* and Jackeline Barragán**

Introduction

As the twenty-first century begins, the problem of illicit drugs has gained a high priority in national and international agendas. This industry, which encompasses peasant farmers, squatters, indigenous groups, dealers, distributors, money launderers, the military, politicians, consumers, and others, has not only been the source of fantastic fortunes but has also had lasting impacts on economies, political institutions, and societies in many countries.

At the world level, the production, processing, distribution, and consumption of psychoactive substances have been one of the most dynamic and prosperous economic activities over the last thirty years. Estimates put world retail sales somewhere between 100 and 400 billion (Falco 1997, 12); the upper of these figures is not far from total public sector spending in the developing countries. The war on drugs consumes large amounts of resources. The U.S. government alone recently allocated about US$2.1 billion to prosecute this war inside its national boundaries and outside them (UNDCP 1997).

The profits from the drug industry are a significant item in world income flows but have had destabilizing effects in many countries; thus far the efforts of national and international agencies to undermine the industry have been unsuccessful. A number of Asian and Latin American economies have suffered: (1) a decline in production of regular (legal) tradable goods, especially agriculture and manufacturing, due to the appreciation of their currencies as drug revenues flow in; (2) bursts of speculative investment which constitute a disincentive to productive investment, both national and foreign; (3) perhaps the most serious, the disincentive effect on investment from the climate of uncertainty and violence which has accompanied the evolution of this industry and raised the cost of many legitimate activities.

Some analysts, however, have argued that in a number of countries the economic resources generated by this industry have helped to prevent or reduce social, political, and economic decline brought on by the negative aspects of industrialization and globalization, on the one hand by providing needed resources to these economies and on the other by opening a space for social mobility in societies otherwise characterized by social and political immobility. In the early years, in Colombia, such ideas were heard with some frequency.

In political terms the drug organizations, which initially aspired only to control the regions in which they undertook production, later sought to expand their influence on national and international decision-making processes, either directly or through third parties. Many politicians have become involved one way or another with the drug industry. The most recent widely cited cases in Latin America include those of General Manuel Antonio Noriega of Panama, Ernesto Samper and his campaign group in Colombia, presidents Carlos Salinas and Ernesto Zedillo in Mexico, and Carlos Menem in Argentina. Television and the press daily report cases of corruption, violence, and criminal activity associated with this enormous network which, as well as moving billions of dollars around the world, is also affecting the social and cultural fabric of nations.

Although the above general patterns are clear, the impact of the industry on many of the groups involved directly or indirectly with the industry, or otherwise affected by it, are still only very imprecisely understood. This study represents a first attempt to provide quantitative evidence on some of the gains and losses from the presence of the industry in Colombia over the period 1974–1996, and with especial reference to the mid-1990s. We first present a brief description of the world market for drugs and its recent trends; the second section looks at Colombia's role in that world market and the scope of each of the main segments of the industry in Colombia (marijuana, heroin, cocaine); next comes an estimate of the levels of net income repatriated to the country and how it is distributed among the participants in the industry, followed by an analysis of how receipt of those incomes may affect the distribution of income in Colombia; the chapter ends with main conclusions and recommendations.

Trends in the Illicit Drug Industry at the End of the 1990s

The evolution of the drug activity, like any other, is determined by the actions taken by producers, consumers, and government. This particular industry has been notably dynamic, changing, and adaptable to varying conditions. The principal trends observed in the 1990s have been a significant shift in consumer preferences, a continued upward trend in supply, and a blurring of the distinction—previously fairly clear—between producing and consuming countries.

Although total consumption of illicit drugs does not appear to have grown significantly in recent years, its composition has undergone considerable change. The consumption of synthetic drugs has risen dramatically, while that of organic drugs has remained relatively constant, with a resulting decline in their wholesale price (though not in the street price, which instead has stabilized) and an increase in the purity of the products (UNDCP 1997). De Rementería (1997) points out that this behavior may indicate that the drug export industry has reached a stage of maturity and stability similar to any other tradable agricultural product, in the sense that with time the price has come to approximate the costs of production and distribution. Meanwhile, on the criminal side of the business, as of the late 1990s the drug lords continued to enjoy a high level of impunity, reflected in falling costs of protecting those criminal activities.

In spite of the attempts at interdiction and eradication, and of the tendency of demand to stabilize, leading to falling farm-gate prices of the products, the area under cultivation of each of the organic drugs continued to rise through the 1990s, as did the number of producing countries.

Production and consumption of illegal drugs are in constant change. Figures made available by United Nations International Drug Control Programme (UNDCP) for 1997 reveal that in the 1990s the number of "permanent" consumers was around 227 millions, of whom 11 million used marijuana, 30 million amphetamines, 26 million hallucigens, 13 million cocaine and 8 million heroin or other opiates (UNDCP 1997, 32). For many years the United States was considered to be the main consumer of psychoactive drugs, but the current figures indicate that it accounts for only 6.1 percent of the world total, thus implying that the major drug consumption problem lies elsewhere.[1]

On the production side, the picture is more complex, and the global scenario continues to evolve. The United States heads the list of producers of synthetic substances (especially ecstasy) and of marijuana (UNDCP 1997, 23), while Latin America continues dominant in the production of cocaine, and has moved recently into the heroin industry, once almost the exclusive domain of the Asian countries.

These recent trends have put paid to the once reasonably clear separation between consuming and production countries, which had become a key element in the definition of international policy against drugs. The blurring of that line implies new challenges for governments and for international agencies dedicated to the eradication of psychoactive substances.

In spite of the efforts made thus far by communities, governments, and international agencies, neither the supply nor the demand for illicit substances has been reduced. In many cases punitive actions have been counterproductive. Failure is equally evident on the side of criminalization of consumers, with the enormous pressure this puts on the prison system, and in the attempts at eradication, which contribute to the destruction of ecosystems that are important for humanity (like the Amazon Basin) through the resulting invasions and deforestation in areas increasingly remote and fragile.

Colombia in the International Drug Market

Among the prominent occurrences of the last 30 years in Colombia have been a continuation of the rural–urban population shift, a pattern of stable economic growth by the standards of the region, few significant reforms in terms of access to productive resources, the appearance of such new groups as the paramilitaries, popular militias and hired killers, an increase in the average living standards of both rural and urban dwellers though with continuing high levels of poverty, inequality, and violence. Perhaps the most significant event for Colombia over this period was its entry into the international drug business. In political, social, and economic terms Colombia has suffered a transformation through the penetration of the major institutions by the drug industry.

Colombia's entry into the international drug trade dates from the 1970s, with the production of marijuana in the Atlantic Coast, especially the Guajira and the region of the Sierra Nevada de Santa Marta. This opportunity arose when Mexico, which had supplied the American demand until the mid-1970s, was eliminated from the picture. Colombia was in a good position to take over this trade by virtue of its proximity by air and by sea to the United States, its long contraband tradition, and a strong endowment of the entrepreneurial skills needed to adapt to this new industry (Zamosc 1986, 137).

Cocaine burst on the consumer scene in Colombia during the 1970s, especially among the middle and upper classes, a factor that encouraged both the expansion of the traditional production zones, especially in Peru and

Bolivia, and later the launching of production in Colombia itself around 1975. The country had already begun to play a role in the world market as a processor of the coca leaf from Peru and Bolivia; the repression of production in those two countries and the adoption of high-yielding varieties in Colombia turned it into a major producer.

Heroin production began in the 1990s in response to three basic factors: (1) an increase in demand in the United States; (2) the chance to use the same distribution channels already employed for marijuana and cocaine; and (3) the alliances that Colombian traffickers established with other international organizations (from Asia and Europe) and which have given all actors a chance to expand their markets.

Various factors have been cited as contributing to the development of the drug industry in Colombia (Thoumi 1997; Thoumi and Mújica 1997), including an increasing world demand for psychedelic drugs; a favorable geographic setting; a crisis in Colombian agriculture, making other crops less attractive to producers; an effective interface with world narcotraffic networks; the weak control by the Colombian state over the country's territory; a lack of state monopoly on the use of force; a weak judicial system; lack of moral strength; a civil society with low levels of organization and with high levels of economic and social marginalization; and bad policy choices with respect to the control of the production of the illicit drugs.

The Production of Illicit Substances in Colombia

The principal producers of *coca leaf* are now Peru, Colombia, and Bolivia. Colombia has been prominent in the processing of coca paste and the distribution of cocaine, while Peru and Bolivia are essentially suppliers of paste, although in recent years they have entered into processing and distribution. Colombia's share of coca leaf production rose from 20 percent at the beginning of the 1990s to 53 percent in 1998. Gross revenues from cocaine sales in 1995 (the year selected for our benchmark calculations) were somewhere in the low billions of dollars. Based on the estimated area under cultivation in that year (see table 6.1) and an average yield of 0.8 metric tons per hectare, deducting 20 percent for losses through confiscation and excluding from consideration the processing of Bolivian and Peruvian leaf, one comes to a lower-limit estimate of about 85 metric tons. At an average price of US$20,000 per kilo on the street (and assuming a conversion rate of 450 kilograms of leaf to 1 kilogram of cocaine), this would imply revenues of about US$1.7 billion (table 6.2). At the other end of the spectrum, assuming that all of Peruvian and Bolivian production was processed by Colombia and that the confiscation ratio was only 10 percent, the total revenue would

Table 6.1 Area Dedicated to Production of Coca Leaf, 1989–1998 (Hectares)

Country	1989	1990	1991	1992	1993	1994	1995	1996	1997	1998
Peru	121,685	121,300	120,800	129,100	108,600	115,300	115,300	95,600	68,800	51,000
Colombia	**43,040**	**41,000**	**38,472**	**38,059**	**40,493**	**49,610**	**59,650**	**72,800**	**79,500**	**101,800**
Bolivia	55,400	58,400	53,386	50,649	49,600	48,630	54,093	55,600	45,800	38,000
World	220,125	220,700	212,658	217,808	198,693	213,540	229,043	224,000	194,100	190,800

Source: Bureau for International Narcotic and Law Enforcements Affairs. 1997. *Worldwide Illicit Drug Cultivation Totals.*

Table 6.2 Colombia's Gross Revenue from Sale of Cocaine, 1995: Range of Possible Scenarios

Alternative Scenarios	National Production (Metric tons)	Cocaine Produced Using Leaf Imported from Bolivia and Peru (Metric tons)	Confiscations and Losses (%)	Wholesale Price in U.S. Port (US$)	Gross Income (Millions of Dollars)
Minimum	106	0	20	20,000	1,700
Maximum	106	301	10	20,000	7,326
Intermediate	106	240	20	20,000	5,540

Source: Authors' calculations.

have been US$7.3 billion. A middle (best) estimate, based on the assumption that Bolivia and Peru process 20 percent of their leaf and that confiscation losses are at 20 percent, is about US$5.5 billion.

The main sources of *opium* are the golden Triangle (Myanmar, Thailand, and Laos) of Southeast Asia, the Golden Crescent (Pakistan, Afghanistan, and Iran) of Southwest Asia, and Mexico. Colombia began producing opium in the 1990s and quickly reached a high level of penetration of the U.S. market. According to available data on area cultivated (table 6.3), and assuming a conversion factor of 10 kilograms of latex per hectare of poppy and two crops per year, production in 1995 would have been 130,800 kilograms of latex, equal to 13 tons of heroine[2] which, estimated to have a value of 59,000 per kilogram in the American port, comes to a total value of US$650 million.

Marijuana generates a much lower gross income, probably in the range of US$150 million. This estimate is based on an average yield of 1.5 tons per hectare[3] (and an average of between two and three crops per year), implying an annual production of 7,500 tons per year. The wholesale price in the United States in 1995 was about US$20,000 per ton.

Thus the total gross estimated income in the American port for the drug industry as a whole (cocaine, marijuana, and heroin) in 1995 would have fallen somewhere between a minimum of around US$2.5 billion and a maximum of around US$8.1 billion; a reasonable middle estimate would be about US$6.3 billion.

The economists who have estimated Colombia's net income from the drug industry judge that raw materials are not very important in the cost structure, but that processing, transportation, bribery, security, and, above all, the laundering of dollars add up to between 40 and 60 percent of gross value. Thus the net income generated by the industry in 1995, based on our best estimate of gross revenues would fall between US$2.5 billion and US$3.8 million.[4] Not all of this, as discussed below, is repatriated to the country. Many factors affect the repatriation decision such as the absorptive capacity of the Colombian financial system, the investment options available within the country, the risk associated with such investment, and the need for resources to reinvest in the drug industry itself.

Though it is of interest from the perspective of the national economy to know the level of economic assets that the drug lords keep outside the country (in part because they can be the source of future flows back into the country), the estimation of this stock is not a simple task. Steiner (1996, 50) reports that it is virtually impossible to get an accurate reading, not only because the information produced by the Bank for International Settlements is in any case unreliable for this sort of assets, but also because it does not

Table 6.3 Area Dedicated to Production of Poppies for Opium, 1989–1998 (Hectares)

Country	1989	1990	1991	1992	1993	1994	1995	1996	1997	1998
Southeast Asia	25,510	20,775	25,835	28,617	25,480	35,144	50,440	44,450	45,300	44,750
Southwest Asia	189,943	184,835	194,837	184,155	195,324	172,540	176,745	190,520	184,950	157,750
Colombia	n.d.	n.d.	**2,316**	**32,715**	**29,281**	**24,676**	**6,540**	**6,300**	**6,600**	**6,100**
Others	15,595	15,230	15,431	11,370	13,624	12,615	13,775	16,240	10,150	8,500
World	**231,048**	**220,840**	**238,419**	**256,857**	**263,709**	**244,975**	**247,500**	**257,510**	**247,000**	**217,100**

Source: International Narcotics Control Strategy Report Data. (1997). *Worldwide Illicit Drug Cultivation Totals.*

include the funds kept in banks in the "tax shelters." Faced with the inability to estimate net repatriation as the difference between gross revenues and money held abroad, various researchers have undertaken direct estimates of the amount of money returning to the country, based on the various mechanisms most frequently used to effect that transfer (tourism, private transfers, underinvoicing of imports, contraband) and have thereby come up with calculations of the percentage that these flows constitute of the total drug income.

Net Income from the Export of Illegal Drugs

Two of the more recent studies of the production and sales of illegal drugs in Colombia give a glimpse of the data and methodological difficulties in reaching a plausible estimate of the size of the industry (Steiner 1996; Rocha 1997). Steiner (1996), using official statistics complemented by calculations of other analysts, estimates that the net repatriated income from the external sales of these drugs fluctuated around 5 percent of Colombia's GDP in the 15-year period 1981–1995, while Rocha (1997) estimates a range from a minimum of 2.3 percent of GDP to a maximum of 8.5 percent, the latter case corresponding to the assumption that almost all of the production of Bolivia and Peru was processed in Colombia. The main differences between these two studies seem to come from differences in conversion factors, assumptions about the number of crops per year, the weight of heroin in the total drug industry, the extent of losses suffered in the chain of production–sales, quantum and price of exports to the American and European markets, the volume of imports of leaf from Bolivia and Peru, the costs of laundering funds,[5] security, and transportation.

A comparison of the estimates for the cocaine market in 1995 allows us to appreciate in detail the differences between the authors (table 6.4). Rocha's estimate of quantity exported was three times Steiner's,[6] while the difference in assumed prices went in the opposite direction. Both assumed costs in the neighborhood of 60 percent of gross revenues, but the assumptions about their composition were quite different; for example, Rocha assumed that inputs represented 23 percent of total costs and Steiner put them at just 8 percent. Steiner (1997, 104) argues that, apart from a bleep in the early 1980s, the revenues from the industry have been relatively stable over time and that this, together with its modest size in the total economy, renders it quite difficult to judge its economic impact on the rest of the economy by trying to relate fluctuations in the one with fluctuations in the other.[7] Rocha reaches the opposite conclusion—that the Colombia economy is quite

Table 6.4 Alternative Estimates of Net Income from Cocaine Sale: Colombia, 1995 (Values in millions of U.S. dollars)

	Steiner	Rocha
Quantity Exported (metric tons)	238.7	764.3
Price per kilo (U.S.$)	16,500	10,500
Gross Income	3,938	8,025
Cost of Purchased Inputs	321	1,613
Other costs	1,811	2,866
Net Income Before Laundering	1,806	3,546
Costs of Laundering	360	533
Net Repatriated Income	1,446	3,013

Source: Steiner (1997) and Rocha (1997).

sensitive to inflows of illegal funds, which can have important impacts even when their magnitude is relatively small. Another difference of interpretation between these authors is that Steiner (1997), on the basis of econometric analysis, concludes that the bulk of the dollar earnings of the industry have been repatriated in recent years, partially through the exchange market and principally through contraband, while Rocha (1997) is inclined to believe that the repatriated resources have been declining; according to him, laundering the money has become more difficult in Colombia, due in part to the structural characteristics of the industry, in part to the increasing difficulties of using contraband as the vehicle since the markets for items like computers have become flooded, and in part to the scarcity of agricultural land of good quality in regions of weak state presence (Thoumi 1997, 23). He thus judges that an increasing share of revenues has been left abroad rather than repatriated.

Despite the significant differences in the estimates of these two and other studies of the drug industry in Colombia, between them they do give a reasonably clear picture of the size and possible effects of the industry in the country.[8] As noted above, the repatriated net income is probably in the range around 5 percent of GDP; total net revenues, including money kept outside the country, would thus be somewhat greater. The lower-limit estimate (from Steiner) comes on average to about a third of legal registered exports during the early 1990s (table 6.5) while the upper limit (from Rocha) averages close to one half. Even the former exceeds coffee exports throughout these years and all of agricultural exports in some of them. Meanwhile the areas dedicated to the production of illegal drugs, which doubled in the short period

Table 6.5 Net Repatriated Income from Export Sales of Illicit Drugs in Relation to Other Exports, 1981–1995 (Values in Millions of U.S. Dollars FOB)

| Year | Registered Exports | | | Net Repatriated | | Net Repatriated Drug Income | |
	Total	Agricultural	Coffee	income from illicit drugs*	As percentage of registered exports	As percentage of registered agricultural exports	As percentage of registered exports of coffee
1990	6,765	2,078	1,415	2,389–6,455	36.3–95.4	115–311	169–443
1991	7,244	2,210	1,336	2,239–4,037	30.9–55.7	101–183	168–302
1992	7,065	2,175	1,259	2,667–3,538	37.7–50.1	123–163	212–281
1993	7,123	2,034	1,140	2,487–3,410	34.9–47.9	122–168	218–299
1994	8,461	2,999	1,990	2,261–3,232	26.7–38.2	75–108	114–162
1995	9,763	2,859	1,832	2,535–3,576	25.9–36.6	89–125	138–195

*The range is defined by Steiner's lower limit estimate and Rocha's upper limit estimate.
Sources: Rocha (1997); Steiner (1997); DANE, Exportaciones Colombianas por Sector Económico.

between 1991 and 1996 from 43,000 to 84,000 hectares, rose from just 1.2 percent to 2.5 percent of all cultivable land in Colombia.[9] The workers involved directly in the drug industry consist of farmers, processors, transport workers, exporters, and distributors. Based on the estimated hectares cultivated over the period 1990–1996, and assuming a permanent labor input of 1 man year/hectare of coca (De Rementería 1995; Rojas 1995) and 2 man years/hectare in the cases of poppies and marijuana, one deduces that the total number of workers rose from 11,400 in 1990 to 95,400 in 1996, and an average of 85,000 over this period. To these figures must be added the seasonal jobs required for the harvesting and processing of leaf to paste, the other direct activities along the product chain plus those employed indirectly in the production and sale of inputs, which raises the estimate to an average of 129,000 or almost 5.5 percent of the agricultural labor force in 1996. Of these, 57 percent were dedicated to the production and processing of coca leaf into paste, 34 percent to the cultivation of poppies and the remaining 9 percent to the production of marijuana. About 20,000–25,000 were involved in processing, 94 percent of these in that of coca leaf. The number of refiners ("chemists") was about 1,500. The exporters, defined as those who manage the process, contracting with transporters and arranging for financing, were about 1,200 (Zabludoff 1994). The transport function varies in character according to the destination and the contractor. Part of this task is carried out by "mules," who assume the risks of moving the merchandise; the majority is handled by people dedicated exclusively to the activity and who use airplanes, boats, and other sophisticated means of getting the goods into the consuming country. Along the chain from producer to consumer there are large groups of workers dedicated to security and communications, together with falsifiers, financial advisors, lawyers, murderers, and launderers of funds.

Incomes by Group

A first approximation of the distribution of earnings among the various groups involved in the drug chain is presented in table 6.6. The largest group are the *cultivators*—the *campesinos*, squatters, or indigenous people who produce the crops and undertake the first stages of processing, dedicating part or all of their time to the activity and sometimes with the participation of the whole family. Our figures suggest that in 1995 nearly 74,200 people fell into this category (constituting about 2.5 percent of the agricultural labor force,[10] and about equal to the employment in the flower industry), a figure reduced by about 8,500 due to the eradication and fumigation carried out by the authorities. The opportunity cost of this labor depends to a large extent

Table 6.6 Direct Income from Participation in the Illicit Drug Industry, by Groups, 1995

Activity	Number of participants	Output	Price per Kg (US$)	Income (mill. US$)	Costs, % (mill. US$)		Profits (mill. US$)
Coca–Leaf–Cocaine							
Coca–Leaf	51,107 farmers	40,886 MT of leaf 273 MT of Paste	2 700	82 191	20%	38	153
Base	22,500 processors	91 MT of base	1,200	109	20%	21.8	87.2
National Production HCL of Cocaine	5,400 refiners	85	2,000	554	20%	110	444
National Production Using Imported Base Exporting	900 exporters	192 277	20,000	5,540	30%	1,662	3,878

Activity	Number of participants	Output	Price per kg (US$)	Income (Mill US$)	Costs (Mill US$)		Profits (Mill US$)
Poppies–Heroin							
Poppy–látex	13,080 farmers	131 MT latex	650	85	40%	34	51
Latex–morphine Factor M	800 processors	13 MT	12,500	163	40%	65	98
Morphine–heroine	100 exporters	13 TM	50,000	650	30%	195	455

Table 6.6 *continued*

Activity	Number of participants	Output	Price per Kg (US$)	Income (Mill US$)	Costs (Mill US$)		Profits (Mill US$)
Marijuana							
Marijuana	10,000 farmers	7,500 MT	10	75	20%	15	60
Exported Manjuana	200 exporters	7,500 MT	20	150	30%	45	105

Source: Authors' calculations.

on the region where the crops are located. When the industry was young, coca-producing regions were characterized by high rates of unemployment and/or underemployment and subsistence agriculture only required a modest share of the farmer's time (perhaps as little as 25–30 percent); thus the opportunity cost of labor often was low. With the expansion and consolidation of the industry the situation of these *campesinos* has changed. There has been considerable immigration from coffee zones and other small farm regions and also of unskilled urban workers. In these cases, it is reasonable to assume that the opportunity cost of the labor corresponds to its productivity in the agricultural or urban activities from which the workers came; it may be approximated by the cost of unskilled urban labor like basic construction workers and the minimum wage in agriculture. Note also that, in general, drug production uses land that was not previously employed for agriculture.

The earnings for the average farmer producing coca leaf in 1995 were about US$2,995; the corresponding figures for producers of poppies and marijuana were $3,890 and $6,000, respectively. From the production of such legal crops as flowers and coffee the average incomes were considerably less, at US$1,560 and $1,975, respectively. Coca producers averaged slightly less than the average construction worker. For many of the participants in drug production, nominal incomes may thus be as much as three to four times greater than in their previous activity. The real income differential is considerably less however, since the cost of living tends to be high in the drug-producing areas (rather parallel to the oil-producing areas), due to high food prices and either high prices and/or lack of access to good quality education and health services.

Although the above figures point to higher average incomes from production of marijuana and heroin than from coca, neither of these two has shown the growth dynamic that coca has. Colombian marijuana is not highly favored in the international markets so most of the production is for local use, at quite low prices. The market share of Colombian heroin has been stable at about 1.5 percent.

Processors

Coca paste is converted to cocaine in two separate steps: first, processing to "base;" then refining to hydrochloride of cocaine, the latter step being undertaken in more sophisticated laboratories and larger quantities. The average output (value added) per processor appears to have been about US$3,900, while that of the refiners was much larger—around US$82,000. The corresponding figure for the processors and refiners of morphine latex was about US$122,000. If individuals in these latter categories were to compete for regular employment as medium level professionals they might expect incomes of about US$10,500 per year. Probably those engaged in processing of coca paste received earnings fairly close to their average productivity, while for the higher-skilled categories one can only treat their average productivity as a ceiling above which earnings could not rise. Since the drug lords control the whole process in greater or lesser degree, the earnings of each group are the result of a process in which those at the top have great influence and may in fact take the bulk of the "rents" involved. For present purposes it is less important for us to know how income is distributed between the drug lords and the relatively highly paid groups in the product chain than to know the share of those at the bottom (mainly cultivators).

Income of those engaged in transportation is hard to estimate on a per person basis for lack of information. Rocha (1997) puts the figure at US$3,000 per kilogram of cocaine or heroin. As for exporters, the available estimates suggest that the approximately 1,000 people engaged in the export of cocaine and heroin took in an average of US$4.3–4.5 million per year. Those in the marijuana business earned a much smaller but still substantial US$525,000. The first two groups would be earning about 20 times the average income of persons classified as "employers" in the Departamento Administrativo Nacional de Estadística's (DANE) household income surveys (Sánchez 1998, 348).

The Distribution of Income in Colombia and How the Drug Industry Has Affected It

The income figures just reviewed paint a picture of enormous inequality in the distribution of drug incomes. Taken literally, they imply that the 1,200 "exporters," who constitute only a little over 1 percent of the people involved, reaped over 80 percent of the income. Even if the figures substantially exaggerate the actual level of inequality within the industry, they still create a strong presumption that income earned directly in the drug industry is substantially more unequally distributed than is national income in Colombia overall.[11] This in turn creates a presumption that the presence of the drug industry probably raises overall inequality; this is not a certainty, however, since the indirect effects of the industry need to be allowed for. A variety of other types of evidence (see below) do tend to confirm this hypothesis, but some tend to cast doubt on it. And there is the possibility that the drug sector is simply too small to have a very noticeable impact on inequality or poverty at the national level. It is in any case desirable to review the relevant information in some detail.

Evidence on the Level and Trends in Inequality in Colombia

The level of inequality has always been high in Colombia, as in most countries of the region. Most students of this feature of Colombian society believe that there was a degree of improvement in the urban distribution between some point in the 1970s and the end of the 1980s (Londoño 1995; Berry 1997; Sánchez 1998). There is no consensus on what happened to rural distribution (on which the data are much sparser and less comparable over time), or on changes in overall-to-overall distribution. For Londoño (1998) inequality and poverty are no longer the dominant social problems of Colombia, having been replaced by educational inequality and the spiral into violence. He believes that poverty and inequality fell in the 1970s and the 1980s due to the overall economic growth, to increases in social spending and to the rising participation of women in the labor force. Ocampo et al. (1998) conclude that, although indicators of social welfare have indeed improved between the 1950s and the 1990s, the evolution of inequality and poverty over the last three decades is worrisome. Over 1978–1988 they estimate that rural poverty rose while its urban counterpart fell up until the early 1990s due to the improved opportunities for women in the labor force; after 1991, however, the situation of the urban poor was affected negatively by a bias on the demand side in favor of skilled workers and against the less skilled and by an increase in nonwage incomes in the urban areas. In 1978 the top decile renewed 47.9 percent of all income and the bottom half got just 12.4 percent. In 1995 the former ratio had risen to 51.0 percent while the latter stayed constant, implying that the intermediate deciles, representing the middle and upper middle classes had suffered a decline in their share from 39.7 percent to 36.6 percent. Meanwhile Berry and Tenjo (1998), who look only at urban distribution (three of the largest cities) agree that urban distribution had improved prior to the early 1990s, but find a sharp reversal of that process in the early 1990s, which they suspect may be related to the liberalization of the economy (including that of the labor market) and to the effects of globalization.

One of the few studies of rural income distribution (Leivovich 1998) finds some improvement over 1988–1995 in a still quite regressive distribution. The distribution of land has been affected by the guerrilla presence in many parts of the country, by the limited activity of the Colombia Agrarian Reform Institute (INCORA) in the process of land redistribution. The purchase of land by the drug lords might be expected to skew its distribution further, only partly alleviated by the possibility of expropriation of land owned by drug lords through the Confiscation Law (Ley de Extinción de Dominio). Leivovich emphasizes the low levels of education as a factor in rural poverty. Since one might have expected the accumulation of land by the drug lords to increase the concentration of rural income, Leivovich's findings in the opposite direction may appear surprising; given the limitations of the data it must be considered tentative. The fact that the drug lords who receive high incomes from the drug industry do not generally live in the rural areas makes the finding less surprising (as does the fact that income surveys may be unlikely to record the families involved in that business in any case). More relevant is what has been happening to the agricultural wage and the overall earnings of the lower-income rural groups. That wage for the country as a whole has fluctuated without clear trend since the late 1970s, after rising sharply at that time. It hit a trough in the early 1990s (when agriculture did badly), and then rose over the period 1992–1997 (Jaramillo and Nupia 1998, 13). Rural poverty incidence seems to have changed little during the 1990s (ECLAC 2000).

None of the cited studies considers the role of drugs as a determinant of income distribution. In this paper we attempt a first modest step toward a better understanding of that role. When the drug industry was in its first growth phase during the 1970s most economists judged that its impact in the labor market was small. Urrutia (1985, 119) noted that since coca paste was not produced locally "this line of business only produced very high earnings for a few underground entrepreneurs and their employees, but had little impact on the overall demand for labor."

Drug Production, Land, Migration, Violence, and Displacement

During the 1980s and 1990s the situation changed considerably, as evidenced by the above-cited figures on land under cultivation and net incomes repatriated, which reflect the country's position as a diversified, integrated, and dynamic drug producer. Through its effect on the ownership of land and capital the drug industry has affected economic structure not only via the primary distribution of income but also in terms of power relations within the country. It is part of a complicated political process that had led to the displacement of almost 1.5 million people by the mid- to late 1990s. Such large movements of people naturally have an impact on local labor markets; they also stand as a stark reflection of the unresolved problem of land rights in Colombia, aggravated by the presence of armed groups financed by the drug trade. These displacements are linked both to land conflicts and to conflicts over territoriality (Conferencia Episcopal de Colombia 1996; CODHES 1998). The former have been present throughout Colombian history, linked to the high degree of land concentration and to the competition for it among *latifundios, minifundios*, and commercial agriculture. The

Table 6.7 Population displaced by year in Colombia, 1985–1998

Year	Number of families	Number of people
1985–1994	108,301	586,261
1995	21,312	89,510
1996	36,202	181,010
1997	51,400	257,000
1998	71,613	308,800
Total	288,828	1,421,781

Sources: DNP/Conpes 2840, September 13, 1995; CODHES 1999.

second are a manifestation of the desire to control territory as a strategic space by the key actors—guerrillas, paramilitary, popular militias, the state, and sometimes others. Although both conflicts cause great damage to the rural poor, the impact, at least as measured by the number of displaced persons, is greater from this second phenomenon. The number of displaced has jumped dramatically since 1995 (Table 6.7). According to Osorio and Lozano (1997), about two-thirds of the displaced population is of rural origin, and the majority of these are small owners, sharecroppers, squatters, or agricultural laborers, with low levels of education. Only one in three displaced families interviewed expected to return to their point of origin and of those only 38 percent have returned to their former homes (i.e. about 13 percent of all those displaced). Each of the groups vying for territorial control is responsible for the displacement of victims. Over 1984–1994 the guerrillas were blamed by 32 percent and the paramilitary, military, and national police lumped together for 46 percent; by 1995–1996 the guerrilla share had dropped a little to 29 percent while that of the other three groups had risen to 49 percent; in particular, the share attributed to the paramilitaries jumped from 21 percent over 1984–1994 to 33 percent in 1995–1996 (Table 6.8).

The large migratory flows toward the drug zones has helped sustain or increase agricultural salaries in legal activities and also acted as a muffler against urban unemployment. Jaramillo and Nupia (1998) show that agricultural salaries have been higher in the regions with significant production of drugs. The population flows have been toward the drug zones in the eastern part of the country and away from northern departments with their historic land tenure problems and from other regions with serious territorial conflict. The relatively high wages in the drug zones cannot, as they would under more normal circumstances, be interpreted as a fairly clear positive indication as to the impact of the industry on workers. They reflect in part

Table 6.8 Who are responsible for the displacements of people in Colombia 1984–1996(%)

Groups	1984–1994	1994–1995	1995–1996
Guerrilla	32	26	29
Paramilitaries	21	32	33
Armed forces	20	16	14
National police	5	3	2
Drug industry	5	2	1
Popular militias	4	2	6
Others	13	19	15

Source: CODHES (1999).

high prices, as noted, but also the fact that, other things equal, wages tend to be higher in difficult and dangerous contexts like these; this was earlier reflected in the high wages reported from the zones of conflict during *La Violencia*[12] of the 1950s.

Land Conflict

Key to the way in which the presence of drug production has played itself out in Colombia is the background of land inequality, unsettled property rights to land and the related conflict over it. "In their own way, the drug lords carried out an Agrarian Reform, for two reasons: first in order to imitate the tradition of large holders and thus convert their fortunes into haciendas; and second, because the majority were dispossessed immigrants who had fled to the cities from other episodes of violence and now, with pockets full, felt the need to return to the places from which they had been earlier evicted" (Castro Caycedo 1996, 254).

The degree of concentration has long been the most striking feature of Colombia's agrarian structure. Over the last several decades there appear to have been two distinct patterns of change. Between 1960 and 1984 there was, at least according to some figures, a tendency favoring middle-sized productive units (20–100 hectares) thereby diminishing the role both of the very large units (over 500 hectares) and the small ones (5–20 hectares); there was also some metamorphosing of traditional *latifundia* into commercial farms or into large cattle ranches. A subsequent period, 1984–1996, has been characterized by Mondragón (1998) as one of "*relatifundization*," and of fragmentation of the smallest farms (under 5 hectares) whose number rose without any change in their total area. This reconcentration has not been accompanied by a general agricultural modernization. There has been a decrease in the area under cultivation, characterizing all sizes but was most marked in those of above 200 hectares, where share cultivated fell from 7.5 percent in 1988 to 1.7 percent in 1996. Among the reasons adduced for this trend have been the rising share of land in the hands of the drug lords and the economic liberalization which led to a major surge of agricultural imports. The drug lords saw land not only as an economic resource but also as a means of achieving social and political influence. Their increased control of land has raised overall land concentration, reinforced a traditional ineffi-ciency in Colombia's agricultural system—the tendency to dedicate the best lands to cattle raising, contributed to the displacement of peasants to fron-tier zones and the cities, and fueled an overvaluation of land which discour-aged legitimate agricultural enterprise (Reyes 1997). It has also financed the counterinsurgents who dispute territory with the guerrillas and often terror-ize the local populations. Reyes concludes that, overall, agriculture has lost much more than it has gained from the presence of the drugs.[13]

Colombia has, over the years, attempted to address problems of inequality and lack of access to land by agrarian reform and by colonization. The former has had little presence or impact in the country in spite of the various laws enacted; the power of large holders and their allies has always outweighed any forces for reform. Law 4 of 1973 basically closed the door on expropriation of land in the populated parts of the country, by establishing very easy condi-tions of ineligibility for expropriation. And Law 6 of 1975, ostensibly designed to protect the sharecroppers, wound up decimating them through the fear it created on the part of the landholders of losing their land.

After the passage of these laws, the importance of INCORA diminished and it limited itself mainly to distributing unused public lands and to solv-ing occasional land disputes using land it had acquired earlier. Over the period 1962–1982, when the land frontier incorporated 6,543,000 addi-tional hectares, INCORA had purchased only 425,000 hectares, expropri-ated 62,000 and received 335,000 through extinction of private domain through lack of use (Ruiz 1987, 491). INCORA has thus been marginal to the process of changing land use in Colombia.

Colonization by aspiring smallholders has been the preferred alternative of the Colombian governments since it does not threaten the interests of the landed elite (Rojas 1990, 414), but it too has been a relatively ineffective tool for resolving problems of land access and rural poverty. Often it does little more that transfer the poverty to a more isolated area; worse, the land conflicts from which the *campesinos* escape as they move to the frontier reap-pear there as well, due to the weakness of the state and its inability or unwill-ingness to impose order on land claims. The agrarian structures of the traditional agricultural zones reappear on the frontier partly because land quickly passes from those who first settle it through bankruptcy, by original arrangement, or in other ways, and partly due to the shift to large-scale ranching in response to low-quality soil and a lack of easy integration into national and international markets (Molano 1987; Mora, Jaramillo, and Cubides 1989). The presence of drug production affects this process in several ways. In some regions, the production of coca appears to have slowed or even suspended the process of land concentration in the hands of traders or speculators, who often wait for the settlers' failure in order to buy the land. The higher income from coca has allowed some settlers to be able to jump to the next level, either in cattle or as modern (nonsubsistence) farmers. In attracting urban unemployed as well as *campesinos* from other zones of conflict, the coca industry has relieved the pressure in those zones, while raising land prices in the frontier areas and unleashing violence there.

Although, as just mentioned, drug production has been the vehicle of upward mobility for some peasants, the general pattern still favors the powerful. One reflection of this is that about half of coca land is in commercial units and produces 65 percent of the crop while the subsistence plots covering an equal area produce only 35 percent of it. A striking similarity with earlier periods is the continuous conflict between large holders and squatters in the frontier zones. Although in some areas the presence of the guerrillas has slowed the march of the large holders, the process of appropriation of land improvements continues.

To this basic and historic conflict has been added the presence of the paramilitaries, created not only to fight the guerrillas but also to secure the territorial control of the large holders and drug lords. Armed conflicts have been a continuing characteristic of the land frontier in Colombia, a reflection of the state's weakness to respond to social, judicial, economic, and political needs generated in the process of economic development.

The guerrilla groups have benefited from the presence of the drug sector, not only because it has widened their zones of influence and their offensive capabilities, but also because their ranks are swelled by the waves of migrants coming to the colonization zones, having been expelled from other regions due to land concentration, dense population, and conflict. In part, the guerillas have substituted for the absent state, exercising control over the labor market, the disposition of land, and the provision of credit, for example, and generally establishing the rules of collective life. In short, colonization has generated a process that is outside state control, with economic links to the production of illegal drugs and with political and social links to the warring groups.

Winners and Losers from the Sectoral Impacts of the Drug Industry

The previous sections have reviewed the evidence on who earns income directly from the drug industry. The incomes of many others are affected indirectly, through the way the drug sector affects other sectors.

A distinguishing feature of the drug industry is its vulnerability. Within that general condition, the financial resources earned in, and related to, the industry respond to the same economic forces, as does capital in general, albeit sometimes in ways that differ in detail. Its impacts on the national economy are hard to sort out, partly because of their being interwoven with other illegal activities and partly because many of its effects are of a regional character and thus vary from place to place. The main impacts traditionally identified involve contraband, the black market for foreign exchange, construction, the financial system, agriculture, and parts of the service sector. Attempts to identify the effects on winners and losers, thus focuses on these sectors.

Contraband and Underinvoicing of Imports

Kalmanovitz (1995) has estimated that contraband imports have amounted to between 5 and 12 percent of legal imports; this would imply an average value of US$536–1,287 million (CIF) for the 1990s (1990–1998).[14] If all of this contraband had been drug related, it would still only correspond to 14–33 percent of the net repatriation of funds estimated by Steiner, leaving at least about 70 percent for the other mechanisms. It is recognized that some export contraband is drug related, but this is generally believed to be much smaller in scope.

Contraband imports have had significant impacts on Colombia's manufacturing sector, especially textiles, clothing, tobacco products, electrodomestics, with the associated loss of jobs and entrepreneurial incomes.[15] The direct beneficiaries of the contraband trade are likely to fall in the middle and upper deciles of the income distribution, consisting of medium and large-scale traders who have hired workers to take care of their business in the San Andrés contraband market, as well as a chain of small street distributors which fall in the middle and lower parts of the distribution.

The Black Market for Foreign Exchange

The arrival of foreign exchange through black market channels has a variety of impacts on the domestic financial system. Since drug money constitutes the bulk of this flow it is the main determinant of the parallel exchange rate and the parallel interest rate and affects the total domestic supply of credit (Laserna 1997, 66). Perhaps the flight of capital and the presence of hot money are the two most distorting effects. The drug industry, while it brings capital into the country also contributes to capital flight through the resulting climate of uncertainty that it creates (Frank 1991). To some degree, therefore, it contributes to a replacement of capital in the hands of those who elect to take theirs out of the country by capital in the hands of or guided by the drug lords. The net effects, apart from simply who owns the capital, are hard to judge. One result is that, according to authors like Rocha (1997), the parallel financial market has reached the magnitude of the legal financial market. Illegality does impose certain additional costs on intermediation in this market.

According to studies by Castro (1996) and Hernández (1997) it appears that the foreign exchange houses financed by the drug lords have been managed by a range of professionals who often move into laundering and exporting. In this phase of the business a network of friends and relatives of the lords seems to develop, people who do not feel they are engaged in dirty business and who benefit without taking the high risks of those directly engaged in the drug industry itself.

Construction

The preferred sectors in which drug money is invested are construction, agriculture, and services. Construction underwent an impressive boom in most of the major cities of Colombia during the 1980s and early 1990s. The supply of funds through this use contributed to large amounts of employment of less-skilled workers and had multiplier effects on other sectors; on the demand side the drug industry contributed to the demand for luxury housing, offices, hotels, warehouses, and commercial establishments. This boom came to a sudden halt in 1995 due to pursuit and threatened confiscation of the assets of the drug entrepreneurs. The collapse affected construction in general and the sectors linked to it. Cali and Medellin quickly suffered recessions, with unemployment reaching the neighborhood of 20 percent, accompanied by increases in violence. Thus, in Cali the level of construction fell from 9,701 square meters in 1994 at the peak of the boom to 2,688 in 1998 (*Revista Cambio* 1999). The effect was strongly felt among small and medium enterprises. Between 1998 and 1999, according to the Cali Chamber of Commerce, over 11,000 of the 60,000 companies registered were in liquidation. The number of taxis (nearly 15,000) exceeded that in New York.

The Financial System

Colombia's financial system has been permeated by drug money. To a large extent the economic stability of the 1980s was due to this supply of financial resources in the face of the pullback of international lending at that time.

Through sophisticated financial operations, the illegal entrepreneurs have been able to maintain their capital in the legal financial system and reap the various benefits of that system. They have employed highly qualified financial advisors (national and foreign) to manage their portfolios both inside and outside the country. The advantages offered by the international banking and financial systems, especially the tax havens, have been a major factor in the fact that much drug income remains outside Colombia. The controls established in Colombia in recent years, and the pressure exerted by the United States on the laundering process have had a similar effect. It was no accident that, in the wake of the international scandal caused by the channeling of drug monies to the presidential campaign of Ernesto Samper, the financial system suffered; many financial companies went bankrupt, others had to scale down their operations significantly and others were intervened by the *Superintendencia Bancaria*.

Agricultural Sector

Agriculture has been hard hit by the drug industry, in part through the increasing concentration of land and the low intensity use of much of it, and in part through the fall in production of food crops, unable to compete with the profitability of the drug crops.[16] Though agricultural wages have been pulled up in the drug zones and indirectly in the regions from which the migrants to those zones come, other elements of rural welfare have worsened given the lack of permanent and stable jobs with social security benefits, the inability of small farmers to accumulate, the climate of violence, and the resulting lack of investment in many normal lines of agricultural activity.

The Service Sector

The informality of much of this sector has made it easily permeable by the drug monies. Commerce, especially that linked to contraband, the hotel industry, tourism, transportation, and computers are the most relevant. The expansion of these sectors has created a significant number of lower-skill jobs though they are not sectors with obvious or large positive multiplier effects.

Fiscal Resources

The growth of the drug industry has not contributed to public sector revenues. Its links with other sectors of the economy have contributed to the spread of tax evasion practices to the great majority of businesspeople. The properties confiscated from the drug lords have become unproductive and in the process have generated costs to the state.

Losses From Drug-Industry Induced Violence

In no other among the drug-producing and consuming countries have the links among poverty, drugs, and violence taken on the dimensions found in Colombia. Violence is by no means a new product of the drug industry, but it has accentuated the problem. Studies by Uprimny (1995) and others have concluded that the majority of acts of violence in Colombia are more related to social and political conflicts than directly with the drug industry. In 1989–1990 at the peak of directly drug-related violence only 227 deaths were directly attributed to the actions of the cartels, compared to 2,969 caused by the "dirty war" and over 20,000 in each year attributable to non-political causes. Drug-related deaths are, however, much higher in Colombia than in either Bolivia or Peru. Colombia suffers from inequality roughly equal to those two countries, but has long suffered from an institutional and ethical crisis, which impedes the resolution of conflicts by peaceful means.

Drug money has become one of the principal sources of finance for both the guerillas and the paramilitary forces, who have entered into a period of bloody struggle for territory where the drugs are produced, processed or exported from. This is the most damaging activity of the drug industry, in terms of its negative effects on the population. The power attained through this process has allowed the industry to broaden its social and territorial bases.

Recently the cost of this web of drug money and violence and its impacts have begun to be studied in a more systematic way. Bejarano et al. estimate the costs to society as follows:

> Taking account of public and private spending, not only to confront the insurgency challenge, together with the losses to robbery, kidnapping, etcetera., the Colombian society is paying about 4.5 percent of GDP during the last five years to just deal with the armed conflict (without including common criminality), of which about 30–40 percent corresponds to public sector expenditures, 10–15 percent to private sector spending and the rest to the loss of human capital. (1997, 250–51)

The National Department of Planning (*Departamento Nacional de Planeación*) (1994) also concluded that the armed conflict and criminality cost the country between 1.5 percent and 4 percent of GDP yearly during 1990–1994. Rubio (1994) estimates that, had criminality remained at its level of the early 1970s, the 1993 GDP would have been 22 percent higher than it was.[17] He estimates that 15 percent of GDP is transferred from the productive sector as a result of pressure from extralegal agents or as protection against them, including items for kidnapping ransom to government support for security costs. Londoño (1996), on the basis of the estimated impact of the industry on life expectancy in Colombia comes to an estimate of lost human capital equal to 2 percent of GDP in the early 1980s and to almost 5 percent in the 1990s.

On another front, the government has had to raise expenditures to combat the production, trade, and consumption of drugs and the laundering of money from their sale; although no estimates are available, given the number of agencies and expenditures involved, it is clear that the sums are large. Contributing to difficulties in the estimation of costs is the fact that many funds used to fight the industry are from international sources. And many resources used to fight consumption of drugs and to support employment viewed as an incentive for people to shift out of production are not included. Colombia and the United States are involved in a costly war against the drug industry involving programs of alternative development, eradication and substitution, repression and control, strengthening of the judicial system, and prevention.

Summing Up

The range of views as to the impact of drugs on the social and economic development of Colombia goes from those who believe it to have been quite positive—even to have supplied the funds which allowed import substituting industrialization to occur in the country (Molina 1995) to those who believe its impact has not been very large, as evidenced by the fact that when war was declared openly on the cartels, the economy did not appear to behave very differently from before (Urrutia 1985). Some believe the main impacts have not been economic but social and political, through the influence of the drug lords on state behavior and on the popular movements using violence and terrorism (Thoumi 1994). In any case, by now its effects have been clearly felt in all corners of Colombian life.

In terms of the effects on different groups, there is no doubt that the industry has raised incomes of a considerable number of small farmers and workers, but at the same time the industry has led to an increase in the concentration of land, and a disincentive to manufacturing production in various sectors. The gap between country and city may have widened as so many of the fruits of the industry have been transferred to the cities as investment and consumption. At a social and political level, the producers have been stigmatized as delinquents. The funds entering the financial sphere have played an important role in speculative activities of no social value. This combination of factors has become unsustainable since 1997 leaving the country in its deepest economic and social crisis.

Although both benefits and losses from this industry have accrued to people at all levels of income, our guess is that the overall impact of its presence has been to widen the gap in economic welfare between the better off and the less well off. The evidence pointing in this direction includes the following:

1. The bulk of drug incomes have gone to high-income individuals. The associated labor income has been too little and not sufficiently progressively distributed to imply a decrease in income inequality. Whether the industry has made any contribution to the income of poorer Colombians is hard to judge since it involves a weighing off of the direct earnings of those involved in the industry, the positive indirect effects (e.g., on construction worker incomes) and the negative indirect effects (e.g., on workers in manufacturing and other agricultural activities that have suffered). Thus it is hard to gauge whether the net impact on poverty has been positive or negative for Colombia as a whole.

2. The enormous cost in terms of loss of life, insecurity and other effects of rural violence and displacement have been principally borne by the poor. It is arguable that these costs dwarf the effects, whether positive or negative, on the monetary incomes of this group. Though other groups have also suffered severely, it is unlikely that the impact on them is anywhere close to that on the poor. The enormous costs of displacement fall very disproportionately on the latter.

3. The proposition that the drug sector made important contributions to the overall Colombian economy and through that to the poor has never had much plausibility and has none at all now. Unlike some other developing countries, Colombia was not lacking in alternative productive activities or sources of export revenues. What drugs did was to push some of those other activities down the competitiveness scale, adding at best to a modest and short-term income gain for the country when the opportunity costs of pulling resources into the sector are taken account of. The events of the 1990s have made the national economics of the drug sector look much more negative as it has fostered the economically and socially costly rural struggles, helped to impoverish the state and contributed finally to the most severe recession in a century.

The most interesting bits of evidence, which might point to a positive impact from the drug sector, are those on agricultural wages and rural income distribution in the 1990s. At face value these suggest considerable improvement, at least from the low around 1992 to just before the economic crisis at the end of the decade. It remains unclear, however, how reliable the rural distribution data are, since they show some implausibly large changes year-to-year. Only when a more thorough analysis of rural incomes over the decade has been undertaken will it be possible to know whether the story of this decade was in fact more positive than the above discussion would suggest.

Both logic and comparisons with neighboring countries do strongly suggest that the impact of the drug industry could have been much more positive or less negative than it was, had the context been different—in particular had that context not involved the long-standing processes of land and territorial conflict.

Notes

* Albert Berry is a professor at the Division of Social Sciences (International Development Studies) and Research Director of the program on Latin America and the Caribbean, Centre for International Studies at the University of Toronto.

** Jackeline Barragán has conducted research in Colombia and Canada on the illegal economy, local development, and the labor market.

1. The figures on heroin addicts in China rose to 400,000, while the consumption of basuco and cocaine in Latin America has exploded. In Bolivia, for example, the number of cocaine users jumped from 25,000 in 1979 to 300,000 in 1994 (Task Force Report 1997, 17).

2. The area cultivated in poppies has been estimated by other authors at close to 15,000 hectares, with average yield of 6 kilograms of latex/hectare and a total production of 18 tons (Vargas 1997, 54). To produce 1 kilogram of heroine requires 10 kilograms of latex.

3. Yields can vary from 0.56 metric tonssolidushectare to 1.13 metric tons/hectare per crop.

4. Note that our estimate matches the range established by Steiner and Rocha for that year. For that reason we use their estimates as a point of reference throughout this study.

5. Costs of money laundering via the importation of contraband are generally related to the differential between the official exchange rate and the black market rate. Although contraband is financed by drug money, different people are in charge of the two activities. The complementary relationship between them permits both to minimize the risks to their investment.

6. Steiner's figure appears the more consistent with estimates of world consumption (UNDCP 1997).

7. Steiner estimated that the net repatriated revenue from the industry fell from a peak of 7% of (legal) GDP and around 70% of legal registered exports at the beginning of the 1980s to about 3% and 25%, respectively, by 1995. But the decline was gradual as total repatriated income showed no trend while GDP was rising.

8. A review of earlier studies (Barragán and Vargas 1994; Kalmanovitz 1995) led us to the conclusion that these two authors had taken account of earlier studies and that their figures bracket a reasonable estimate of the range from lower to upper plausible limits.

9. Based on data from the Bureau for International Narcotic and Law Enforcements Affairs (1997) and from DANE (Sector Real).

10. Based on the calculations of Balcázar (1998, 10).

11. This same presumption is implicit in the fact that an industry which may be generating say 5% of the legal GDP creates jobs for less that 1% of the labor force. Note that the figures used here refer to repatriated income; that which is kept abroad also accrues mainly to the kingpins, so its inclusion would further skew the distribution of income generated in the sector.

12. For more about the period of *La Violencia*, see Thoumi and Rojas in this volume.

13. He also, however, believes that it opens the door to a genuine agrarian reform, since if all drug lands could be expropriated this would provide a large base from which to supply land to smallholders.

14. Other authors, among them Junguito and Caballero (1980) have estimated for various periods that the contraband represented in the 1980s between 5% and 10% of the legal imports.

15. The drug industry is like any other export industry; by making more foreign exchange available it discourages other export industries and import-competing ones. It would not be legitimate to characterize it as a Dutch disease industry since it does generate a relatively large number of jobs per dollar repatriated. With the latter figure in the range US$2.5–3.5 billion in the early 1990s and the number of jobs at say 100,000, the exports per person come to 25–35 million per person.

16. Another view is that the presence of the drug industry forced competing subsectors to become more efficient in order to compete with that industry. Most likely, however, this effect would at most partially offset the negative effect just cited.

17. This was based on Scully's (1995) estimate that countries which respect laws and property rights grow at 1–2 percent faster than those that do not.

References

Balcázar, Álvaro. 1998. *Las transformaciones agrícolas en la década de los noventa*. Unpublished manuscript, Bogotá.

Barragán, Jackeline and Ricardo Vargas. 1994. Economía y violencia del narcotráfico en Colombia: 1981–1991. In *violencia en la región andina. El caso Colombia* (2nd ed.), edited by Fernán González et al., 265–86. Bogotá: Cinep-Apep.

Bejarano, Jesús Antonio et al. 1997. *Colombia: Inseguridad, violencia y desempeño económico en las areas rurales*. Bogotá: Fonade/Universidad Externado de Colombia.

Berry, Albert. 1997. The Inequality Threat in Latin America. *Latin American Research Review* 32: 3–40.

Berry, Albert and Jaime Tenjo. 1998. Trade Liberalization, Labour Reform and Income Distribution in Colombia. In *Poverty, Economic Reform, and Income Distribution in Latin America*, edited by Albert Berry, 155–78. Boulder, Colorado: Lynne Rienner Publishers.

Bureau for International Narcotic and Law Enforcements Affairs. 1997. *International Narcotics Control Strategy Report*. February. Washington, D.C.: U.S. Department of State.

Castro Caycedo, Germán. 1996. *En secreto*. Bogotá: Planeta.

Conferencia Episcopal de Colombia. 1996. *Desplazamiento y Derechos Humanos en Colombia 1993–1995*. Bogota: Conferencia Episcopal de Colombia/CODHES.

Consultoría para los Derechos Humanos y el Desplazamiento (CODHES). 1998. *Un País que Huye. Desplazamiento y Violencia en una Nación Fragmentada*. Bogota: UNICEF/CODHES.

———. 1999.

Departamento Nacional de Planeación (DNP). 1994. *Lineamientos de política para el desarrollo alternativo*. Documento Conpes. Bogotá: DNP.

De Rementería, Iván. 1995. *La elección de las drogas. Exámen de las políticas de control*. Lima: Fundación Fiedrich Ebert.

———. 1997. La economía política de las drogas en la década de los años 90: una nota de síntesis. In *La grieta de las drogas. Desintegración social y políticas públicas en América Latina*, edited by M. Hopenhayn. Chile: Naciones Unidas/Comisión Económica para América Latina y El Caribe.

Economic Commission for Latin America and the Caribbean (ECLAC). 2000. *The Equity Gap: A second assessment*. Santiago, Chile: ECLAC.

Frank, Gunter. 1991. Colombian Capital Flight. *Journal of Interamerican Studies and World Affairs* 33 (Spring): 123–47.

Jaramillo, Carlos Felipe and Óscar Nupia. 1998. *Salarios rurales, agricultura e integración: una evaluación de los cambios recientes en el mercado laboral rural*. Unpublished manuscript. Bogotá.

Junguito, Roberto and Carlos Caballero. 1980. La economía subterránea y la política monetaria. *Economía Colombiana* 125 (February–March).

Kalmanovitz, Salomón. 1995. Análisis macroeconómico del narcotráfico en la economía colombiana. In *Drogas, poder y región en Colombia*, edited by Ricardo Vargas. Bogotá: CINEP.

Laserna, R. 1997. La economía de la coca en Bolivia: cinco preguntas y una duda. In *La grieta de las drogas. Desintegración social y políticas públicas en América Latina*, edited by M. Hopenhayn, 65–71. Santiago, Chile: Naciones Unidas/CEPAL.

Leivovich, José. 1998. Análisis de los cambios en la distribución del ingreso rural: 1988–1995. In *La distribución del ingreso en Colombia. Tendencias recientes y retos de la política pública*, edited by Fabio Sánchez. Bogotá: Tercer Mundo Editores/Departamento Nacional de Planeación.

Londoño, Juan Luis. 1995. *Distribución del ingreso y desarrollo económico. Colombia en el siglo XX*. Bogotá: TM Editores/Banco de la República, Fedesarrollo.

———. 1996. Violencia, psiquis y capital social. *Revista Consigna* 420:20.

Londoño, Juan Luis. 1998. Brechas sociales. In La distribución del ingreso en Colombia. Tendencias recientes y retos de la política pública, edited by Fabio Sánchez. Bogotá: Tercer Mundo Editores/Departamento Nacional de Planeación.

Molano, Alfredo. 1987. Selva adentro. Bogota: Áncora Editores.

Molina, P. 1995. Illegal Drug Trafficking and Economic Development in Colombia. Ph.D. Thesis, Urbana, Illinois.

Mondragón, Héctor. 1998. Relatifundización, megaproyectos y campesinos. Unpublished manuscript, Bogotá.

Mora, Leónidas, Jaime Jaramillo, and Fernando Cubides. 1989. Colonización, coca y guerrilla. Bogotá: Alianza Editorial Colombiana.

Ocampo, J.A., M.J. Pérez, C.E. Tovar, and F.J. Lasso 1998. Macroeconomía, Ajuste Estructural y Equidad en Colombia: 1978–1996. In La distribución del ingreso en Colombia. Tendencias recientes y retos de la política pública, edited by F. Sánchez, 37–86. Bogotá: Tercer Mundo/DNP.

Osorio and Lozano. 1997.

Revista Cambio 1999.

Reyes, Alejandro. 1997. La compra de tierras por narcotraficantes. In Drogas ilícitas en Colombia. Su impacto económico, político y social, edited by Francisco Thoumi et al. Bogotá: PNUD/Ariel Ciencia Política/DNE.

Rocha, Ricardo. 1997. Aspectos económicos de las drogas ilegales en Colombia. In Drogas ilícitas en Colombia. Su impacto económico, político y social, edited by Francisco Thoumi et al. Bogotá: PNUD/Ariel Ciencia Política/DNE.

Rojas, Humberto. 1990. Economía campesina y recursos naturales en zonas de colonización. In El campesinado contemporáneo, edited by Fernando Bernal. Bogotá: Ceres/Tercer Mundo.

Rojas, Maritza. 1995. Los campesinos cocaleros del Departamento de San Martín. Perú: Cedro.

Rubio, Mauricio. 1994 Los costos económicos del conflicto armado en Colombia 1990–1994. Bogotá. Colombia. Departamento Nacional de Planeación.

Ruiz, Juan Pablo. 1987. Expansión de la frontera agrícola ¿un sustituto de la reforma agraria? In Seminario internacional de economía campesina y pobreza rural, edited by Jorge Bustamante. Paipa: Ministerio de Agricultura/Fondo DRI.

Sánchez, Fabio, ed. 1998. La distribución del ingreso en Colombia. Tendencias recientes y retos de la política pública. Bogotá: Tercer Mundo Editores/Departamento Nacional de Planeación.

Scully, Timothy R. and Scott Mainwaring, eds. 1995. Building Democratic Institutions: Party Systems in Latin America. Stanford, California: Stanford University Press.

Steiner, Roberto. 1996. Los ingresos de Colombia, producto de la exportación de drogas ilícitas. Coyuntura Económica 27.

———. 1997. Los dólares del narcotráfico. Bogotá: Tercer Mundo Editores/Fedesarrollo.

Thoumi, Francisco. 1994. The Size of the Illegal Drug Industry. In Drug Trafficking in the Americas, edited by Bruce M. Bagley and William O. Walker. Miami: North–South Center.

————. 1997. *Economía, política y narcotráfico*. Bogotá: Tercer Mundo Editores.

Thoumi, Francisco and M. E. Mújica. 1977. Negociación: ¿una alternativa política para el narcotráfico? *Revista Ensayo y Error* 2: 116–35.

United Nations International Drug Control Programme (UNDCP). 1997. *World Drug Report*. United Kingdom: Oxford University Press.

Uprimny, R. 1995. Narcotráfico, régimen político, violencias y Derechos Humanos en Colombia. In *Drogas, poder y región en Colombia* (vol. I), edited by Ricardo Vargas. Bogotá: CINEP.

Urrutia, Miguel. 1985. *Winners and Losers in Colombia's Economic Growth of the 1970s*. New York: Oxford University Press for the World Bank.

Vargas, Ricardo. 1997. "Drogas en Colombia" los efectos de una economía gansteril. In *La grieta de la drogas. Desintegración social y políticas públicas en América Latina*, edited by M. Hopenhayn. Santiago de Chile: Naciones Unidas/CEPAL.

Zabludoff, Sid. 1994. *Colombian Narcotics Organizations as Business Enterprises*. In U.S., Department of State and Central Intelligence Agency Economics of the Narcotics Industry, Washington, D.C.

Zamosc, León. 1986. *The Agrarian Question and the Peasant Movement in Colombia*. Cambridge: Cambridge University Press/UNRISD.

CHAPTER 7

Why a Country Produces Drugs and How This Determines Policy Effectiveness: A General Model and Some Applications to Colombia

Francisco E. Thoumi[*]

Introduction

Criminal impunity combined with rampant violence has created an environment in which vigilante justice and retribution has replaced legal recourse. Human rights abuses are pervasive. Violent deaths are only one indicator of this problem. Colombia today accounts for about one-half of all kidnappings reported in the world and extortion from businesses and "vaccines," or fees paid to prevent kidnappings, are common occurrence. The actors of the country's "ambiguous war" benefit from these schemes but also do common criminals.[1] Kidnapping is frequently a private business. Its development has spurred the growth of a "secondary" market in which common delinquents operate, abducting hostages who are then sold to guerrilla fronts. A kidnapping negotiation industry has also sprouted to serve the victims' families and employers.

During the last 35 years the illegal drug industry has become entrenched in Colombia. Illegal drugs are not the only illegal industry that has flourished in the country. Colombia is also the first producer of counterfeit U.S. dollars; the only place I know where people march to claim their right to engage in contraband (in the city of Maicao in the Guajira peninsula); the first or second Latin American exporter of prostitutes to Europe (competing with the Dominican Republic); the country where the term "disposable" was coined to refer to beggars, gays, prostitutes, and other undesirable members of society to be cleansed. All these events reflect the fact that the rule of law is not only weak but absent in many areas of the country.

Colombia has had a continuous political and armed conflict since the 1930s that has alternatively simmered and erupted. *La Violencia* of the 1940s and 1950s ended with a peculiar political agreement (the National Front) between the two traditional parties (Liberals and Conservatives) who agreed to share power. The National Front directed politics toward a distribution of government spoils to co-opt partisans. This depoliticized the parties and generated a feeling of political exclusion for those who wanted to promote political and social reforms from without the two traditional parties that monopolized power (Leal 1989; Leal and Dávila 1990; Martz 1997). The National Front eliminated overt partisan conflict but failed to address the most important grievances of many Colombians, particularly those relating to rural land tenancy, to the high levels of inequality of income, to the distribution of wealth and access to opportunities, and to the widespread feeling of political exclusion. After *La Violencia* ended, most insurgent actors relinquished their weapons. Some, however, who remained profoundly distrustful of the state and highly committed to social reforms, kept their weapons, and withdrew in hiding to isolated jungle areas where the state had at best a very marginal presence. Those groups provided the roots for Fuerzas Armadas Revolucionarias de Colombia (FARC), the largest current guerrilla organization, formed in 1964 (Pizarro 1991). A group influenced by the liberation theology of the 1960s, which included some prominent Catholic priests, founded the Ejército de Liberación Nacional (ELN), the second largest current guerrilla (Medina-Gallego 2001). Some urban intellectuals and university students formed the M-19 after the 1970 election in which Misael Pastrana (1970–1974), father of former President Andrés Pastrana, was elected in a highly questionable election (Lara 1986; Noriega 1998). Smaller guerrilla organizations like the Native American based Quintín Lame also appeared. The activities of these guerrilla groups have varied through time. Beginning with the Belisario Betancur administration (1982–1986), successive Colombian governments have attempted to negotiate with the armed insurgency. These negotiations have achieved some successes and some guerrilla groups disarmed and integrated themselves into mainstream society. Most significantly many FARC insurgents joined the Unión Patriótica (UP), a legal political movement founded during the Betancur administration. However, current insurgency groups are very reluctant to give up their arms because the UP experience proved disastrous. After guerrillas reinserted themselves into society, they were systematically decimated by right-wing groups. Indeed, a very large number (over 2,000) were assassinated. On the other hand, the M-19 which also attempted reinsertion did not succeed in offering a political alternative although some former M-19 members have become successful congressmen and mayors. As a result, FARC, ELN, and the Ejército Popular de Liberación (EPL) (a marginal group of Maoist tendencies) have persisted in their activities.

Since 1990 the production of illegal crops has grown exponentially changing the role of the illegal drug economy in Colombian society. A combination of factors has promoted this growth:

• The successful break-up of the Medellin and Cali cartels disrupted coca markets in Bolivia and Peru and led to a dispersion of the illegal industry and its atomization into many small groups for whom it was not profitable to go abroad to buy supplies.
• The agricultural sector recession and peasant migration encouraged settlements in vacant areas of Colombia where the state had no concrete control. The increased competition of cheap coffee from Vietnam has been a key factor in this.
• The collapse of Communism encouraged guerrilla organizations to find new sources of income and promote coca and poppy plantings.[2]

The aggressive coca eradication campaign undertook by the Hugo Bánzer regime in Bolivia after 1998 reinforced the incentives to develop large coca plantings in Colombia.

The development of illegal plantings allowed guerrilla and paramilitary groups to exploit the industry in order to finance and broaden their activities. Today illegal drugs are a main source of funding for the "ambiguous war" that the country is experiencing. Indeed, the role of illegal drugs in Colombia evolved from that of spurring an illegal economic boom that was tolerated, even tacitly welcomed by most Colombians in the 1970s and 1980s, to that of fueling the war thus becoming a main obstacle to peace. Unfortunately, today illegal drugs and internal war have become imbricated and together have generated a complex phenomenon that requires a concurrent solution of the illicit crop, guerrilla and paramilitary problems. Colombian attitudes toward the illegal drug industry have changed as a consequence. Today, a majority recognizes it as the cause of the deep current crisis (Thoumi 2002).

Illegal drugs have also changed the nature of Colombia's internal conflict. They have allowed right and left wing warring guerrilla factions to improve their military capabilities. They also created new reasons to fight since both right- and left-wing guerrillas now contend for control of coca-and poppy-growing areas and export routes. This has depoliticized the conflict as the warring groups have become more interested in profiting from the illegal industry than in their stated political goals. Drugs weakened centralized control within guerrilla and paramilitary organizations as well as individual armed fronts have become increasingly financially independent from their head organizations. Moreover, coca- and poppy-growing peasants have become actors of the armed conflict. Illegal drugs' funding of the Colombian conflict has enhanced the American and European participation in it and has been a reason for the internationalization of Colombia's internal conflict.[3]

Illegal drugs have also compounded the weakness of the state. The Colombian state has never controlled the country's territory,[4] and illegal drugs have heightened the need for control, while making it considerably more difficult. Illegal drugs have corrupted a weak political system (Lee and Thoumi 1999). Drug traffickers have funded political campaigns and influenced politicians since at least the late 1970s. The scandal over the 1994 campaign of President Samper only underscored this phenomenon. The 1991 Constitution, which was a flawed attempt to improve the democratic process, introduced electoral changes that increased costs and made the political system more dependent on those with vast financial assets: drug traffickers and large financial conglomerates.[5] The illegal drug industry has also promoted a culture that values wealth over anything else and a "get rich quick" mentality with scant regards as to where wealth originates. It is significant that during the last few years the number and magnitude of scandals about fraud, bribery, and misuse and misappropriation of public funds have increased dramatically. The illegal industry has forced the state to divert very scarce resources from infrastructure, social sector, and other development projects to law enforcement and unproductive investment in coca- and poppy-growing areas.[6] Finally, the violent tactics of drug traffickers, drug-funded guerrillas and paramilitaries against public officials have been a substantial obstacle to the conduct and effectiveness of honest public service. Public servants who engage in antidrug activities are well aware that they are risking their lives and those of their relatives.

When President Álvaro Uribe took office in August 2002 he changed to a more proactive and aggressive policy against subversive actors and illegal drug producers. His antidrug policies have focused on extraditing drug traffickers and a controversial coca and poppy fields aerial spraying campaign. According to official and UN data, coca plantings have declined by about 30 percent. The United States and a large number of other countries have recognized left- and right-wing guerrilla groups as terrorist organizations and the war against them has become intertwined with the war on drugs. The aerial spraying program is implemented by an American company and the number of American advisers has increased to the point that some warn about a possible "Vietnamization" of the Colombian war.

While the Uribe administration can show some significant results in its fight against drugs, retail prices in the main markets have not increased significantly, raising questions about policy effectiveness. Indeed, it appears that plantings have spread to many areas of Colombia and that illegal crops are coming back in Bolivia and Peru. Today Colombian society has very few objections to extraditing drug traffickers but many have substantial questions about aerial spraying. Only the future will tell whether Uribe's hard hand policies will make a significant dent on the illegal industry.

The developments of the last 20 years show that it is impossible to understand Colombia's social, economic, and political development without defining the role that the illegal industry has played in the country. For this reason it is imperative to understand why the international illegal drug industry developed in this particular country, and why this country became one of its major actors.

The Competitive Advantage in Drugs[7]

In order to understand the development of the illegal drug industry, to evaluate current policies, and to determine whether it is possible to formulate and implement successful policies, two central questions must be answered: first, why do some countries produce illegal drugs while others do not? And second, why does a country produce illegal drugs at some periods in time and not at others?

Among the most frequently mentioned causes for the development of the illegal drug industry are poverty, inequality, economic crises, and state corruption. The relationship between poverty and the illegal industry is however very difficult to determine. It is a fact that all laborers and most farmers in the coca fields are quite poor, yet many needy farm workers do not participate in illegal crop cultivation. It is also true that coca and poppy grow in poor countries, but most of those countries do not cultivate illegal crops. In the Andes, Colombia is richer than Bolivia, Ecuador, and Peru, yet it is the main illegal drug actor. Furthermore, in Colombia there is no correlation between peasant poverty levels and illegal crops.[8] Moreover, some large coca farmers are financially at ease, and many participants in illegal manufacturing and smuggling have relatively high levels of education and could have sought employment alternatives in the legal economy.

Illegal drug activity does not vary through time with poverty levels and inequality, which compounds the difficulty of establishing a strict correlation in this matter. The record of Colombia is also quite clear in this respect. During the 1980s, a decade when illegal drugs grew at a fast pace in Colombia, the measures of inequality and poverty actually declined in the country and the standard of living of most Colombians increased. It cannot be inferred from this that poverty and extreme misery do not play causal roles in the development of the illegal drug industry, but rather, that the relationship is indirect and quite complex. Poverty and inequality are likely to contribute to the growth of the illegal industry, but they are not *per se* determining factors.

Observing the impact of economic crises points toward a similar conclusion. During the 1980s Colombia was the only country in Latin America and the Caribbean that avoided the external debt crisis faced by the region, and the only one in which GNP did not decline in a single calendar year. The crises experienced by Colombian regions were much milder than those faced by other Andean countries, and yet it was precisely in Colombia where international trafficking organizations developed.

There is no doubt that poverty and crises create incentives for illegal behavior, but we cannot derive from them a one-to-one relation. This is consistent with criminological paradigms showing that chronic poverty is a lesser motive of crime than sharp declines in income, failed expectations of income increases, or the perceived impossibility to compete in the job market with others with apparently similar credentials and skills. In informal conversations, one will frequently hear spontaneous statements such as: "he had to commit a crime to feed his children." Granting extreme cases in which the head of a family commits a crime to avoid family starvation, why is it that in some countries these parents just steal food, while in other countries they kidnap, extort, abuse, and even kill their victims?

Alongside poverty, corruption is frequently associated with the illegal drug industry. Several factors that make the relationship between illegal drugs and corruption difficult to evaluate must be taken into account. First, there is no agreement on the definition of corruption, and behaviors considered as corrupt in some environments are perceived as sound in others. Second, corruption and drug trafficking are difficult to measure and their size, scope, and importance are difficult to establish. Third, corruption is a multidimensional phenomenon, so that various types of corruption can have different effects on the drug industry. Fourth, the relationship between illegal drugs and corruption is circular, which means that corruption may attract the illegal industry, but illegal drugs are also a main source of corruption.

Fifth, corruption and drug trafficking are generally symptomatic of deeper social problems.

A look at the country Corruption Perceptions Index elaborated by Transparency International shows the difficulty of correlating illegal drugs and corruption. This index varies from year to year, but in most years Ecuador and Bolivia have been ranked as more corrupt than Colombia. Venezuela and Peru are also frequently lower than Colombia. It is clear that this most frequently used corruption index[9] is very volatile and, moreover, not directly related to illegal drug activity.

According to conventional wisdom, profitability is another essential motivation behind the production of illegal drugs. A careful look at the geographical distribution of the world's illegal drug industry leads to an interesting paradox: the search for profit can explain why a particular individual participates in the illegal business, but it does not account for why some countries produce illegal drugs and others do not.

Legal economic activities and the illegal drug industry are similar in their search for profit, but the illegality of cocaine, heroin, and other psychoactive drugs introduces significant differences. There are remarkable differences between the economic geography of illegal drug production, marketing and consumption, and that of legal goods.

To illustrate this, let us focus on licit agriculture products like coffee, banana, tobacco, rice, sugarcane, cocoa, soy beans, potatoes, wheat, and corn. For these products the availability of natural resources determines whether a country can produce them, and indeed the list of countries that have the capacity to produce them overlaps almost perfectly the producer country list. Virtually every country that can produce them does. Some countries produce higher-quality goods than others, some produce at low and others at high prices, some are net exporters and others are net importers, but every country produces some amount of them. Only very small economies that are unable to diversify their production because of lack of economies of scale fail to produce all the goods allowed for by their natural resource endowments.

A look at footloose industries, those that require little capital and use well-known technologies that do not require scarce skills or a location near its demand or input supply sources, shows similar patterns. For example, clothing, wood furniture, leather shoes, soap and cosmetics, and other simple manufacturing products are found in virtually every country. As in the case of primary agricultural products, nonproducing cases are exceptional.

In contrast to common goods, virtually all countries can produce and traffic in illegal drugs and launder drug profits, but most do not. Coca is produced mainly in parts of the Andes Mountains and the Amazon basin, but it can be produced in many other places in Africa and Asia, Latin America, and even in small areas of the United States (Puerto Rico, Virgin Islands, Hawaii, and Guam). Indeed, a century ago, Peru suffered one of its frequent export busts when the Dutch developed large coca plantations in Indonesia and Malaysia and flooded the market.[10] Until 1940 coca also grew in India and Taiwan. Since the 1970s, in South America coca has been produced mainly in Bolivia, Colombia, and Peru, while Ecuador, Venezuela, and Brazil have produced only marginal amounts.

The geographical distribution of opium poppy, a crop with a market comparable in size to coca, is even more puzzling because it can grow in more regions of the world than coca. Poppy can grow in parts of Europe, large portions of Asia and Africa, parts of North America, tropical highlands of South America, and other parts of the Southern Hemisphere. Nonetheless, relatively few countries grow opium poppy.

The patterns of coca- and poppy-based drugs are also peculiar. Coca leaves must be processed into coca paste and opium latex must be produced at or very near the planting sites. Cocaine base, cocaine, morphine, and heroin can be refined anywhere as they are archetypical footloose industries: they require very little capital, few labor skills, the needed technologies are extremely simple and well known, the chemical inputs used are common and all have possible substitutes.

From a purely economic perspective, the narrow geographical distribution of illegal drugs is quite remarkable since the industry's extremely high profits should provide very strong incentives for their widespread production. On this basis, one could reasonably expect a more disperse production pattern that of legal goods.

To understand the economic geography of the coca–cocaine and poppy–opium–heroin industries one cannot escape the fact that they are illegal. Making an economic activity illegal does not eliminate it globally unless the rule of law prevails everywhere. Since this is not the case, the prohibited industries will tend to locate themselves where the rule of law is weakest. To understand why a country produces illicit drugs, it is necessary to focus on the differences between licit and illicit industries, particularly in the tasks required by the illicit drug industries that are not required by licit activities. Some of these are:

1. To trade in illegal inputs, which are frequently controlled substances and have to be smuggled and/or obtained in a black market;
2. Growing illegal crops;

3. Developing clandestine drug manufacturing systems;
4. Selling illegal products in the domestic market;
5. Smuggling the final products out of the country;
6. Developing illegal marketing networks abroad;
7. Transporting illegally obtained currency across international borders and to exchange these funds from one currency to another without revealing their origin; and
8. Laundering and invest illegally obtained funds, and to manage portfolios of illegally obtained capital.

An economics approach to illegal economic activities would be based on the premise that many criminal operations are motivated by expected gains and that they can be analyzed in similar ways to other activities. From this point of view, the decision to commit a crime is based on the criminal's evaluation of the operation's costs, benefits, and risks. The simple economics approach to crime has proven quite useful in many contexts as it can explain variations in crime through time in a particular locality, as long as the social structure and social constraints to crime remain constant. This is the model's main strength. However, when the underlining social structure changes, the model loses its explanatory power. Specifically, it does not account for some important and specific characteristics of the international illegal drug trade and markets. A few examples illustrate this point:

• Colombia is deeply involved in the cocaine industry while Ecuador is not. On the other hand, the costs and revenues of the illegal drug industry are similar in both countries. Following the economics model, one should conclude that Ecuador is not involved in the illegal drug industry because the risks of punishment by the authorities in that country are much higher than in Colombia. Therefore, to validate the model, it is necessary to state that Ecuador has efficient police and justice systems that totally discourage the illegal drug industry while Colombia's systems are inferior. In reality, however, both countries have weak central governments that suffer from widespread corruption. Local authorities are controlled by economic and political elites. They are highly vulnerable to bribes and prone to power abuses. Economic power is concentrated in a group of conglomerates that exert great influence on the political system and succeed in bending and manipulating laws and regulations to create and capture economic rents, and politicians and the State apparatus have a reputation of being easily bought.
• Since the 1980s wholesale cocaine prices in Europe have been substantially higher than in the United States. Here again one must conclude that either

punishment is much higher in Europe than in the United States to limit supply and increase prices, or that smuggling cocaine into the United States has been significantly easier than into Europe, in spite of the "war on drugs" followed by the U.S. government. Evidence contradicts both of these statements.

• Curiously, while cocaine prices have been significantly higher in Europe than in the United States, the opposite has happened with heroin. Since both products are imported by similar criminal organizations, if their price differences were determined by repressive policies only, both would be expected to be higher in the most repressive country and lower in the least repressive ones.

• Cocaine and heroin are distributed in the United States, among others, by ghetto-based gangs like the "crips" and the "bloods" and groups of Colombians, Dominicans, Jamaicans, Haitians, and Mexicans. It is true that strong loyalty ties among the members of criminal organizations increase crime return and lower the risk of punishment, but there are other immigrant and nonimmigrant groups with strong internal loyalty ties like the Koreans, the Vietnamese, and the Irish, which have not developed illegal drugs' distribution networks.

In conclusion, economic profitability plays a relevant role in promoting crime, but other important factors affect it, including social controls and each individual's internalized constraints to behavior.

The Role of Moral Values, Social Capital, and Social Behavioral Constraints

Some individual behaviors can have undesirable social effects. However, the definition of what constitutes deviant and damaging action varies among societies and through time. These include conducts related to political activity, sex and gender relations, religious activity, violence, gambling; private property accumulation and use, and the production, commerce, and consumption of certain goods and services.

To control and regulate behavior, societies rely on norms that are enforced by many institutions—family, religion, the state, peer groups, schools, and others. Justifications for behavior control have been diverse. They have been based on moral, ethical, political, or practical grounds. Ideologies, religions and other institutions have influenced behavior, regulations, and legislation in all societies.

Diverse social institutions have played a role in psychoactive drug control. Religion has often times banned or ritualized their use. The family and social groups have established conditions and environments for their consumption, thereby minimizing negative externalities. In modern democracies where executive, legislative, and judicial powers, as well as state and religion are separated, behavioral controls are imposed by the same institutions that impose them in traditional societies (state, family, religions, and schools). Because legislation is formally separate from religion, the main controls appear to emanate from the state, which is seen as responsible for their production and enforcement. As modernization has proceeded, extended families have become weaker, people have moved away from native localities where local institutions restricted behavior; religion has lost much of its dominion. Traditional social norms have become increasingly elusive and the task of constraining deviant behaviors has shifted to the state.

Humans are social beings and their position in society influences their behavior and productivity. "Social capital," defined as the set of relations among individuals and the reciprocity and trust networks and norms that develop as a result have a significant influence on the way in which people behave, and impact their attitude about the social repercussions of their actions. Individuals who originate from environments with high levels of "social capital" (two parent and extended families, sound relations with parents, relatives, and friends, good schools, active religious and sports participation), develop a strong sense of belonging, trust other community members, and weigh the socially positive and negative effects of their actions in their decision-making processes. Social capital contributes to the development of civic responsibility.

Productive and extensive networks within a particular community undoubtedly generate social capital, a key factor in the production of solidarity and trust. When societies are segmented, and individuals express loyalty and show solidarity with subgroups but not with society as a whole, the social capital of some groups can be detrimental to others. Indeed, there are several kinds of social capital and it is important to consider at least two: bonding and bridging (Putnam 2000). It is essential for any society to balance both types of social capital. Bonding social capital generates great loyalty within a group but may spur great antagonism toward outsiders. A disproportionate amount of this social capital can be divisive and lead to conflict. On the other hand, social capital that bridges differences among groups promotes coexistence. When there is only this type of social capital, people are not bound to their groups and life in them tends to be unattractive. It may be posited that social capital in Colombia is scarce and most of what exists is of the bonding type. It is not then surprising that Colombia suffers a dramatic lack of solidarity: "Colombians do not aspire to be loved, only to be respected" (Lemoine 2000, 26).

In segmented societies, personal attitudes toward crime within and without a particular community or group can seem discrepant. For instance, stealing from the poor may be perceived as condemnable, while killing the rich may seem almost innocuous and justified. A network of relationships that generates strong social capital within a marginal community can become perverse and produce negative effects for society at large. The social constraints and norms of such a group can become very detrimental to society at large.

Many recent analyses of Colombia identify the weakness of "civil society" as a cause of violence and other social problems. Civil society refers to organizations separate from the state that in many instances contribute to the development and strengthening of social capital. However, they are not social capital in and by themselves, and on occasions they may not contribute to its formation or strengthening. The myriad NGOs that have developed in Colombia are unquestionably very important institutions, which often accomplish positive roles and functions. Their existence *per se*, however, does not automatically guarantee their integrity. There remains the risk that old or newly created NGOs may be misused to divert and squander funds.

Internalized Constraints

A norm may be internal to the individual who will evaluate, sanction or restrict the individual's behavior accordingly (Coleman 1990). Every citizen has its own distinctive "criminal threshold" that stems from nature and is fashioned by socialization. In every society therefore some people are more scrupulous than others. The "price" of a particular individual's honesty depends on the individual's own endowment of natural attributes and on the internalized behavioral constraints developed through his socialization and life experience.

External Constraints

The state and other institutions can encourage and discourage behaviors and their policies can lower or raise the costs and punishments faced by would-be criminals. Civil societies generate peer pressure and can sanction individuals in many positive and negative ways (e.g., praising, granting status, shunning, shaming, excommunicating, executing). The state can pass and implement laws promoting, regulating, outlawing, and punishing behaviors, and establish market as well as nonmarket incentives to achieve its goals.

Civil societies and the state impose varying constraints and punishments on different people depending on their social status, race, gender, religion, political affiliation, and other variables. Even though higher crime rates can be generally associated with individuals who share some socioeconomic characteristics (e.g., low income), most members of those groups *do not commit crimes.*

Government and social institutions are not monolithic in their attitudes toward crime and punishment. Several agencies formulate and implement crime-related policies. Frequently, coordination among them is lacking and they may even work at odds (crosswise). They may quarrel over budgets and jurisdiction over policy formulation and implementation. The same happens with institutions outside government: many may chastise crime, but others may actually encourage it. For instance, in the U.S. ghettos, going to jail can be a "rite of passage" that increases the status of young males. Tax evasion in many Latin American countries faces a very low risk of government punishment, is widely condoned by society, and frequently represents a source of pride.

Finally, in the medium- and long-term, social and government institutions also have an effect on criminal behavior. Failure by the government and society to punish deviant behaviors weakens the incentives for the development of strong internalized constraints, which then increases the proportion of individuals willing to break the law. The long-term dynamics initiated by weakened external behavioral constraints can be devastating. They first increase the profitability of criminal actions, and as those become widespread and increasingly accepted by society, honest behavior becomes more costly. Internal constraints weaken as a result. In addition, when criminal behavior is tolerated and accepted, the socialization process eventually produces a generation of individuals with damaged internalized constraints. In these cases it may be argued that a society falls into a "dishonesty trap" from which it is very difficult to escape (Thoumi 1987).

The Causality of Illegal Drugs

As discussed above, profits are one of the variables that promote crime, but other factors also play important roles: social restrictions and attitudes toward crime, and the strength of internalized controls of the citizenry. The effectiveness of law enforcement efforts, the level of discipline that the state can apply, social sanctioning, and the all-out (general) effectiveness in inculcating internal behavioral constraints on individuals play causal roles, and are institutional causes. However, the knowledge about most of these variables is quite imperfect and if the magnitude and interaction of each and all of these are not known, it is impossible to predict the effects of a particular policy. Unfortunately, this is not recognized by policy makers and other analysts who propose policies as "solutions." When policies fail to achieve unrealistic goals, shortcomings are attributed to "lack of commitment or political will," or/and to "corruption." Few underscore the existence of institutional constraints in society that make it impossible for policies to succeed even if governments were "committed, had political will and were not corrupt."

The illegal drug industry development in a particular country requires a social environment characterized by institutions which impose minimal if any behavioral restrictions, and which tolerate or condone deviant behaviors. In this respect, institutional evolutionary processes are important. Criminal activity responds not only to illegal profits, but also to changes in the institutions that weaken behavioral controls, including those within the state. When the controls imposed by a particular institution weaken, other mechanisms must be set in motion to prevent crime increases. However, these changes are hardly ever smooth or even feasible. For example, when changes in family structure or other civil institutions weaken social controls, the state may not be effective in staying the trend because of conflicts with other of its functions, and/or because it is seen as contradicting professed goals such as protection of individual rights.

One clear-cut implication of this analysis is that crime levels reflect social structures, institutions, and values. In this sense, the illegal drug industry is symptomatic of changes in those social variables. The evolutionary processes that generate an environment where crime can thrive take time to develop. Conversely, reversing them is also likely to require patience. There is no "silver bullet" type of policy that can squarely eliminate the "drug problem" in the short run.

The determining role played by weak state, social, and internal controls in fostering illegal activity does not exclude other factors from being taken into account. Variables such as extreme poverty, lack of social mobility channels, inequality, and economic crises which, as discussed above, have frequently been used to explain and justify the development of the illegal drug industry in Colombia do play a role. They can be considered as latent causes that in most cases and most of the time *do not* result in the development of illegal economic activities. However, when the social structure slackens, it does become a trigger for the development of the illegal industry.

Economic crises are also secondary factors. Colombian regions experienced economic declines during the 1980s but Colombia was the only country in Latin American and the Caribbean that escaped the external debt crisis of that decade and the only one where GNP did not decline in any year. During the 1980s, coca plantings grew in Bolivia, Peru, and Colombia, and Colombians developed and controlled the cocaine industry. The crises of many Latin American countries were very acute compared to the ones in Colombia, yet did not lead to the development of the illegal drug industry. Relatively mild crises acted as a trigger in Colombia during the 1980s because the institutional social changes that the country had experienced made it vulnerable. Without a social and institutional environment conducive to such developments, the industry would not have grown.

This has important implications on policy formulation. If the growth of the illegal drug industry is caused by institutional changes that have weakened social and state controls, repressive policies might not be effective. The effectiveness of antidrug polices has often been overestimated, leading to unrealistic expectations. It must be pointed out, however, that shortcomings need not necessarily lead to an abandonment of policy, only that expectations should be reasonably lowered. It should be stressed that the long-term solution to the "drug problem" is institutional and requires significant changes in society, not simple short-term policies. Current policies could play important roles in mitigating some of the main negative effects of the "problem," but if there is no real social change, very little will be accomplished in the long run.

How Different is Colombia?

The above analysis posits that the illegal drug industry develops in societies with weak state and institutional presence ineffectual in generating social controls and where social capital is deficient. This raises an interesting question: are those traits distinctive enough in Colombia in comparison with other Latin American countries to explain this country's key role in the illegal industry?[11] The following section explores this hypothesis.

A main difference between Colombia and the rest of Latin America stems from geography. Colombia emerged from colonial periods as an ensemble of distinct regions with scant communication and trade exchanges among them. Physical obstacles were (and remain) very great so that regions tended to develop as fairly self-sufficient units. In many of them small urban centers grew and today Colombia, in contrast to other Latin American countries, is a country of many cities that are regional centers.[12] Geographical heterogeneity does account somewhat for the breaking off of Ecuador and Venezuela from Colombia a few years after independence. Because of its geography, Colombia was until the early twentieth century the Latin American country with the lowest per-capita international trade.[13] Only the development of the coffee industry modified this condition. Furthermore, export production generated infrastructure that linked a few Colombian regions with the coast and foreign markets, but contributed little to national integration. Geography was also an obstacle to taxation because it increased its costs enormously. Hence its collection was frequently privatized through auctions that permitted private citizens to profit from it. Until the mid-twentieth century most central government revenues originated in international trade taxes.[14] Thus, a very poor central state was a corollary of the country's regional diversity. Because of its geography, Colombia had the greatest need for investment in infrastructure to integrate the country into a nation. But because of financial constraints and the need to respond to urban constituencies, the central state's presence has traditionally been precarious in large portions of the country. Indeed, the Colombian state has never controlled its territory.[15]

Geography was an obstacle to economic integration not only because of very high transportation costs, but also because near most urban centers there was a variety of weathers that promoted a variety of food and other rural products. This encouraged regional self-sufficiency and discouraged the formation of a national market since most regions produced the same products.

Throughout history Colombia has been a country with abundant natural resources, particularly fertile land. Until the mid-twentieth century Colombia had a relative scarcity of labor. During colonial times the Spanish faced a political problem: in order for the *Hidalgos* to enjoy a "decent" life of leisure, it was necessary to create institutions that tied down peasants to the land. This led to limitations to peasants' movement and access to land. Abundant unsettled lands offered opportunities for peasants and run-away slaves to flee to isolated regions where they could subsist independently of the state. Tropical illnesses were probably the main obstacles to these movements. During the eighteenth and nineteenth centuries "palenques" or settlements of run-away slaves were established out of the control of the state, church, and other dominant social institutions. By the late nineteenth century, population in the *minifundia* areas of Cundinamarca and Boyaca had increased beyond what those smallholdings could support and peasants migrated mostly to the opening coffee-growing regions where they settled. These migrations led "to the spontaneous formation of societies marginalized from the social, family, religious, and political controls that characterized their original locations" (González 1998, 151). In other words, throughout history the Colombian state and society have had difficulties establishing controls to individual behavior and many Colombians have lived without them.

Regional heterogeneity found its expression in cultural diversity. Regional behaviors, accents and values tend to be very distinctive. Area loyalties are strong and the conformation of a national identity has been slow and incomplete.[16]

During the first 110 years after independence (until the 1920s)·Colombia suffered a chronic external debt crisis caused by Simón Bolivar's large foreign borrowing to finance his campaign to liberate Bolivia and Peru (Junguito 1995). When the Gran Colombia (Colombia, Ecuador, and Venezuela) broke down in 1830, the external debt was distributed proportionally to each country's population, irrespective of each country's capacity to pay that was conditioned by its exports. Colombia, that had the lowest exports per capita, lived with a chronic balance of payments crisis and had to renegotiate its share of the debt several times during the nineteenth century. Because of this, the government did not have access to foreign capital markets to develop the infrastructure needed to integrate the country (Junguito 1995).

During the nineteenth and part of the twentieth century, Colombia had a series of primary product export booms and busts: indigo, quinine, cocoa, rubber, and bananas. These booms generated short-lived prosperities in different places, which did not allow for the development of stable institutions and communities. Only the development of coffee from the 1920s on was conducive to those developments. This contrasts with the export booms and busts in Bolivia, Peru, Chile, Argentina, and Uruguay that repeated themselves in the same places.

The structure of Colombian political parties is atypical. The main parties in Latin America are organized centrally and attempt to present a distinct political agenda. Others respond to a leader with a strong personality. In both these cases, the structure is organized from the top–down. In contrast, the two Colombian traditional parties—Liberal and Conservative—are organized from local groups-up. They tend to be organizations of local leaders who unite to influence the central government. In many regions they have substituted for the state and mediated between the central state and the citizenry. Many Colombians developed toward their parties the sort of loyalties that people develop toward the nation state. Until recently, many Colombian were Liberal or Conservative by birth rather than choice. "That sense of belonging represented a transcendental element of civil life that marked and defined personal identities" (Acevedo-Carmona 1995, 41). For this reason, traditional Colombian parties have been pluriclassist and spread throughout the country. Moreover, strong party allegiance has represented an obstacle for the development of other parties. These may meet with occasional success, but will fail to sustain themselves in the medium term. Diverging political views are most frequently expressed as dissident factions of the traditional parties or as independent, nonparty movements.

The National Front contributed to the depolitization of the parties. They became electoral machines that organized themselves at times of elections but achieved little beyond that. It is significant that from the postwar period until the late 1990s politics remained very distant from the formulation of many economic policies. These were relegated to highly trained professionals who formulated them and responded more to pressures of the economic elite than to the concerns of the majority. Hence the dictum "the country is in bad shape but the economy is doing well" which reflected public perceptions of Colombian reality for many years. The political system in Colombia has not been responsive to the need for social and economic reforms. Colombia has been the only country in the region where the political left never achieved an electoral success that allowed to experiment with policies different from those advocated by the traditional establishment.[17] This has had a positive effect to the extent that, in contrast to most of Latin America, macroeconomic stability was able to prevail and extreme inflationary episodes as well as economic crises were averted (Urrutia 1991). However, lower-class grievances have not found channels to express themselves; significant needed reforms were frustrated and their supporters led to advocate the resort to violent nonpolitical means.

Native communities were weaker and did not generate, as in other Andean countries, social behavioral constraints in the majority of the peasant population. In Bolivia, Ecuador, and Peru native communities have a strong identity, their members develop a sense of belonging and the community generates important behavioral norms. In Colombia, the largest native groups were organized enough to be exploited by the Spanish *Colonizadores*, but weak enough to survive as a community. In addition, those communities experienced a very fast process of *mestizaje*, blended into the mainstream and lost their identities (Jaramillo-Uribe 1991, Chapter 3). Colombia still has some native communities where social norms are strong and *deviant behaviors* punished. However, these are a minority. Most Colombian peasants are the result of *mestizaje* and have weak communal ties. Colombian native communities are the exception in rural Colombia. A few subsist in isolated areas or in the southern highlands that marked the northern limits of the Inca Empire.

The "white" or/and *mestizo* community is also different. Colombia is the Latin American country that has had the most limited exposure to non-Spanish influences. It has had the fewest number of non-Spanish immigrants relative to the size of its population, especially non-Catholic ones. Colombia was settled by Spaniards who came shortly after seven centuries of warring with the Arabs. They came from one of the most medieval regions of Europe and the regional isolation discussed above allowed them to maintain many of their traits. Their values have influenced Colombian society throughout its history. For instance, the 1886 Constitution that remained in force with some amendments until 1991, aimed at strengthening *Hispanidad* and some have argued that it attempted to replicate the Spain of Philip II. This constitution was very hostile to non-Spanish non-Catholic immigrants since the Church monopolized many civil procedures and controlled education. It is significant in this respect that Colombia is one of the countries where it is most difficult to become a naturalized citizen. These factors explain why until recently Colombia remained remote from modernizing ideas and technologies. In the words of former president Alfonso López-Michelsen, Colombia was the Tibet of Latin America. Traditional premodern Spanish values were not conducive to respect of central government laws or authorities and the isolation of many of the descendants of the *Conquistadores* allowed them to remain fairly autonomous from the central government. In the early twentieth century, Colombia was a very stratified society in which landlords retained a great deal of autonomy. Their local power was strong and they could frequently abuse it. In other words, their societies did not impose strong behavioral constraints.

Colombia experienced during the twentieth century a dramatic expansion of the agricultural and ranching frontier. This process was highly influenced by rural violence and population explosion.[18] Individual settlers spontaneously undertook most of this expansion with little if any state support. Most settlers were armed and many were displaced by rural violence in other regions. These settlements were violent and unstable. In many cases guerrilla organizations were welcome as they imposed order in the existing power vacuum.[19]

La Violencia also generated large rural–urban migrations to urban slums. One salient effect of violence-induced migration is the loss of links between migrants and their original communities, which are often destroyed. Many urban–rural migrants lost whatever social links and constraints they had, and their predicament caused them in turn to be extremely resentful. Furthermore, there was a significant rural–rural migration that went into the "empty lands" that established many settlements outside the state control.

The Colombian military is also distinctive. Colombia had not experienced military coups (the 1953 military government was the result of an "opinion coup" in response to a social clamor to halt *La Violencia*). The armed forces have been traditionally weak. They have never controlled the territory and lacked in particular a significant presence in large border areas. In addition, they are not representative of Colombian society: military service by elite children has been exceptional. Finally, Colombian military personnel have generally not been active in politics, even after retirement (in 1999 only one of about 250 members of the Colombian Congress had military experience).

Colombian citizens have had life-long experience with violence and insecurity. It can be argued that every Colombian has been a victim and many others victimizers. Post-trauma stress syndrome is rampant and untreated. One can only speculate about the implications that this may have on social development prospects, but in a society in which everyone is leery, developing social trust is a considerable feat.

Available studies show that the levels of solidarity and trust in Colombia are low. In contrast to the countries mentioned above, social capital in Colombia has characteristically been of the bonding type within small social circles. Bridging social capital has been extremely scarce. This has led some scholars to argue that Colombians act using a remarkable individual logic but a disastrous social one (Gómez-Buendía 1999). Furthermore the state has particular weaknesses that differentiate it from that of other countries. All these factors not only have made Colombia a very fertile ground for the development of the illegal drug industry but also for the high level of violence, corruption, and other social ills. These forces have been at work in Colombia for a long time, yet they had not brought about before social crises comparable to the current one. But as Colombia evolved from a traditional rural society and population grew, urbanization exploded, the rural frontier expanded spontaneously, education increased, income levels raised, women's roles changed, the vulnerability of the Colombian social structure made it the best location for the illegal drug trafficking industry. Once established, this industry acted as a catalyst that accelerated a process of social change and continued to devastate traditional social controls (Thoumi 1995).

The Colombian political system tolerated a "state as a bounty" mentality that allowed the system to co-opt many critics and potential dissenters and maintain political stability. Unfortunately the dynamics of this system are vicious, as they require an ever-growing bounty to satisfy an increasing number of people who need to be co-opted. The system allowed state justice mechanisms to become increasingly inefficient, which elevated the costs of doing business. Police and security systems became increasingly privatized as personal bodyguards, house guards, and other paid protection became common. In other words, the rule of law had weakened significantly. These changes increased the dead weight of predatory behaviors on the economy and finally brought down economic growth. By the end of the twentieth century the country was in a deep crisis, and so was its economy.

Many Colombians currently place the roots of their troubles in the illegal industry but they do not perceive the societal weaknesses that allowed the illegal industry to develop. They tend to refer the illegal drug industry as a scourge that fell on them because of bad luck, an unjust international system or evil forces. Not surprisingly, they blame international drug demand for their troubles.

Drug Policy Implications

Illegal drug policies have been designed to lower the industry's absolute and relative profitability. At best, they have succeeded in making illegal drugs unprofitable at particular locations. Antidrug policies in Colombia use a carrot and stick approach. Alternative development represents an incentive, while repressive policies such as various forms of interdiction, destruction of the industry's productive infrastructure (including aerial fumigation), anti-money laundering measures, and the capture and incarceration of drug actors constitute the policies' coercive aspect. These policies are formulated on the implicit assumption that social institutions and values do not determine or have scant bearing on policy effectiveness. In other words, they are assumed to work effectively in every society if there is "political will" to enforce them. The arguments developed in this essay show first that such expectations are unrealistic, and second that such a strategy will not eliminate illegal drugs without a profound change in the social institutions and values. Antidrug policies encounter several types of obstacles. First, at the social level, prerequisites for success include strong communities that generate social behavioral constraints, as well as a strong accountable state that controls its territory and responds to the citizenry's needs. In other words, the rule of law must be strong. Second, policies confront technical limitations of various kinds. The effectiveness of aerial fumigation, for instance, requires the use of pesticides against which peasants cannot devise protective methods. Furthermore, locating the illegal plantings is usually done through satellite photography that would be thwarted by cloud covering. Alternative development requires at a minimum that soil quality be high enough for noncoca crops to be sustainable. Third, many policies work at cross-purposes. Antidrug policies must fight market forces and aim at achieving an economic incongruence: to maximize retail drug prices while minimizing coca and opium poppy prices. Thus, many policies increase economic incentives at various stages of the production and trafficking networks, undermining other policies.

Given both policy requirements and limitations, Colombia is predictably a particularly difficult country for traditional antidrug policies to succeed. Colombia presents more obstacles than other Andean countries. Consider first Alternative development. Understandably, the most positive alternative development experiences have taken place in native communities where there are social controls on behavior.[20] The effectiveness of the policies promoted and implemented need to be weighed against the context in which they are introduced. Coca- and poppy-growing regions are often located in areas where communities are very weak. In many of these settlements, peasants have been displaced there by violence, and are armed. In most coca- and poppy-growing areas there is virtually no state presence. An occasional public representative (sporadically paid teacher or health worker) hardly represents a surrogate for a government that is largely absent, and therefore does not accomplish its duties. Hence, concrete power often lies in guerrilla and paramilitary groups that have substituted for the state. The Amazon basin soils in Colombia are very poor and on average, poorer than those of Chapare and the Upper Huallaga Valley. In these areas, it is technologically impossible to harvest sustained agricultural production different from coca. Many coca-growing areas in Colombia are very distant from markets and infrastructure is badly lacking.

Aerial fumigation is of doubtful worth in Colombia. The lack of state control largely explains why Colombia is the only Andean country where fumigation is allowed; less radical measures, such as manual eradication, could otherwise have been implemented. Fumigation is an indiscriminate weapon that can impact nontargeted crops. It can, in addition, technically fail. Fumigation is not eradication; its effectiveness can be reduced by weather conditions and/or by protective measures taken by peasants. Also, because of lack of government control, there is always a danger that ground fire impact fumigation airplanes. Therefore, these must fly higher than required for precise targeting. There have been frequent reports that alternative development projects and subsistence crop have been fumigated. Lack of coordination between fumigation and alternative development authorities have undermined the latter's projects. In the long run fumigation is successful if there are no replantings on site or in other places (balloon effect). Reports of replanting suggest that fumigation has been less effective than desired and that persistent treatment (spraying) is required. The long-term health and environmental effects of this policy in one of the most fragile ecosystems of the planet are worrisome. Furthermore, in many areas, fumigation represents the main state presence. "State presence by fumigation" increases resentment against the government and undermines any other of its activities in those communities. Manual eradication in Colombia is more difficult than in Bolivia and Peru (and probably impossible in most places) because of the lack of state presence in producing regions, and the lack of organized stable communities in most illegal crop zones.

Interdiction has different effects depending on what element it targets in the production-trafficking chain. A policy to seal coca- and poppy-growing areas lowers crop prices and has less disruptive effects than fumigation on peasant communities. On the other hand, interdicting finished cocaine and heroin at export ports that seizes only a proportion of intended exports has the opposite effect. If traffickers estimate that approximately 15 percent of their exports are captured, they will then consider seizures as a cost of doing business and proportionally increase their demand for coca and poppy and their cocaine and heroin production to maintain the quantity they want to supply their customers.

Antidrug policies require coordination among executing agencies. Coordination is key to making sure efforts do not cancel each other out. In Colombia it is particularly important that alternative development programs and projects not be fumigated. The weakness of state institutions allows parts of the government to act autonomously in ways that may neutralize other agencies' actions. A war-driven mentality or any frustration-based reaction among those in charge of fumigation can render alternative development useless.

The effects of current programs on democratic development are important. Alternative development together with local governance programs, when implemented in organized communities, offer a very positive opportunity to strengthen democracy. These programs can bolster local institutions and increase stability. In effect, many indigenous communities feel threatened by illegal crops because these undermine traditional social structures, and have welcomed alternative development programs. Not surprisingly, the most positive experiences have taken place in indigenous communities where there are social controls on behavior.

When alternative development and local governance initiatives are carried out in areas where loose communities subsist they can be used to create or strengthen them. In these cases they can promote community organization through physical infrastructure, education, and other investments always in consultation and negotiation with local partners. Alternative development/local governance projects must be predicated on the assumption that eradication sustainability requires strong community bonds able to enforce crop bans. These organizations have to be representative and organized from the bottom–up. In other words they must genuinely reflect community values and interests. The community-building aspects of alternative development and local governance initiatives are a key and irreplaceable element if these are to succeed.

Most alternative development programs have regional components as water use, highways and other infrastructure. Such undertakings affect several communities. Strong local governance and democratic communities are necessary to cooperate with neighboring localities in the formulation and implementation of regional programs.

The communal effects of fumigation differ widely from those of alternative development. One issue is whether it bonds the communities against the state. Vargas-Meza (1999) has studied in detail all cases of aerial fumigation during the last 25 years in Colombia and concludes that they have contributed to delegitimating of the state and have increased the peasantry's distrust of it. One basic problem is caused by the bluntness of fumigation that makes it difficult for the state to use a "carrot and stick" approach because the stick frequently destroys the carrot (see Vargas-Meza 1999).[21] This makes it difficult for the state to follow a "good cop–bad cop" approach.

Whether aerial fumigation fosters loyalties toward the guerrilla and paramilitary groups depends on the treatment these extend to the peasants. There are reports that peasants frequently resent guerrilla and paramilitary intrusions and do not have strong allegiance to them. In support of this statement one can mention the lack of massive rural protests to the recent widespread fumigation, in contrast to the guerrilla-sponsored marches of 1996.

Traditional antidrug policies in Colombia have a role, but they cannot be expected to succeed if weak state and institutions persist. In other words, if the social environment characterized by lack of trust, weak and only bonding social capital, and premodern weak state persist, those policies would not be able to achieve any lasting results. President Richard Nixon declared the "war on drugs" over 30 years ago. It is high time to declare the "war on illicit drug causes."

Characteristics of an Antidrug Strategy

A successful antidrug strategy should be two pronged. It should rely on some traditional policies, but it should also be grounded on the awareness that success depends on strengthening the state so that it can enforce its policies, and the community so that it develops social controls. In other words, it is necessary to establish the rule of law. These caveats underscore the necessity of a long-term approach to complement short-term measures. This could be concretely problematic since political governance generally shows a heavy short-term bias that favors quick results. For this reason, effective antidrug policies should be state and not government policies. That is to say that they must transcend a particular administration.

Alternative development policies should be coordinated with democracy and community development programs and should be implemented in areas where there exist strong communities or where other programs contribute to their development.

The strengthening of the state should include developing its capabilities to control the territory. This requires strong armed forces with two characteristics. First, they should have sufficient numbers and equipment. Second, and more important, they should represent a cross-section of society (fighters should not only come from the lower social strata) and their actions should lead them to gain community support. A strong state should not be a blunt efficient authoritarian machine but one with increased legitimacy and community acceptance. Local governments need to improve how to respond to the citizenry instead of a limited constituency of a few local rich or influential people. Any state strengthening program should be complemented with the development and strengthening of grassroot level organizations able to express citizens' priorities and demand accountability. In other words the long-term policy should have these two components to ensure stable democracy, promote bridging social capital and develop social behavioral controls.

Only a combination of a strong state and democratic community institutions will guarantee the success of antidrug policies. Some traditional short-term policies could be continued, but they should be implemented having in mind their effects on the necessary changes in Colombian society to achieve long-term sustainable success. Thus, they should be applied with extreme care since they can backfire in the long run. They should be looked at as temporary measures while long-term solutions develop.

Notes

*   Visiting Professor, Department of Economics, Universidad del Rosario, Bogotá. This essay was originally prepared for USAID but has been revised to take into account recent evidence and debates. The opinions stated herein are the author's own and do not necessarily reflect the views of the U.S. government. The author thanks the comments of Álvaro Camacho-Guizado, Laura Garcés, Cristina Rojas, and Sergio Uribe-Ramírez to an earlier version of this essay and exonerates them from any intellectual responsibility.
1. The Colombian conflict is difficult to classify, as it does not fit into any of the war classical categories. The term "ambiguous war" was coined at a December 1998 seminar in the U.S. Army War College, and is meant to convey the complexity of the Colombian conflict. For a report of this conference's proceedings see Downes (1999). For a thorough and perceptive analysis of this conflict as one in which Colombian society is trapped as hostage, see Pécaut (2001).
2. In earlier publications, accepting assertions by the Peruvian government, I argued that Peruvian program to shot down trafficking airplanes contributed to

large expansion of Colombian coca plantings (Thoumi 2003a). However, official data from the Peruvian Air Force show "that the program to down airplanes began in 1990 when 3 were neutralized. These figures were 11 in 1991, 11 in 1992, 25 in 1993, 15 in 1994, 20 in 1995, 3 in 1996, 10 in 1997, 0 in 1998 and 1999 and 2 in 2000 and 2001" but "coca prices remained relatively stable and total coca acreage increased somewhat during the years in which more airplanes were neutralized. These facts support the contention that Montesinos controlled the market. Airplanes of traffickers that competed with his organization and a few others were neutralized to show results. These figures indicate that this program did not have a significant effect on illicit acreage and that other factors were relevant. Indeed, the illegal industry appears to have adapted quite well to the Air Force program" (Thoumi 2003b).

3. Garcés (2003) analyses in detail the effects of internationalization on the various actors of the Colombian conflict.

4. The Colombian state presence in very large portions of the territory has been precarious at best. Its administrative agencies have been ineffective and the military and police functions have not been exercised. State control in those regions should be entirely built, not just regained.

5. It established a second round for the presidential election when the winner of the first one did not obtain over 50% of the vote, it made senatorial constituencies national which require campaigning outside the candidate's region and, more important, allowed paid political advertising in the media, particularly onerous TV ads. All these changes resulted in a several-fold increase in campaign costs.

6. Alternative Development and other development projects are implemented to eliminate illegal crops, not because they are profitable. Indeed, a normal entrepreneur seeking to produce hearths of palm or other products would likely never choose the coca- or poppy-growing regions for his or her investment. It may be argued that there are compelling moral and political reasons to do so. Independently of whether they are justified, they do hinder economic growth and are tantamount to a forced transfer imposed on the formal economy.

7. The model used in this section is developed in Thoumi (1999; 2003c).

8. There are many very poor rural areas that do not grow illegal crops and the percentage of the rural population involved in illegal crops is small: less than 4%.

9. See index at Transparency International's Internet web page: http://www. transparency.org/

10. From 1900 to 1939, when cocaine was still legal, Indonesia was the largest world exporter of coca leaves (Gootenberg 1999).

11. See Thoumi (1999, 2003c). Yunis (2003), a first-rate genetist and a former President of the National University devoted a book to this issue and arrived to similar conclusions.

12. The 1993 census estimated Bogota's population at about 5 million. There were two metropolitan areas of 2 million each and one of 1.3 million, two others had over 600,000 one about half a million, three were in the 300,000–400,000 range, nine in the 200,000–300,000 range, and six in the 100,000–200,000 range.

13. Palmer (1980, 46) shows that as late as 1910 Colombian exports per capita were 77% of the second lowest country (Honduras), 67% of those of Peru, 52% of those of Venezuela, 12% of those of Argentina, and 9% of those of Uruguay.

14. Colombian low taxes were a constant throughout all the nineteenth century (Deas 1982).

15. It may be argued that this has also been the case in other Latin American countries. Colombia, however, is different because of the dispersion of its population among small urban centers. In countries like Peru, Bolivia, or Brazil, the state did not have presence in large parts of the territory, but most of the population lived in areas where the state did have presence.

16. This is what Yunis (2003) calls regional "cultural endogamy."

17. The October 2003 election of Luis Eduardo "Lucho" Garzón as Bogota's mayor may be an important milestone for change.

18. From the end of post–World War II to the mid-1970s, Colombia had one of the highest population growth rates in Latin America. Since then it has had one of the sharpest declines. This was achieved through a quiet government-funded campaign after the Catholic Church agreed not to oppose it as long as the government did not promote it openly. The effects of this decline on the labor force growth began to be felt only in the 1990s and were partially compensated by an increase in female labor force participation rate.

19. This process is in stark contrast with the Chapare settlements in Bolivia where many peasants migrated communally and where the state promoted migrations and had some presence. Indeed, today Chapare has the best rural infrastructure of any Bolivian region while the Colombian coca- and poppy-growing zones have almost none (Thoumi 2003c).

20. The best example of policy success is Thailand where there was a confluence of positive factors: organized communities that had a profound respect for the a king who took it as a personal crusade or jihad to eliminate opium, fertile soils that can produce many regular crops, infrastructure development to link isolated poppy-growing regions to Bangkok, a country whose economy grew at over 10% per year over a decade, and communities where opium was consumed and people were aware of the social costs of addiction. Yet, under such propitious circumstances, it took 30 years to eliminate opium and even though this was a success from the point of view of Thailand, plantings simply moved to Myanmar and there was no real effect on world heroin prices (Renard 2001).

21. Vargas-Meza (1999) cites many examples of fumigations of alternative development projects and legal crops and of lack of coordination between fumigating and other antidrug agencies.

References

Acevedo-Carmona, Darío. 1995. *La mentalidad de las elites sobre la violencia en Colombia (1936–1949)*. Bogotá: IEPRI/El Áncora Editores.

Coleman, James. 1990. *Foundations of Social Theory*. Cambridge, Mass.: Harvard University Press.

Deas, Malcom. 1982. Colombian fiscal problems during the XIX Century. *Journal of Latin American Studies* 14 (November): 287–328.

Downes, Richard. 1999. Landpower and Ambiguous Warfare. The Challenge of Colombia in the 21st Century. Conference Report, March 10. http://carlisle-www.army.mil/usassi/ssipubs/pubs/pubs99/colombia/

Garcés, Laura. 2003. Pastrana and the internationalization of the Colombian conflict. In *El conflicto colombiano y su impacto en los países andinos*, edited by Álvaro Camacho-Guizado. Bogotá: Ediciones Uniandes.

Gómez-Buendía, Hernando. 1999. La hipótesis del Almendrón. In *¿Para dónde va Colombia?*, edited by Hernando Gómez-Buendía. Bogota: TM Editores-Colciencias.

González, Fernán, S.J. 1998. La Guerra de los Mil Días. In *Las guerras civiles desde 1830 y su proyección en el siglo XX*. Bogotá: Museo Nacional, Memorias de la II Cátedra Anual de Historia "Ernesto Restrepo Tirado".

Gootenberg, Paul. 1999. Reluctance or resistance? Constructing cocaine (prohibitions) in Peru, 1910–1950. In *Cocaine: Global Histories*, edited by Paul Gootenberg. London and New York: Routledge.

Jaramillo-Uribe, Jaime. 1991. *Ensayos de historia social* (vol. I). Bogotá: TM Editores/Ediciones Uniandes.

Junguito, Roberto. 1995. *La deuda externa en el siglo XIX. Cien años de incumplimiento*. Bogotá: Tercer Mundo Editores and Banco de la República.

Lara, Patricia. 1986. *Siembra vientos y recogerás tempestades: la historia del M-19, sus protagonistas, sus destinos*. Bogotá: Planeta Editorial Colombiana.

Leal, Francisco. 1989. El sistema político del clientelismo. *Análisis Político* 8 (September–December): 8–32.

Leal, Francisco and Andrés Dávila. 1990. *Clientelismo: el sistema político y su expresión regional*. Bogotá: Tercer Mundo Editores/IEPRI.

Lee III, Rensselaer W. and Francisco E. Thoumi. 1999. The Criminal-Political Nexus in Colombia. *Trends in Organized Crime* 5 (Winter): 287–328

Lemoine, Carlos. 2000. *Nosotros los colombianos del milenio*. Bogotá: Tercer Mundo Editores.

Martz, John, D. 1997. *The Politics of Clientelism: Democracy and the State in Colombia*. New Jersey: Transaction Publishers.

Medina-Gallego, Carlos. 2001. *ELN: una historia de sus orígenes*. Bogotá: Rodríguez Quito Editores.

Noriega, Carlos Augusto. 1998. *Fraude en la elección de Pastrana Borrero*. Bogotá: Editorial Oveja Negra.

Palmer, David Scott. 1980. *Peru: the Authoritarian Tradition*. Westport, Connecticut: Praeger Publishers.

Pécaut, Daniel. 2001. *Guerra contra la sociedad*. Bogotá: Editorial Planeta.

Pizarro, Eduardo. 1991. *Las FARC (1949–1966): de la autodefensa a la combinación de todas las formas de lucha*. Bogotá: IEPRI/Tercer Mundo Editores.

Putnam, Robert D. 2000. *Bowling Alone: the Collapse and Revival of the American Community*. Washington, D.C.: Simon and Schuster.

Renard, Ronald D. 2001. *Opium Reduction in Thailand 1970–2000: a Thirty-Year Journey*. Bangkok, Thailand: Regional Center for East Asia and the Pacific, UNDCP.

Thoumi, Francisco E. 1987. Some Implications of the Growth of the Underground Economy in Colombia. *Journal of Interamerican Studies and World Affairs* 29 (Summer): 35–53.

————. 1999. The Role of the State, Social Institutions, and Social Capital in determining Competitive Advantage in Illegal Drugs in the Andes. *Transnational Organized Crime* 5, 1 (Spring): 67–96.

————. 2002. Illegal drugs in Colombia: from Illegal Economic Boom to Social Crisis. *The Annals of the American Academy of Political and Social Science* 582 (July).

————. 2003a. ¿Por qué razón un país produce drogas y de qué manera esto determina la eficacia de la política?: un modelo general y algunas aplicaciones al caso colombiano. In *El conflicto colombiano y su impacto en los países andinos*, edited by Álvaro Camacho-Guizado. Bogotá: Ediciones Uniandes.

————. 2003b. Illicit drugs in the Andes five years after UNGASS-98. In *Global Organized Crime: Trends and Developments*, edited by Dina Siegel, Henk van de Bunt, and Damián Zaitch. Dorddrect: Kluwer Academic Publishers.

————. 2003c. *Illegal Drugs, Economy and Society in the Andes*. Baltimore, Maryland: Woodrow Wilson International Center for Scholars, Johns Hopkins University Press.

Urrutia, Miguel. 1991. On the Absence of Economic Populism in Colombia. In *The Macroeconomics of Populism in Latin America*, edited by Rudiger Dornbush y Sebastián Edwards. Chicago: The University of Chicago Press.

Vargas-Meza, Ricardo. 1999. *Fumigación y conflicto: políticas antidrogas y deslegitimización del estado en Colombia*. Bogotá: TM Editores/TNI/Acción Andina.

Yunis, Emilio. 2003. ¿Por qué somos así? ¿Qué pasó en Colombia? Análisis del mestizaje. Bogotá: Editorial Temis.

PART 4

Cultural and Local Consequences

CHAPTER 8

Colombia's Indigenous Peoples Confront the Armed Conflict

Jean E. Jackson*

Introduction

In the last third of the twentieth century, Colombia's indigenous peoples emerged as a political force in the national arena. This chapter discusses the indigenous movement's surprising degree of clout—surprising because only 2 percent of the nation's citizens are indigenous—and the ways the current crisis is affecting them. Following an overview of the country's indigenous communities (*pueblos*[1]) and a brief history of indigenous mobilizing, I examine indigenous participation during the National Constituent Assembly (*Asamblea Nacional Constituyente*, henceforth ANC) and the crafting of the 1991 Constitution. The constitution's successes and failures are then taken up, focusing on indigenous matters, followed by a discussion of the situation of the country's indigenous *pueblos*, focusing on the intractable and intensifying problems the country is currently facing. The chapter ends with some comments on the role of U.S. policy.

Background

Overview of Colombia's Indigenous Communities

Colombia's indigenous people form at least 81 distinct *pueblos*[2] and speak 64 different languages. The 1996 national census gives a figure of 638,606 Indians,[3] roughly 2 percent of the total population (Roldán 2000, 128).[4]

From the comparatively densely populated Andean communities to the smaller and more dispersed communities in the plains and tropical forests regions, the nation's indigenous people have always been extremely marginalized, socially, politically, and economically. In the second half of the fifteenth century, the Crown created a system of *resguardos* in New Spain, collectively owned indigenous reservations,[5] in part to protect the communities from exploitation so rapacious that they were in danger of totally disappearing. *Resguardo* inhabitants were to work the land and pay tribute to the Crown. Sixty-six contemporary *resguardos* trace their title back to this era. Independence from Spain and Portugal ushered in an ideology of nation-building, which required forging a unified national citizenry, homogeneous, Spanish (or Portuguese) speaking Catholic, and patriotic. State policies of *indigenismo*, directed at incorporating Indians into the general population through racial mixing and cultural assimilation (Ramos 1998, 5–6), were developed in all Latin American countries with indigenous populations. In Colombia, indigenous communal landholding came to be seen as especially inimical to the nation-building project, and legislation intended to dismantle the *resguardos* was promulgated in the nineteenth century. However, Law 89 of 1890, passed by the Conservatives then in power, slowed down this process, for it acknowledged the official status of the *resguardo*, and legalized the indigenous councils, known as *cabildos*. These councils, which governed the *resguardos*, were part of the Crown's attempt to centralize and urbanize the scattered "uncivilized" indigenous populations. They continue to be the legal institution governing the internal affairs of each indigenous community, in accordance with its values and customs (*usos y costumbres*). Law 89 reversed the previous "progressivist" legislative trend toward eliminating payment of tribute and privatizing collectively owned lands. This law was often cited during the repossession campaigns of the 1970s and 1980s in highland areas. In 1988 Decree 2001 defined the *resguardo* as a special kind of legal and sociopolitical institution made up of an indigenous community or entire indigenous *pueblo*.

During most of this century, the Colombian state left much of the job of governing and civilizing its indigenous population to the Church. In 1962, the Summer Institute of Linguistics/Wycliffe Bible Translators was permitted to begin placing linguist missionaries in indigenous communities (Stoll 1982, 165–97). The Division of Indigenous Affairs (*División de Asuntos Indígenas*), the official government agency representing the state to the country's *pueblos*, was founded in 1960. Presumably an advocate for indigenous interests, it has consistently been criticized for implicitly supporting an indigenist[6] approach, only gesturing to the need to respect cultural difference (Jimeno and Triana 1985; Jackson 2002). Needless to say, traditional vested interests continue their attempts to control indigenous lands, promote their own version of development, and find ways to exploit indigenous labor.

History of Indigenous Mobilizing

During the first half of the twentieth century, indigenous communities in the Andean region of the country began to organize to fight for land rights. In the 1920s, several indigenous activists involved in the effort came to question the assimilationist positions held by both the left and right, and spoke of an "indigenous proletariat." The most famous leader of that time, Manuel Quintín Lame, a Páez from Cauca (a *pueblo* now known as Nasa) eventually came to support indigenous separatism (Pineda 1984; Rappaport 1990; Gros 1991). Indigenous communities and nonindigenous peasants continued the land struggles during the 1930s and 1940s. The beginning of the insurgent groups of the 1980s and 1990s are found in the Marxist and liberal guerrilla groups that fought against the Conservative government of the 1950s by forming "independent republics" as part of the *Movimiento Agrarista* (Agrarian Movement) in the southern part of the department of Tolima. In addition to land rights disputes, peasants, initially organizing to protest harsh working and living conditions in the large coffee-producing estates, found their concerns expanding beyond labor demands to broader political concerns (Vargas Meza 1998, 23). Encountering brutal repression, armed "self-defense" peasant groups began to emerge. Those that fled the repression, many Indians among them, migrated to lower-altitude regions to the south and east and began the process known as "armed colonization" (Ramírez 2001).

Indigenous mobilizing during this period focused on repossessing lands that had been illegally expropriated by large landowners. The National Association of Peasant Users (*Asociación Nacional de Usuarios Campesinos*, ANUC) had been formed in 1970 to ensure enactment of the land reform laws passed in the early 1960s. Its indigenous members, from Cauca, Nariño, Putumayo, San Andres de Sotavento, and Antioquia, after realizing that ANUC was only interested in "peasantizing" (*campesinar*) its indigenous members, formed a National Indigenous Secretariat (*Secretaría Indígena Nacional*) within one faction when ANUC divided. In early 1971, members of the Secretariat formed the Regional Indigenous Council of Cauca (*Consejo Regional Indígena del Cauca*, CRIC), whose mission was to fight for land rights and to defend local communities against the severe repression from both the guerrilla armies and the national armed forces. Demanding implementation of agrarian reform laws passed in the early 1960s, which mandated expansion of indigenous *resguardos*, and continuing to press for the return of *resguardos* established during the colonial era, CRIC's activism was opposed not only by local landowners and the government, but also the church, one of the largest landowners in some areas. Other indigenous organizations were subsequently formed, modeling themselves on CRIC's institutional structure. By 1986, 16 regionally based indigenous organizations had appeared (Avirama and Márquez 1995, 84). When it became clear that land repossessions were going to continue, despite imprisonment, assassinations and other forms of repression, the state reversed its position and began to explore ways to ensure that land recovery occurred within a legal framework. Although land reform legislation was passed, and the Colombian Institute for Land Reform (*Instituto Colombiano de Reforma Agraria*, INCORA), was established in the early 1960s, Colombia would never undergo a full-fledged land reform. Certainly implementation of INCORA's recognition of indigenous communities' traditional notions of communally held land would require further struggle (Jimeno and Triana 1985; Findji 1992, 119–21).

Although designating itself indigenous and made up of mostly Nasa members, CRIC has never identified itself with a particular *pueblo*. Notions about how to organize along indigenous lines, and whether this was a good idea, were fiercely debated in the early days of the movement. CRIC's original organizing principle was social class (Findji 1992, 118), but very soon the organization began to move toward a more culturalist mission, modifying its charter to include the defense of "indigenous history, language and customs" in the fall of 1971 (CINEP 1981, 12).

CRIC's own version of its history acknowledges that at the very beginning "we ourselves believed that being *indio* was not good, and that in order to progress we had to copy what came from outside" (CINEP 1981, 11). CRIC has maintained links with other sectors of the rural society, helping amplify its potential for mass mobilization. In 1974, CRIC began *Unidad Indígena*, a newspaper currently published one or more times a year.

During 1976–1981, the government attempted to pass a repressive "Indigenous Law" which in effect would give the state extensive power over the *pueblos*, including the authority to decide who was and was not indigenous (Triana 1978). But the organizing efforts were kept alive, aided by several scandals that received national and international attention,[7] and by activists' successful alliance-building with peasant groups and other left organizations. Eventually the government gave in and recognized the indigenous organizations, and a nationwide umbrella organization: National Organization of Colombian Indians (*Organización Nacional Indígena de Colombia*, ONIC) was founded in 1982. From 1983 on, ONIC officially participated in several governmental programs concerned with indigenous affairs.

Beginning with the concerted land repossessions in the Andean regions in the 1960s and 1970s, and the activism around pressuring the state to enforce the land reform legislation begun in 1961, Colombia has been handing over territory, at times very large tracts of it, to its indigenous communities. Today the *pueblos* collectively and inalienably own one-fourth of the national territory, approximately 28 million fully demarcated hectares, located mostly in the plains and tropical forests.[8] The 1991 Constitution confirms their collective ownership and the *pueblos*'s right to decide the disposition of their territories, including what has come to be called ethno-development. Unfortunately, the Constitution is vague and ambiguous, perhaps deliberately so, in several places. The current U'wa crisis, in which the government wishes to explore for oil under land collectively owned by an indigenous *pueblo* adamantly opposed to it, reveals one of the more glaring contradictions: in such a situation a state will have problems defending its oil policies, despite the fact that the constitution has granted it subsoil rights.[9]

One consequence of the organizing was Colombia's Indians beginning to see the collectivity of the nation's *pueblos* as an "imagined community" (Anderson 1983). As is true for many other Latin American nations with indigenous populations, however, a tension remains between a nationally based indigenous identity and *pueblo*-specific ones. For example, when the Andean Guambianos began to organize, they explicitly stated that they were struggling to eradicate the "*indio*" identity that had been imposed on them, and replace it with one based strictly on the notion of a "people"—the *pueblo* of Guambía (Findji 1992). The Wayúu, who live in both Venezuela and Colombia on the Guajira Peninsula, are another example of the tension between *pueblo* and national indigenous identity, for they have often evinced a lack of enthusiasm for the national movement and its goal of developing a nationally based indigenous identity. The effort by the nation's Indians to retain their otherness but reverse its negative valorization has been successful in many respects. But indigenousness, especially with regard to its generic meaning, continues to be an unstable and contested concept, and by no means has it been able to totally cast off its pejorative connotations within certain sectors of Colombian society.

Certainly the processes of change and restructuring that began in the 1970s in Colombia and elsewhere in Latin America substantially influenced the evolution of indigenous identity. New incentives and opportunities for the development of a generic indigenous identity emerged. Political liberalization reduced repressive responses to indigenous demands, which resulted in broader organizing efforts and more inclusive demands. The indigenous movements in the United States and Canada, as well as the environmentalist movement, contributed to this revision and expansion of goals.

A resignification of "indigenous" occurred during this time, its meaning increasingly relying on the interplay between negotiated otherness and cultural continuity. What had been a stigmatizing identity for those Guambiano turned into symbolic and political capital during the 1970s and 1980s, becoming what political scientists call a political opportunity structure. Indigenous demands moved away from a discourse of minority rights toward one of rights as a people. The Colombian movement, as elsewhere in Latin America, continued its efforts to gain access to the political institutions of the state, but also realized it needed to pay much more attention to developing strategies for strengthening the traditional institutions of each *pueblo*. Cultural recovery projects began to assume great importance, both for the *pueblos* themselves, and in their interactions with the outside (for a Cauca example, see Gow and Rappaport 2002).

These evolving notions and new strategizing possibilities had far-reaching effects. The meaning of indigenous territory, and, consequently, of land claims, shifted. Territory came to be envisioned more comprehensively as land, and also as the underpinnings of self-determination, a "fundamental and multidimensional space for the creation and re-creation of the social, economic, and cultural values and practices of the communities" (Grueso, Rosero, and Escobar 1998, 20). Indigenous claims to a core, intrinsic, positively valenced indigenous identity, and for autonomous jurisdiction, were increasingly validated by performances of cultural distinctiveness by drawing on a *pueblo*'s repertoire of traditional rituals, sacred and secular. Increasingly, collective land rights were secured by winning debates about just what indigenous identity consisted of. Of course, the state had for a long time been denying claims to specific lands by denying the applicants' indigenous identity; what was new was the latitude it was increasingly delegating to the *pueblos* themselves to establish the criteria and make the decisions.

In sum, new parameters emerged for indigenous participation in state institutions at the national, regional, and municipal level. The country was coming to see itself in pluralist terms, terms enshrined in the 1991 Constitution[10] that mandated that indigenous *pueblos*'s autonomy be respected to a degree unthinkable in earlier periods.

Although in some quarters indigenous identity retained its negative meaning, in others its recently acquired positive significance resulted in its becoming a strategy.[11] What the concept meant, never fixed, became much more unstable as all actors repeatedly modified their discourses in response to interactions within the new multiculturalist frame. And in addition to becoming a political resource, the ANC deliberations revealed that indigeneity had become a moral reproach to *status quo* hegemonic institutions such as the state and the Church; indeed, to some degree it had taken on the role of a critique of Western society as a whole.

The 1991 Constitution

The old 1886 Constitution was extremely rigid, inefficient, and overly centralized. Although its authors, principally Rafael Núñez, spoke of it as a democratic foundational charter, it favored the Conservatives and, more generally, the privileged and powerful—a characterization that has been leveled at the Colombian state ever since (de la Calle November 13, 1994). Colombia has been called a "façade" democracy: as Álvarez, Dagnino, and Escobar (1998, 9) note, in such countries the majority of citizens have come to regard politics as the private business of the elites.

The push for constitutional reform arose from perceptions that the current social order, in which access to the government was gained exclusively through political parties via an entrenched system of patronage, was incapable of adapting to changing social conditions (Van Cott 2000, 63–89). All other attempts to participate politically ran the risk of being ignored or treated as subversion. The political and moral crisis resulting from the insurgency, the increase in violence as landowners and security forces attempted to root it out, and a pervasive distrust of a state controlled by the oligarchy also impelled the will toward constitutional reform (Assies 2000, 3). Corruption was very pervasive; in 1990 *The Economist* described Colombia as one of the five most corrupt countries in the world (Buenahora 1991, cited in Van Cott 2000, 49). Especially during the 1980s, the unending states of siege and the havoc wreaked by the drug cartels at times seemed to paralyze the state, revealing its inadequacies in a shocking manner.

As well as create a more open and legitimate political system, constitutional reform was intended to advance the neoliberal and decentralizing processes already in motion. The original agenda had not included benefiting the country's minorities, but during the ANC deliberations, several political interests, not just indigenous and Afro-Colombian, discovered that championing pluralism furthered their own ends. The debates opened up new spaces for democratic participation and for an emergent civil society (Van Cott 2000). The reforms began a process of reconfiguring the relationship between state, market and civil society, and notions of participation and empowerment, previously limited to oppositional social movements and NGOs, began to make an appearance in governmental discourse, notably in the constitution itself (Assies 2000, 2–3).

Indigenous *Pueblos*, and the Constitution

In its recognition of indigenous rights, Colombia's new constitution is the most far-reaching in Latin America. The remarkable media focus during the ANC on the three indigenous representatives, Francisco Rojas Birry, Lorenzo Muelas, and Alfonso Peña Chepe, was not an indication of any real political clout that had suddenly coalesced; rather, it was because the *pueblos* had, to a remarkable degree, come to symbolize tolerance and pluralism, a rediscovered national identity, historic reconciliation, justice, political effectiveness, and participatory legitimacy (Cepeda 1995, cited in Van Cott 2000, 72). The three men's participation in the ANC conveyed the promise of a new sociability based on respect and dialogue rather than violence. Murillo (1996, 22) suggests that the indigenous representatives helped legitimize the government and the entire process of constitutional reform. The Gaviria administration (1990–1994) "offered the protection of ethnic minority rights as a highly visible emblem of the new regime of rights protection" (Van Cott 2000, 74). A government previously closely associated with assimilationist policies reversing its stance and conspicuously guaranteeing the rights of its most marginalized population would illustrate democracy's extension to the most peripheral sectors, so that for the first time they would be considered not only citizens in good standing but also citizens belonging to unique communities whose distinctiveness the state recognized, valued, and promised to protect (Van Cott 2000, 74). The reconstitution of state-indigenous relations, by moving from a paternalistic, assimilationist stance to one recognizing the right to autonomy, dignity, and self-determination, in effect valorizing difference itself, became an emblem of the overall goal of reconstituting relations between the state and society as a whole.

Constitutional Reforms Especially Important to Indigenous *Pueblos*
The Constitution recognizes both ethnic differences and regional cultural differences. It defines the nation as a unitary, decentralized republic, its territory arranged into "territorial entities" to which it transfers a significant degree of political power. The Constitution most significantly benefits Colombia's indigenous *pueblos* in its mandate that the new territorial ordination legislation[12] will include "Indigenous Territorial Entities"—*Entidades Territoriales Indígenas* (ETIs) (Jackson 1996; Padilla 1996; Roldán 2000, 33–59). Note, however, that the ETI legislation has yet to be written, and, given the current crisis, territorial units following this model are very unlikely to materialize. The Constitution's recognition of customary law (*usos y costumbres*) allows indigenous communities to settle their internal affairs as they see fit, even criminal cases, so long as the basic law of the land is not violated (Sánchez 1998, 71–120).

Among the legal mechanisms set up by the Constitution, the writ of protection—*acción de tutela*—has definitely benefited the nation's *pueblos*, for it "empowers citizens to appeal for immediate court action when their fundamental constitutional rights are violated and no other judicial means are available" (Van Cott 2000, 87). The Constitutional Court, another reform, defended the rights of many citizens, including Indians, during the subsequent decade (Ministerio de Justicia y del Derecho/Ministerio del Interior 1997).[13] Van Cott (2000, 112) notes that the Court has issued an accumulated jurisprudence on indigenous rights and jurisdiction far more extensive than anywhere else in Latin America.

In addition, ethno-education programs in indigenous communities legislated during the 1980s (for instance, in health and bilingual education) were strengthened, and a greater share of state resources through transfers began to be made directly to *resguardos*, as was constitutionally mandated (Dirección General de Asuntos Indígenas 1998).

Post-Constitution Difficulties

Intractable Problems

Several long-standing extremely serious problems ensured that the constitution would not accomplish many of its creators' goals. The reforms simply were not nearly extensive enough to resolve the various crises, which had impelled the country to undertake the reform process. First, the traditional parties, the legislature, and post-constitution administrations have successfully restricted access to effective participation in many arenas. Second, while much has changed, the state still has not penetrated a significant part of Colombian society: military and police are the sole representatives of the state in too many rural areas, and the total absence of the state in others leaves the local population under the rule of guerrilla forces or local elites and their illegal paramilitaries.

The violence now gripping the country has deep roots. Bloody encounters throughout the first half of the twentieth century culminated in "*La Violencia*" (1948–1957), a decade of horrendous interparty warfare in which an estimated 150,000–200,000 people died (Van Cott 2000, 39).[14] The governments of Belisario Betancur (1982–1986) and Virgilio Barco (1986–1990) began reaching out with peace initiatives aimed at establishing a more democratic political system and reforming the 1886 constitution. Such measures, it was hoped, would defuse the situation and decrease the armed left's appeal.

Since the 1990s violence has escalated. The carnage and terror are documented by human-rights groups and journalists, who themselves end up targeted for assassination as a consequence. Civilian massacres occur all too frequently, by far most of them the work of the paramilitaries.

Other remaining problems include the inability of the neoliberal economic model to democratize the distribution of the nation's wealth. Van Cott (2000, 49, 248) notes that if one were to use conventional economic measures (e.g. balance of payments debt, yearly growth), the Colombia of the early 1990s could boast about its robust and stable economy. Soon, however, the economic dislocations caused by *la apertura*, the neoliberal opening legislated during the decade, increased the sense of crisis, for it aggravated already serious income disparities. Even at the beginning of the 1990s, approximately 50 percent of the population was already living in absolute poverty.

The Constitution is totally mute regarding these ever-increasing inequalities of wealth, and subsequent court decisions have not taken such reforms as their mandate. The judicial system continues to be paralyzed with respect to prosecuting criminals and enforcing sentencing. Assassinations of human-rights activists, politicians, journalists, and judges continue, maintaining a climate of intimidation and, in many rural areas, sheer terror. Between 1986 and February 2002, 3,500 trade unionist leaders had been murdered by state and parastate forces.[15]

Colombia's drug problem remains extremely serious. Because the U.S.-dominated international market virtually guarantees that vast sums of narcodollars will continue to flow into the country, it is no surprise that both guerrillas and paramilitaries quickly stepped into the spaces left by the dismantling of the cartels during the Ernesto Samper administration. The constitutional reforms did not touch the military, either in its structure or in its abysmal human-rights performance, which meant that there was no hope of achieving the reform's main goal, ending the cycle of violence.

The Crisis and the Pueblos

During the ANC, indigenous activism was weakened by divisions within the movement, some of them the result of organizations with a national presence like ONIC having sponsored their own candidates for election. Although the movement comes together during times of crisis, such as the two-year negotiation with various government agencies that culminated in the final 1995 proposal over legislating the ETIs, and during the series of strikes that occurred during the summer of 1996 (Jackson 2002), divisions had been forming earlier during the 1980s, even as the movement was gathering strength. The same events—participating in the ANC and in the 1994 elections—that led to the movement's achieving a new degree of maturity also, perhaps inevitably, led to factionalization within ONIC. The

Colombian Traditional Indigenous Authorities (*Autoridades Indígenas de Colombia*, AICO)—which had grown out of the Indigenous Association of the Southern Andes (*Asociación Indígena del Sur de los Andes*)—created in 1990, had previously challenged ONIC's procedures and decision-making. These two organizations have been likened to labor unions, in that their mandate is to protect and further the interests of their constituencies. Both ONIC and AICO put up candidates in the 1990 elections, and Rojas Birry and Muelas were elected, as we have seen, becoming extremely visible figures during the ANC. Continuing processes of factionalization resulted in the subsequent emergence in 1992 of another organization, the Indigenous Social Alliance, the product of an alliance between the Quintín Lame movement (indigenous guerrillas from Cauca who demobilized to participate in the political process), CRIC, and several other regional organizations (Triana 1992). Antonio Quirá was its leader. Then in 1993, the senator elected on the ONIC slate, Gabriel Muyuy, left the organization, his supporters forming the Movimiento Indígena Colombiano (MIC). MIC, like the other parties, publishes a platform of national issues concerned with Colombia's Indians, the rural poor, and the environment, but its major strength derives from its main constituency, the Inga people. All four organizations have played the role of political parties, although by 1994 electoral politics had proven so disruptive for ONIC that it pulled out.[16] ONIC has always experienced difficulties defining its role in the national political scene, both with respect to its mandate to represent all of the country's *pueblos*, and with respect to the kind of political activism it should adopt (Jackson 2002). It felt shut out during the César Gaviria administration (1990–1994), which dealt mainly with the indigenous senators and congressional deputies, and took away the organization's *personería jurídica* (its status as a legal entity). ONIC's continuing and considerable difficulties notwithstanding, Pizarro (1997, 97–99) reminds us that the achievements of the overall movement are nothing short of extraordinary: it is the most active social movement in the country, and achieved a representation in the senate in the 1994 elections way out of proportion to the numbers of "ethnic" voters, its ostensible constituency. Indeed, to a large extent, nonindigenous votes put these candidates into office.

It is essential to keep in mind the tight connection between democratic reforms throughout Latin America and adoption of neoliberal policies. As Álvarez, Dagnino, and Escobar (1998) point out, implementation of structural adjustment policies requires a concomitant "social adjustment," which includes movement toward a more participatory civil society. The state goal of "minimalist" government, one depending much more on the private sector (including NGOs, which often function as parastate institutions), portends enormous consequences for Colombia's *pueblos*. Decentralization as such does not empower or enhance their participation in civil society. Furthermore, although Colombia has established a "safety net" (Solidarity Network, *Red de Solidaridad*) to ease the burden of structural adjustment on the poorest sectors, public services have been drastically cut. The elimination of price supports and subsidies for the agrarian sector has further disadvantaged both highland and lowland *pueblos*.

The adverse consequences of the neoliberal economic policies of the 1990s did less harm, however, than the violence and terror the *pueblos* are facing. Indigenous communities are targeted by all the armed groups: military, paramilitaries, and guerrillas. Between the early 1970s and 1996 over 400 indigenous leaders had been assassinated, none of their killers brought to justice (Murillo 1996, 21). Although the government has ended its repression of indigenous activists, and no longer assumes that political opposition equals subversion, many authorities in the rural areas continue to assume that Indians are either actual or potential supporters of the guerrillas—due to their geographical location and their poverty—and thus appropriate targets for counterinsurgency measures (Van Cott 1994, 10). Indians living in the Choco, Antioquia, Cordoba, parts of the Sierra Nevada de Santa Marta, Arauca, Vaupes, Guaviare, Putumayo, and Amazonas are the most endangered. Part of the problem is the increased likelihood of an indigenous community being labeled as guerrilla sympathizers, or vulnerable to manipulation by the guerrillas, if the abandonment of its settlements results in the territory becoming available for cultivation or other development by large landowners or corporate interests (Forero May 14, 2001). And part of the problem is the refusal of the armed combatants to recognize communities' publicly stated wishes to remain neutral. As is the case with nonindigenous Peace Communities, such declarations are seen as an invitation for repression from all the armed groups. The Emberá-Katío are among those most affected by forced displacement from their ancestral territories in the Uraba region, especially Riosucio. Paramilitaries order them to leave or be slaughtered, while at the same time Fuerzas Armadas Revolucionarias de Colombia (FARC) prevents movement by setting up roadblocks and prohibits medication and commercial goods from entering (Colombia Support Network August 20, 1999).[17] Emberá-Katío resistance to the Urra hydroelectric dam gave rise to paramilitary massacres, which intensified when members of these communities steadfastly refused to grow coca (Lloyd and Soltani 2001). Emberá leader, Pedro Alirio Domico was murdered in the summer of 2001 by paramilitaries. Nasa leader Cristóbal Secué Escué, a former CRIC leader was killed by the FARC on June 25, 2001. The list goes on and on. The Carib-speaking Karijonas in Amazonas numbered 70 in 2001, down from 280 in 1993 (Forero May 14, 2001). One source estimates that half of Colombia's indigenous peoples face annihilation from the escalating conflict (Lloyd and Soltani 2001).[18]

Guerrillas, paramilitaries, and military detachments occupy large sections of indigenous territory, forcing Indians to serve as guides or informers by threatening their families (Roldán 2000). Forced recruitment of indigenous teenagers by the FARC and ELN has been reported in many regions (Rights & Democracy 2001, 29). The extent of indigenous vulnerability is illustrated by the 1998 meeting between Francisco Rojas Birry, the indigenous senator, Abadio Green, then president of ONIC, and Carlos Castaño, the head of *Autodefensas de Colombia* (AUC) to negotiate a ceasefire of 60 days in the highly conflictive zones of Córdoba and Urabá (*El Espectador* September 25, 1998). Some Indians do voluntarily join the guerrillas, and occasionally even the paramilitaries, to protect their families in areas under paramilitary control, or for the promise of a uniform and pay. In February 2002, a recruit in the AUC, the main paramilitary organization, earned US$180 per month, a very healthy sum in Colombia, given its 20 percent unemployment and up to 60 percent underemployment (Forero February 13, 2002).

Indians have also been involved in other kinds of conflict; in the Chocó region on the Pacific coast, for example, Indians and Afro-Colombians have clashed over land demarcation (Wade 1993, 353; Achito 1997). In this instance, however, attempts have been made to ease the situation: the local indigenous organization has attempted to build alliances in the fight against environmental degradation, and black peasant associations often invite Indians to their meetings to build trust (Wade 1993, 353, 357).

Narcotrafficking seriously imperils indigenous communities in many regions and in many ways. Both highland and lowland Indians grow illegal crops (coca and opium poppies), sometimes by choice, sometimes under duress, with severe impact on the traditional subsistence economy and social order. In addition to intrafamilial and inter*pueblo* disputes,[19] health problems and possible legal penalties, Indians face potential loss of livelihood and health risks from fumigation of fields, as well as a scarcity of essential commodities like gasoline, due to government efforts to decrease production of coca paste. The Kofán, located in the Putumayo region, one of the areas being heavily sprayed, have suffered enormously, first from the state's homesteading program which sent hundreds of *colonos* into their territory, then from drug traffickers who gave them the choice of growing coca or leaving the region, then from armed groups, and now from airplanes spraying fumigants that destroy subsistence crops and sharply reduce fish and game.

Although the United States claims it sprays only large-scale coca cultivation, delegations to the region in 2001, one Canadian and one from the Office of National Ombudsman (*Defensor del Pueblo*), carefully recorded multiple cases of damage (Rights & Democracy 2001, 30). The assassination of Pablo Emilio Díaz, a Kofán leader early in 2001, very likely by paramilitaries, created further disruption and displacement of families, many fleeing to Ecuador (Lloyd and Soltani 2001).

The Role of U.S. Policy

Plan Colombia

After much debate and numerous revisions, the assistance package known as Plan Colombia was signed into law by President Bill Clinton on July 13, 2000. Its stated purposes are to eradicate narcotics production and help restructure the country's economy, in particular ensure delivery of social and economic benefits to its coca- and poppy-growing regions. The document is troubling with respect to possible consequences for human rights and Colombia's ability to restart the peace process. The Plan's counterinsurgency objectives raise the very real possibility of a quagmire or even escalation. Its antidrug strategy has been shown not to work. Finally, the potential of seriously exacerbating the internal refugee problem is very worrisome, for more than 2 million citizens are already involuntarily displaced from their homes. Credible sources report that paramilitary commanders' assertions that they are actually spearheading the government's fumigation offensive in the Putumayo and Caquetá provinces, are backed by reliable evidence (Penhaul March 28, 2001).

In the opinion of many knowledgeable scholars and policy-makers, Plan Colombia will not, because it cannot, solve the problem. Opium poppies are grown in Cauca, and coca in lowland regions in the southeast (Guaviare, Vaupes), and south (Caqueta, Putumayo). The program has been widely protested. Delegations of Colombian officials have traveled to Washington, D.C. to appeal to the U.S. Congress and the public to support their campaign to stop aerial fumigation. Bills to end the program have been introduced in both houses of the Colombian Congress, and Governors in six southern Colombian departments have joined human-rights organizations and some officials of the Pastrana government in opposing it. Monsanto's own instructions to users of the fumigant Roundup Ultra (*glysophate*)—to use protective eye covering and to avoid inhaling the chemical, or spraying it on water, or allowing domestic animals into treated fields for at least two weeks (Vargas Meza 2000)—give the lie to a U.S. Department of State (2002) "Fact Sheet" claiming that reports of harm are not to be trusted. Other health problems reported include respiratory problems, gastrointestinal illnesses, and birth defects (Vargas Meza 2000; *Chicago Tribune* August 14, 2001; Podur 2001, 45). A successful spraying will kill one-fourth of the coca plants at best, but its effects on other cultigens are far more deadly (Forero January 31, 2001). Because of the danger from FARC guerrillas, planes often are forced to fly too high to accurately target the drug crops. Furthermore, Roundup Ultra is always combined with nonregulated chemicals called "surfactants," and despite assurances by Monsanto that its product has been shown to be harmless to people and animals, no studies have been done showing the risks of the actual formula used in spraying. The UN drug control program has called the fumigation program "inhumane" and "ineffective" (DeYoung August 1, 2001). However, the United States considers it so integral to its Colombia policy that a July 23, 2001 order from a Bogota judge that the spraying be shut down (Forero July 30, 2001) was rescinded only a week later, due to pressure from the United States.

Unfortunately, most of the new plots are cleared in virgin forest. Damage to the ecosystem has been widely reported, and the World Wildlife Fund has called for suspension of the program until the "potentially grave environmental impact" on the world's second most biodiverse country can be studied. Ironically, contamination of water supplies and near-total destruction of legal crops mean that some of the government's development programs in the region, most notably pisciculture, have utterly failed.

A little-noticed part of Plan Colombia is a proposed use of "tested, environmentally safe mycoherbicides," a program to develop fungi designed to kill drug crops. All indications are that if developed, such fungi will potentially have the ability to attach to other crops, lie dormant in the soil for years, and pose a danger to humans, in particular the immunocompromised (Bigwood and Stevenson 2000, 8–9).

Clearly, as long as the market for cocaine and heroin continues to grow, stopping drug production at its source will not solve the problem. Studies have repeatedly shown that domestic drug treatment and education programs are much more dollar-effective at reducing U.S. narcotics abuse than foreign military aid.[20]

Who Benefits?

It is most unfortunate that far greater numbers of ordinary citizens than combatants are killed. Many analysts (Krauss September 10, 2000; Klare 2001; Theidon 2001) have concluded that what was once a Marxist revolutionary effort to bring social justice and economic reforms to a country whose claims to be a democracy and to have legislated land reform were false, has deteriorated into a bloody free-for-all over resources, as has happened in the Congo and Sudan. Even if none of the actors can win, the stakes are high enough for all of them to keep trying, and surely if we are to understand the conflict we need to appreciate the combatants' interest in ensuring that the revenues at their disposal will continue and, if possible, create new sources of revenues. At present, these include narcotics, oil, minerals, and rich agricultural land in places like Uraba in the north.

We also need to understand the stakes for the noncombatant actors. Drugs, military expenditures, oil exploration and extraction, and hydroelectric energy production mean profits going into national and international coffers. Klare (2001) draws attention to a stepped-up interest in Colombia's oil reserves following the September 11 attacks and subsequent increase in instability in the Middle East. The announcement was the first acknowledgment that U.S. military involvement is not exclusively aimed at reducing the production of illegal drugs.[21]

Isikoff and Vistica (April 3, 2000, 39) have pointed out that most of the funds supposedly earmarked for Colombia will in fact remain in or quickly return to the United States. For example, between 1992 and 1998 Monsanto received US$24 million from sales of Roundup Ultra for use in Colombia (*Cultural Survival Voices* 2001, 4). Blackhawk helicopters are manufactured in Connecticut, whose senator, Christopher Dodd, lobbied energetically for the Plan. Mercenaries serving as "consultants," such as those employed by Dyncorp earn salaries (which are ultimately paid by U.S. taxpayers). The U.S. military also benefits from an initiative that permits continuing military training exercises, justifies increased expenditures for military equipment, and demonstrates the necessity for continued surveillance of, and interaction with, the U.S. military's Latin American counterparts. Finally, coming across as a high-ranking officer in the "war on drugs" clearly results in air time and other forms of political capital for U.S. government desk warriors inside the Beltway.

In sum, the two main problems with Plan Colombia are its support of a militarized approach to countering narcotrafficking, including forced aerial fumigation of coca and poppy fields; and its large-scale funding of the Colombian military, despite having the worst human-rights record in the Americas, and despite well-documented tacit and active collaboration with paramilitary groups who do the truly dirty work. Along with the guerrillas the United States has labeled the paramilitary groups "terrorists," but the continued military aid in effect sanctions the abuses.[22] The European Union's decision to sharply scale back their promised aid, fearing that Plan Colombia would only inflame the war, would seem to be prescient.

Conclusions

The remarkable emergence of Colombia's indigenous peoples during the past three decades—their success at finding a political voice and gaining recognition as valued citizens, some of that value seen to derive from their otherness—constitutes an impressive achievement. Mobilizing and alliance-building, both national and international, accompanied by democratic reforms and the new pluralist vision, produced changes no one foresaw. However, all these achievements and promising future scenarios appear extremely vulnerable in the current context of the political and moral crisis the country is undergoing, and the increased poverty caused by structural adjustment, shrinking state services, and, worst, the civil war. Despite the possibilities of developing a more participatory citizenry, of a robust civil society finally being born, we have seen that in the last decade the position of most *pueblos* has worsened. Uncontrolled colonization of indigenous territories in the plains and Amazon regions, accompanied by the armed conflict, coca-crop spraying, and incursions into virgin forest make a mockery of indigenous ownership and control of their *resguardos*. Drug trafficking and the daily terrorizing of civilians so characteristic of guerrilla warfare make life a horror for many *pueblos*, as assassinations and forced migration increase. Massive development projects also produce forced migration (at times Indians must run for their very lives, threatened by paramilitaries), and promote disease and death, rather than the benefits touted by multinational corporations in their slick project statements (Brysk 2000, 10). In addition to the communities internally displaced by the violence, economic conditions have forced many indigenous people to move to the "zones of misery" surrounding the urban centers and try to cope with the horrendous conditions there.

Returning to the issue of U.S. involvement in the conflict, in particular following the attacks of September 11, the possibility that the global "war on terrorism" may include increased U.S. support for military operations against Colombia's armed groups is very real, especially given the end of the peace talks in February 2002. But although the FARC and ELN guerrillas and the AUC paramilitaries appear on the U.S. Department of State's list of foreign terrorist organizations, these groups in fact resemble armies more than shadowy terrorist cells. The FARC, most analysts agree, is "the richest and most powerful rebel group in Latin American history, a force of at least 17,000 well-armed fighters dispersed across virtually every province in the country" (Forero February 22, 2002). One of the top leaders of the AUC, Salvatore Mancuso, claimed that by February 2002, the organization had already swelled to 14,000, up from just 850 a decade ago; he spoke of nearly doubling its numbers within a year (Forero February 13, 2002). Combating such armed combatants in the name of counter-terrorism would in fact require an enormous counterinsurgency effort. The country's crisis worsens daily; surely a solution can be found to the extremely complex and wide-ranging crisis the country is facing, which will not involve such enormously high costs.

Notes

* Professor at the Department of Anthropology, Massachusetts Institute of Technology, Cambridge, MA. In Colombia, thanks to all who have helped my research on indigenous organizing, in particular Raúl Arango, Jaime Arocha, Ana Cecilia Betancourt, Guillermo Carmona, François Correa, Martín Franco, Segisfredo Franco, Abadio Green, Leonor Herrera, Víctor Jacanamejoy, Myriam Jimeno, Gladys Jimeno, Hernando Muñoz, Guillermo Padilla, Roberto Pineda, María Clemencia Ramírez, Elizabeth Reichel, Esther Sánchez, María Lucía Sotomayor, Adolfo Triana, Enrique Sánchez, Roque Roldán, Carlos Uribe, Martín von Hildebrand, Simón Valencia, Miguel Vázquez, the Instituto Colombiano de Antropología, the Department of Anthropology at the Universidad de los Andes, various members of the Regional Indigenous Council of the Vaupés—Consejo Regional Indígena del Vaupés (CRIVA), and various officials of the Organización Nacional de Indígenas de Colombia (ONIC). Trips to Colombia (1985, 1987, 1989, 1991, 1992, 1993, 1996, and 2000) have been funded in part by the Dean's Office, School of Humanities, Arts and Social Sciences, M.I.T. For help thinking through the ideas presented here, thanks to Cristina Rojas, James Howe, and Donna Van Cott. All translations are my own. The responsibility for the ideas set forth here is entirely my own.

1. *Pueblo* ("people," "community") is the official term for a distinct indigenous group.
2. The actual number of indigenous *pueblos* in Colombia is somewhat uncertain; some authors, like Roldán (2000), listing 81, others (ONIC 1998) as many as 95.
3. Where stylistically possible I use "indigenous" rather than "Indian," but retain the latter term when a noun referring to one or more individuals must be used, despite the term's controversial status.
4. Padilla (1996, 93) gives a total of 972,000 people who consider themselves indigenous.
5. Arango and Sánchez (1998, 23–33).
6. Note that "indigenist" has two well-established, often confusing meanings. The first, negatively valenced and most often used in reference to state policy toward indigenous peoples, indicates an integrationist position; this is particularly the case with the word's Spanish and Portuguese cognates. The second meaning refers to any individuals (indigenous or not), or institutions in favor of indigenous rights.

7. One scandal, following a 1967 massacre of 15 Guahibo Indians in the eastern plains region of the country, was widely cited because one of the assailants, a settler, said in his defense at the trial that he had not seen anything wrong with the killings, because they were Indians. He was acquitted (Bodley 1990, 29). Discussing another massacre that occurred in 1969, one of the killers said that since Indians have no soul they cannot be considered human beings (*El Tiempo* September 18, 1988).

8. Seventy-three percent of these lands are in the Amazon region. On average 85% of the occupants of these lands are indigenous. There are 469 *resguardos* (more precisely, 460 *resguardos* and nine indigenous reserves); 83% of these are new *resguardos* and 81% of Colombian Indians live in territories collectively owned by them (Roldán 2000, xxiii, xxiv, 49–50). See Jimeno and Triana (1985) on the history of *resguardo* creation following agrarian reform in the 1960s.

9. The U'wa case has received a great deal of media attention in Colombia and the United States. See *El Tiempo* (February 5, 1997), Amazon Coalition (April 14, 1998), and Vargas Meza (April 30, 1999).

10. Article 7 of the Constitution states, "The State recognizes and protects the ethnic and cultural diversity of the Colombian Nation" (Constitución Política de Colombia 1991).

11. Laurent (1997) discusses four approaches to analyzing Latin American indigenous movements: the essentialist analysis (focusing on "objective" criteria like language); the internal colonialism analysis (which sees indigenous identity to be based in collective experiences during colonial and neocolonial periods); the instrumentalist analysis (which focuses on ways in which indigenous identity is a strategy that helps indigenous organizations gain access to goods, power, prestige hitherto denied); and the situational analysis (which sees the movement as highly dynamic, whose subjectivity and goals respond to a given situation the movement is currently confronting). She argues, correctly in my opinion, that the situational analysis best fits the Colombian movement.

12. Territorial ordination (*ordenamiento territorial*) refers to the Constitution's mandate that the entire country undergo a radical re-ordering of its political landscape, necessitating a redrawing of its political map. A significant amount of power would then flow from the regions, made up of Territorial Entities, instead of from the capital. The reforms, therefore, recognize local autonomy in a fundamentally new way. The Constitution arranges for follow-up legislation, called the Organic Law for Territorial Demarcation that would specify the process of territorial ordination—the actual distribution of Territorial Entities—and defines in detail these units' actual responsibilities. This law would also regulate dispute settlement between the national government and the Territorial Entities (Betancurt and Rodríguez 1994, 22).

13. The Court has heard a truly remarkable number of cases: by mid-1996 more than 100,000 citizens had exercised the writ of protection (Van Cott 2000, 112).

14. More on the period of *La Violencia* can be found in Thoumi in this volume.

204 • Jean E. Jackson

15. Information from Colombia Solidarity Campaign, PO Box 8446, London N17 6NZ, February 22, 2002.
16. Gros (1996, 259–73) and Laurent (1997) provide analyses of post-constitution indigenous electoral politics and political participation more generally.
17. See Dudley and Murillo (1998, 46) regarding Occidental Petroleum's insinuation that Roberto Cobaría, the U'wa leader, was bending to pressure from the ELN, an accusation tantamount to a "death sentence" given the waves of paramilitary violence in these regions.
18. Esnal (1998); *El Espectador* (December 1, 1998); and *El Tiempo* (November 4, 1998) on a guerrilla attack on Mitu, the capital of the Vaupes, a department that is 85% indigenous.
19. See Abultaif's (October 25, 2001) report on a deadly land dispute between Guambianos and Ambaló.
20. Theidon (2001) reports that a RAND corporation study commissioned by the Office of National Drug Control Policy and the U.S. Army found that for every dollar invested in domestic cocaine treatment US$7.46 was gained in terms of increased social productivity and reduced cocaine consumption, crime and violence. But every dollar spent on coca eradication resulted in an additional loss of US$0.85.
21. Another indication of an increase in U.S. involvement is the U.S. government's decision to share intelligence with the Colombian government in the campaign against the rebels. A restriction established during the Clinton administration in 2000 bars the use of American intelligence for counterinsurgency efforts. In early 2002 an unnamed senior official in the Bush administration confirmed that lawyers were studying ways to circumvent this restriction in order to provide such intelligence by following the administration's post–September 11 directives on intelligence-sharing with respect to terrorist organizations. The U.S. labeled the FARC as a terrorist organization in 1997 (Marquis 2002).
22. Amnesty International (2001); Lloyd and Soltani (2001).

References

Abultaif, Amira. October 25, 2001. Seething Rivals Vow to Aim for Peace. *The Globe and Mail.*
Achito, Alberto. 1997. Autonomía territorial, jurisdicción especial indígena y conflictos interétnicos en el Pacífico. In *"Del olvido surgimos para traer nuevas esperanzas": La jurisdicción especial indígena,* edited by Ministerio de Justicia y del Derecho, Ministerio del Interior/Dirección General de Asuntos Indígenas, 53–62. Bogota: Ministerio de Justicia y del Derecho, Ministerio del Interior/Dirección General de Asuntos Indígenas.
Álvarez, Sonia E., Evelina Dagnino, and Arturo Escobar, eds. 1998. Introduction: The Cultural and the Political in Latin American Social Movements. In *Cultures of Politics Politics of Cultures: Re-visioning Latin American Social Movements,* 1–32. Boulder: Westview Press.

Amazon Coalition. April, 14, 1998. Why Occidental's Oil Project is a Death Sentence for the U'wa. *The New York Times.*

Amnesty International. 2001. Country Page on Colombia. *http://www.iadb.org*

Anderson, Benedict. 1983. Imagined Communities: Reflections on the Origin and Spread of Nationalism. London: Verso.

Arango, Raúl and Enrique Sánchez. 1998. *Los pueblos indígenas de Colombia 1997.* Bogota: Departamento Nacional de Planeación.

Assies, Willem. 2000. Indigenous Peoples and Reform of the State in Latin America. In *The Challenge of Diversity: Indigenous Peoples and Reform of the State in Latin America*, edited by Willem Assies, Gemma van der Haar, and André Hoekema, 3–22. Amsterdam: Thela Thesis.

Avirama, Jesús, and Rayda Márquez. 1995. The Indigenous Movement in Colombia. In *Indigenous Peoples and Democracy in Latin America*, edited by Donna Van Cott, 83–106. New York: St. Martin's.

Betancurt, Ana Cecilia and Hernán Rodríguez. 1994. After the Constitution: Indigenous Proposals for Territorial Demarcation in Colombia. *Abya Yala News: Journal of the South and Meso American Indian Information Center* 8: 22–23.

Bigwood, Jeremy and Sharon Stevenson. 2000. Fungi for Colombia? *Colombia Update* 12 (Summer/Fall): 8–9.

Bodley, John. 1990. *Victims of Progress* (3rd ed.). Mountain View, California: Mayfield Publishing Company.

Brysk, Alison. 2000. *From Tribal Village to Global Village: Indian Rights and International Relations in Latin America.* Stanford: Stanford University Press.

Buenahora Febres-Cordero, Jaime. 1991. El proceso constituyente: de la - propuesta estudiantil a la quiebra del bipartidismo. Bogota: Cámara de Representantes/Pontífica Universidad Javeriana.

Cepeda Espinosa, Manuel José. 1995. Ethnic Minorities and Constitutional Reform in Colombia. In *Ethnic Conflict and Governance in Comparative Perspective*, 100–38. Working paper no. 215. Washington, D.C.: Woodrow Wilson International Center for Scholars.

Centro de Investigación y Educación Popular (CINEP). 1981. *Consejo Regional del Cauca—CRIC: Diez años de lucha: historia y documentos.* Serie Controversia No. 91–92. Bogotá: Editorial CINEP.

Chicago Tribune. August 14, 2001. Editorial: Spraying Poison in Colombia.

Colombia Support Network. August 20, 1999. Please Help Save the Emberá Nation. Urgent Action Appeal. *http://www.csn@pop.igc.org*

Constitución Política de Colombia. 1991. Bogota: República de Colombia.

Cultural Survival Voices. 2001. Fumigation. 1 (Fall): 5.

DeYoung, Karen. August 1, 2001. Colombians Protest Fumigation. *The Washington Post.*

Dirección General de Asuntos Indígenas. 1998. *Los Pueblos Indígenas en el País y en América: Elementos de Política Colombiana e Internacional.* Bogotá: Serie Retos de la Nación Diversa.

Dudley, Steven and Mario Murillo. 1998. Oil in a Time of War. *NACLA* 31 (March/April): 42–48.

El Espectador. September 25, 1998. Tregua indígena con "paras": 60 días para evaluar papel de los indígenas en el conflicto.

———December 1, 1998. En Mitú quieren olvidar la tragedia.

El. Tiempo. September 18, 1988. La historia sí se repite: violencia y comunidades indígenas.

———. February 5, 1997. Habrá decreto para reglamentar consulta con U'wa.

———. November 4, 1998. No habrá cese del fuego, dice "Tirofijo."

Esnal, Luis. November 4, 1998. "Colombia violó nuestra soberanía": Brasil. *El Tiempo.*

Findji, María Teresa. 1992. From Resistance to Social Movement: The Indigenous Authorities Movement in Colombia. In *The Making of Social Movements in Latin America: Identity, Strategy, and Democracy*, edited by Arturo Escobar and Sonia E. Álvarez, 112–33. Boulder: Westview Press.

———. May 14, 2001. After centuries, Colombian Tribes are now Imperiled by a Civil War. *The New York Times.*

———. July 30, 2001. Judge In Colombia Halts Spraying of Drug Crops. *The New York Times.*

———. February 13, 2002. Colombia Militia Chief Vows to Expand. *The Boston Globe.*

———. February 22, 2002. Colombia Attacks Rebel Zone and Leader's Patience Snaps. *The New York Times.*

Gow, David and Joanne Rappaport. 2002. The Indigenous Public Voice: The Multiple Idioms of Modernity in Native Cauca. In *Indigenous Movements, Self-Representation and the State in Latin America*, edited by Kay B. Warren and Jean E. Jackson, 47–80. Austin: University of Texas Press.

Gros, Christian. 1991. *Colombia Indígena: identidad cultural y cambio social.* Bogota: Fondo Editorial CEREC.

———. 1996. Un ajustement à visage indien. In *La Colombie: à l'aube du troisième millénaire*, coordinated by Jean-Michel Blanquer, and Christian Gros, 249–75. Paris: Travaux et mémoires de l'IHEAL.

Grueso, Libia, Carlos Rosero, and Arturo Escobar. 1998. The Process of Black Community Organizing in the Southern Pacific Coast Region of Colombia. In *Cultures of Politics Politics of Cultures: Re-visioning Latin American Social Movements*, edited by Sonia E. Álvarez, Evelina Dagnino, and Arturo Escobar, 196–219. Boulder: Westview Press.

Isikoff, Michael and Gregory Vistica. April 3, 2000. The Other Drug War. *Newsweek.*

Jackson, Jean E. 1996. The Impact of Recent National Legislation in the Vaupés Region of Colombia. *Journal of Latin American Anthropology* 1: 120–51.

———. 2002. Contested Discourses of Authority in Colombian National Indigenous Politics: The 1996 summer takeovers. In *Indigenous Movements, Self-Representation and the State in Latin America*, edited by Kay B. Warren and Jean E. Jackson, 81–122. Austin: University of Texas Press.

Jimeno, Myriam and Adolfo Triana. 1985. El estado y la política indigenista. In *Estado y Minorías Étnicas en Colombia*, edited by Myriam Jimeno, and Adolfo Triana Antorveza, 65–143. Bogotá: Editorial Gente Nueva.

Klare, Michael. 2001. *Resource Wars: Global Geopolitics in the 21st Century*. New York: Metropolitan Books.

Krauss, Clifford. September 10, 2000. War in Colombia Creates a Nation of Victims. *New York Times*.

Laurent, Virginia. 1997. Población indígena y participación política en Colombia: Las elecciones de 1994. *Análisis Político* 31 (May–August): 63–81.

Lloyd, Janet and Atossa Soltani. 2001. *Report on Plan Colombia and Indigenous Peoples*. December. Washington, D.C.: Amazon Watch.

Marquis, Christopher. February 23, 2002. U.S. to Give Colombians Data to Help Fight Rebels. *The New York Times*.

Ministerio de Justicia y del Derecho, Ministerio del Interior/Dirección General de Asuntos Indígenas. 1997. *"Del olvido surgimos para traer nuevas esperanzas": La jurisdicción especial indígena*. Bogota: Ministerio de Justicia y del Derecho, Ministerio del Interior/Dirección General de Asuntos Indígenas.

Murillo, Mario. 1996. Confronting the Dilemmas of Political Participation. *NACLA* 29: 21–22.

Organización Nacional Indígena de Colombia (ONIC). 1998. *Memorias: Los pueblos indígenas de Colombia, un reto hacia el nuevo milenio*. Bogota: República de Colombia: Ministerio de Agricultura y Desarrollo Rural.

Padilla, Guillermo. 1996. La ley y los pueblos indígenas en Colombia. *Journal of Latin American Anthropology* 1: 78–97.

Penhaul, Karl. March 28, 2001. Outlaw Role Seen in Colombia Effort. *The Boston Globe*.

Pineda, Roberto. 1984. La reivindicación del Indio en el pensamiento social Colombiano (1850–1950). In *Un siglo de investigación social: Antropología en Colombia*, edited by J. Arocha and N.S de Friedemann, 197–252. Bogota: ETNO.

Pizarro, Eduardo. 1997. ¿Hacia un sistema multipartidista? Las terceras fuerzas en Colombia Hoy. *Análisis Político* 31 (May–August): 82–104.

Podur, Justin. 2001. A Way Out for Colombia: U.S. Military Assistance and Fumigation Programs. *Z Magazine* (October): 45–8.

Ramírez, María Clemencia. 2001. *Entre el estado y la guerrilla: identidad y ciudadanía en el movimiento de los campesinos cocaleros del Putumayo*. Bogota: Instituto Colombiano de Antropología e Historia.

Ramos, Alcida Rita. 1998. *Indigenism: Ethnic Politics in Brazil*. Madison: University of Wisconsin Press.

Rappaport, Joanne. 1990. *The Politics of Memory: Native Historical Interpretation in the Colombian Andes*. Cambridge: Cambridge University Press.

Rights & Democracy. 2001. *Mission to Colombia to Investigate the Situation of Indigenous Peoples*. May 27 to June 3. Montreal, Quebec: International Centre for Human Rights and Democratic Development.

Roldán Ortega, Roque. 2000. *Pueblos indígenas y leyes en Colombia: Aproximación crítica al estudio de su pasado y su presente*. Bogota: Tercer Mundo.

Sánchez, Esther. 1998. *Justicia y pueblos indígenas de Colombia*. Bogota: Universidad Nacional de Colombia.

Stoll, David. 1982. *Fishers of Men or Founders of Empire? The Wycliffe Bible Translators in Latin America*. London: Zed Press.

Theidon, Kimberly. 2001. Building Peace in Colombia. Briefing from the Institute for Human Rights Policy and Practice. Unpublished document, October.

Triana Antorveza, Adolfo. 1978. El estatuto indígena o la nueva encomienda bonapartista. *Controversia 79*, 29–41. Bogota: CINEP.

———. 1992. Grupos étnicos, Nueva Constitución en Colombia. In *Antropología Jurídica*, edited by Esther Sánchez, 103–14. Bogota: Sociedad Antropológica de Colombia/Comité Internacional para el Desarrollo de los Pueblos/VI Congreso Nacional de Antropología.

U.S. Department of State. September 4, 2002. Report on Issues related to the Aerial Eradication of Illicit Coca in Colombia.

Van Cott, Donna Lee. 1994. Indigenous Peoples and Democracy: Issues for Policymakers. In *Indigenous Peoples and Democracy in Latin America*, 1–28. New York: St. Martin's.

———. 2000. *The Friendly Liquidation of the Past: The Politics of Diversity in Latin America*. Pittsburgh: University of Pittsburgh Press.

Vargas Meza, Ricardo. 1998. The FARC, the War and the Crisis of the State. *NACLA* 31 (March/April): 20–22.

———. April 30, 1999. Oxy realizará inversiones en busca de crudo. *El Espectador*.

———. 2000. Biowarfare in Colombia? A Controversial Fumigation Scheme. *NACLA 34* (September/October): 20–22.

Wade, Peter. 1993. *Blackness and Race Mixture: The Dynamics of Racial Identity in Colombia*. Baltimore: The Johns Hopkins University Press.

CHAPTER 9

Elusive Peace, Elusive Violence: Identity and Conflict in Colombia

Cristina Rojas*

V iolence in Colombia is elusive. Various factors, among them, temporal discontinuity and multidimensionality, make it difficult to comprehend violence and, therefore, to find an adequate solution. Periods of intense conflict are followed by periods of relative peace. The civil wars of the nineteenth century, which culminated in the War of the Thousand Days (1899–1902), were followed by periods of economic prosperity and political stability until the outbreak of *La Violencia* (1946–1957), which initially took the form of a bipartisan conflict between Liberals and Conservatives. Contemporary violence is referred to as *Las Violencias*, the plural expression emphasizing the diversity and changing forms of violence. It has been characterized by its multidimensionality, having socioeconomic, political, cultural, regional, and lately, drug-related dimensions. A warfare between guerrilla, paramilitaries, and the army, and drug-related violence characterize this period.

Violence occurs territorially. In the mid-nineteenth century some department were able to isolate themselves from most of the nation's civil wars. During *La Violencia*, the department of Caldas ranked one in the number of deaths, Tolima was second and Antioquia third (Oquist 1980, 227). In 1994, 56 percent of the country homicides occurred in three departments—Antioquia, Valle, and Bogota (Franco 1999, 86). Violence affects not only large cities but also small municipalities. Between 1990 and 1995, the 20 most violent municipalities in the country, home to only

8.5 percent of the population, contributed 28.8 percent of the violent deaths (Rubio 1999, 40).

This elusive violence is also distributed unevenly across gender, age and race in Colombia. Proportionally, indigenous and black populations have suffered more. It is estimated that in 2002, a third of displaced people were Afro-Colombian and indigenous even though they make up only 11 percent of the total population (Norwegian Refugee Council 2003, 9). In the department of Antioquia, the homicide rate for young people between the ages of 20 and 24 reached 1,044, meaning that one of every 100 young people was killed in 1994 (Franco 1999, 91). There is also a disproportional distribution of violence by gender. Homicides affect mainly men who, on average, account for more than 90 percent of the victims. Women are overrepresented in domestic violence where 93 percent of the cases reported are against women. Two-third of sexual offenses reported in 1996 were girls under the age of 14.

Poverty has been discounted as the explanatory factor for violence (Sarmiento 1999) despite levels of rural poverty that have escalated from 30 percent to 87 percent in the last 30 years (UNDP 2003, 42). Economic factors are also important as violence tends to predominate in areas that are rich in natural resources, highly productive agriculturally and undergoing great economic expansion (Sánchez 2001, 5). There is also violence against labor and social leaders.

Politics engender violence but do not explain it. Furthermore, today's political conflict is responsible of 10 or 15 percent of total homicides.[1] The remainder is the result of intolerance, drug-related conflicts, confrontation among juvenile gangs and common crime. This elusiveness makes it more difficult to trace dividing lines between political and nonpolitical violence, between organized and unorganized violence.

Recognizing violence's elusiveness does not require the abandonment of the search for commonalities among the diverse factors cited above in order to shed light on the causes of violence. I argue that violence is better understood when seen through the process of construction of identities, specifically, the dynamics of recognition. Violence against women, peasants, street children, indigenous, and black populations is preceded by a depreciatory image of the victim on the part of its perpetrator. Their social and economic demands are not recognized as legitimate and claims for justice are criminalized and met with force. Most of the causes of crimes are unknown and most crimes remain unpunished. Further, responsibility for such major acts of violence as the case of the massacre in the banana plantations in 1928, *La Violencia* of the 1950s, the assassination of political leaders in the 1980s and the massacres in the 1990s have not been established. As pointed out by Daniel Pécaut (2001, 246–47), violence in Colombia does not have a history; when the history is narrated, it attributes the causes to the barbarism of the masses and, therefore, legitimizes the domination of the upper classes. Gabriel García Márquez (1978) captures well the elusiveness of violence in his novel, *La mala hora* (*The Evil Hour*), by concluding the search for its causes with the attribution: "It's the whole town and it isn't anybody."

To develop this argument I divide the chapter into three parts: the first section outlines the theoretical foundation for a focus on identity and violence; the second, analyzes the internationalization of the war on drugs from the dynamic of recognition. The third part applies the analysis to Colombia's domestic war on drugs and the strategy of "Democratic Security" put forward by President Álvaro Uribe.

Identity and Violence

I relate violence to process of identity formation, be they by gender, racial, or religious affiliation, and to the formation of collective identities such as party affiliation or feelings of local and national identity. I consider the formation of identity in relationship with others. I know who I am by differentiating myself from others. Following Bakhtin, the self can only achieve self-awareness "by revealing myself to another, through another and with another's help" (Todorov 1984, 96). To ignore this process of mutual recognition and to deny the humanity of others who have equal rights and the ability to respond as equals, is to engender violence.

Violence is engendered in processes of nonrecognition or misrecognition in which a demeaning image is projected on others. Charles Taylor (1994, 26) expresses the relationship with violence "misrecognition shows not just lack of due respect. It can inflict a grievous wound, saddling its victims with a crippling self-hatred. Due recognition is not just a courtesy we owe to people. It is a vital human need." In general, racism and sexism position others in devalued identities. In Colombia, the concentration of violence on indigenous and black population is associated with nonrecognition.

In addition to moral injuries, misrecognition furthers violence when those situated in higher positions authorize force or coercion to keep groups or individuals in a subordinated position, as happens in all forms of slavery and colonialism. Moreover, in situations in which the other is denied human value, the consequence may be physical elimination as in practices of ethnic cleansing and genocide. In Colombia, labeling the homeless, street children, prostitutes, and homosexual as "disposable" precedes and accompanies practices of "social cleansing."

Not all violence emanates from demeaning the image of the other; it also occurs between equals, or doubles: individuals belonging to the same social strata, political party or nationality, and even between couples of the same sex.[2] Violence between "doubles" has its foundation in the lack of recognition. The self fails to recognize "the other in the self."[3] A fragmented self attempt to gain coherence by denying the other, as a consequence, the other is perceived as a threat. Nonrecognition of the other in the self is a source of aggressiveness. To believe in a self-contained identity is a form of violence on the other. Connolly (1995) captures this relationship when he asserts that the main impetus for violence emerges from ways of thinking and political movements that suppress difference. In his view "culture wars do not reflect too much diversity, difference, or variety; they express contending demands to control the exclusive form the nation, state, or community must assume" (Connolly 1995, xxi).

Fundamentalism is an example of violence that originates in the search for a true identity. According to Connolly (1995, 121) a fundamentalist secures the identity of the self by converting differences into dangers that must be eliminated, punished, or reformed. Furthermore, the dynamic behind fundamentalist beliefs is not recognized but is concealed under unquestionable values such as security, nation, God or reason. To assure the true identity of the self, others must be eliminated. War in the name of a true identity provides an opportunity for self-affirmation. War is ontological; its aim is self-recognition (Shapiro 1997, 52, passim).

According to Girard (1995, 152) rivalry between doubles causes their desires to converge over the same object and to see the other as obstructionist, "[t]he subject desires the object because the very rival desires it." By not being able to enjoy the same object, the rivals enter into conflict. Violence between rivals evolves into a vicious circle defined in terms of vengeance and reprisals. It is a self-propagating and imitative violence. In Colombia, this type of violence is demonstrated by conflict between paramilitaries and guerrillas and in the partisan violence between Liberals and Conservatives in *La Violencia* period, when spirals of violence erupted with no cause other than belonging to a particular political party.

Placing identity at the center of violence does not mean ignoring material and political aspects of conflict; on the contrary, lack of recognition, material deprivation, and political exclusion are intertwined together. It is no mere coincidence that poverty and marginality are more prevalent among blacks, indigenous populations, and women. In this I follow Nancy Fraser's (1997) claim that problems of redistribution and recognition are not independent, although one can not be reduced to the other.

Nonrecognition is linked to political exclusion because it silences voices of those assigned a devalued identity. For example, earlier forms of democracy were restricted to white proprietor males. In hierarchical arrangements, only the points of view of those in positions of power are taken into consideration. Devalued identities are denied a position from which to speak. I refer to such situations as monological: the world is interpreted from a single position, generally the position of those in power. Practices of cultural imperialism, in which only the experience and culture of the dominant groups are considered to be worthy, render invisible the perspective of dominated groups (Young 1990, 89). The United Nations Development Programme (UNDP) report on the Colombian conflict summarizes the relations between the elite's perceptions of subaltern groups and the armed conflict:

> On the one hand, elites look at the "other Colombia" (colonization areas, ethnic minorities, etc.) as a strange world, primitive, inferior and threatening, that brings all kind of problems and must be submitted to discipline [. . .] On the other hand, they are submitted to a regimen of "internal colony," subject to the appetite of landowners, traders and venal civil servants that extract the surplus and bring it to the "metropoli" (Bogota) [. . .] This mixture of disdain and scrabbling inspire the wrong strategies and contraindicated actions in the territories more sensible to conflict. (2003, 37–38)

Identities are more than a source of violence. The solution to violence has to be found in a process of reconstitution of identities allowing individuals to participate in public spaces where antagonisms can be solved and voices legitimized. It is through the reconstitution of identities that collectivities seek recognition from others and are legitimized as equal partners. As chapter 7 by Jean Jackson in this volume illustrates, the struggle of indigenous peoples was first of all a struggle to value their identity in order to gain political legitimacy. This is a political process as long as it broadens public spaces where disagreements can be solved. For this to happen, it is necessary to constitute political contenders. In this direction, Young (1990, 82–83) sees the politics of difference as a resource to democratic communication, not an obstacle to democracy. The enhancement of democracy results from the inclusion of different perspectives and from the communication of different experiences to correct the biases derived from monological positions. Differences have the potential to constitute different publics. Fraser (1997, 81) refers to them as *subaltern counterpublics*, defined as parallel discursive arenas invented by subordinated groups in order to formulate oppositional interpretations of their identities and interests.

Last, but not least important, is the role that the constitution of identities has in the process of reconciliation and forgetting. As Elizabeth Jelin (2003, 14) points out, group identity is linked to a sense of permanence in time and space. Identity is a process of encounter between memories from the past and projects for the future. This process involves "complex negotiation about what is acceptable and what is to be silenced, what can and cannot be said, in the disjunctions between private narratives and public discourses." (Jelin 2003, 17). In her view, to define and name what took place in periods of violence and war, to honor the victims and identify the perpetrators are linked to projects of democratization and construction of the future; more important, those are "necessary steps to make certain that the horrors of the past do not recur—*Nunca más* (Never Again)" (Jelin 2003, 3).

The International War on Drugs and the Misrecognition of Others

Drug trafficking in Colombia has added new elements of uncertainty to an already elusive violence. In the words of Ana María Bejarano

> Drug-trafficking in all its ramifications has penetrated the Colombian economy, its politics and society. Together with the fight against drugs, it has helped to fragment the state even further, has caused divisions among the guerrillas, and has led to a growing number of groups who have taken justice into their own hands (it is to these last that Colombians have given the name "paramilitaries"). This fragmentation is like a mirror game, repeating over and over again *at infinitum.* (2003, 229)

Despite these deleterious effects, drug trafficking is not the main or only cause of poverty, inequality, and violence as the chapters in this volume illustrate. As Francisco Thoumi contends, illegal drugs changed the nature of the conflict by strengthening the capacity of guerrillas and paramilitaries, by weakening the state and by diverting scarce resources from development projects to law enforcement. This view is reinforced by Berry and Barragán's conclusion that income from illegal activities worsened problems of income distribution and poverty. In their view, most of the drug money has gone to high-income individuals while the poor bear most of the costs in terms of lost of lives, insecurity, rural violence, and displacement. For the country in general, drug trafficking has meant the lost of life and weakening of the state and it also contributed to the economic recession of the 1990s. Jean Jackson refers to the effects on indigenous population, the environment and human health. Military activity in areas of conflict has increased internal displacement and emigration of the people.

In this section I argue that the war on drugs has been waged from a monological perspective, without recognizing the complexity of the Colombian conflict, the links to social and economic factors or the links to U.S. demand. The war on drugs is ontological in the sense that it has been waged in the cause of protecting the U.S. domestic identity by elevating drug-producing countries to the status of security threat to the United States. As stated by Tickner (2001, 218) "[a]lthough the people of the United States are not exceedingly worried about [the drug] problem . . . this continues to be considered a deadly menace to the United States' identity." This monological vision predisposes a military strategy with detrimental consequences for the countries' capacity to provide a political solution through democratic channels.

This identification of drug trafficking as a threat to American security goes back to the Presidency of Ronald Reagan. Viewing drug trafficking as a security threat led to the involvement of the American military in counternarcotics operations and to the putting in place of measures such as "certification" that allow the U.S. president and Congress to influence drug-producing countries and to evaluate their cooperation in the war on drugs. As it appears in the Center for International Policy's appendix, between 1999 and 2002, 83 percent of U.S. aid to Colombia went to the military and police.

Under George Bush, the war on drugs intensified and new policing mechanisms such as the Office of National Drug Control Policy were created. This one-dimensional identification of the problem led to military and police interdiction to block the entry of drugs into the United States. While President Bill Clinton (1993–2000) questioned the effectiveness of interdiction, he continued the military approach. His strategy, however, centered on crop eradication and substitution in drug-producing areas, as reflected in Plan Colombia and the Andean Regional Initiative. These interventions were consistent with the view of Colombia as a "problem-country" in terms of regional security (see chapter 3 by Tokatlian in this volume). It was General Barry McCaffrey who popularized the vision of an "explosion" of coca production in Southern Colombia (Arnson 2001, 17).

President George W. Bush's conflation of the war on terror and the war on drugs, enhanced the perception of the security risk coming from the

Andean region, particularly Colombia. In the debate on the Andean Initiative in the U.S. Congress, Senator Bob Graham (D-Fl) identified Colombia "as one of the global battle scenes against terrorism" (*Miami Herald* October 26, 2001 quoted in García 2003, 41). Senator Graham observed that extremists

> have committed nearly 500 acts of terrorism against United States interests and citizens in the last year [. . .] and of these nearly 500 incidents, 44 percent in just one country. Was this country Egypt? No. Israel? No. Afghanistan? No. The 44 percent was in Colombia [. . .] it is there where the terrorist war has been in full furor. (*Miami Herald* October 26, 2001 quoted in García 2003, 41)

The war on drugs has also affected relations between countries in the Andean region. Rather than forging common links between neighbors, the war on drugs has intensified distrust between countries in what they identify as the "Colombianization" of the problem. In the words of Adrian Bonilla, neighboring countries "concentrate on containment of the violence within Colombia's boundaries and on prophylaxis to avoid contamination among local actors" (Bonilla 2003, 230). Rather than pursuing a policy common to all countries in the region, the United States has engaged these countries bilaterally. As Ana Sanjuán illustrates in this volume (chapter 5), Venezuela has also defined the Colombian conflict as a "threat to national security," and, as a result, has given its Armed Forces more resources and autonomy. Border areas have become theaters of military operations in which certain constitutional guarantees have been suspended. Furthermore, increasing military strength and stronger ties between Colombia and the United States have increased mistrust among neighboring countries and are affecting the military equilibrium in the Andean region.

Reports by leading foreign policy think-tanks have denounced the U.S. strategy toward the region as "myopic" and predict the potential of a regional collapse and destabilization of the hemisphere (Council on Foreign Relations 2004, 13–15). A misrecognition of the actors in the conflict is shown by what the report refers to as a war of "drugs and thugs" that leaves aside issues of social and economic reforms (Council on Foreign Relations 2004, 3). In March 2004, President George W. Bush requested from Congress authority to increase American presence, both civilian and military, in Colombia, and to strengthen the military capability of the Colombian army. According to Stratfor's Strategic Forecasting (2004), these operations will shift the balance of military power in favor of Bogota. As a result, neighboring countries will likely begin to acquire weapons, the potential for more clashes between the

Venezuelan and Colombian armies will increase, as well as the movement of displaced persons, rebels and drug traffickers between Colombia and Ecuador.

The war on drugs can be characterized as a "desencuentro" between Colombia's domestic policies and U.S. interests in the region. At the same time that President Ronald Reagan initiated a military solution to the war on drugs, Colombian President Belisario Betancur (1982–1986) was exploring the opportunity of a negotiated solution to the Colombian conflict. Betancur marked a turning point in the history of the armed conflict by changing public attitudes toward the need for a negotiated solution to the conflict by attending to the economic and social causes of conflict (Bejarano 2003, 240). President Virgilio Barco (1986–1990) continued the strategy of improving economic conditions as a road to peace; his "National Plan of Rehabilitation" made public expenditures in areas of poverty and conflict a key strategy in finding peaceful solutions to conflict. Rather than supporting economic development, President George Bush continued the emphasis on military assistance ignoring Colombian petitions, and even contributed to the undermining of government legitimacy by announcing through the then Drug Czar, William Bennett, the possibility of sending troops to Colombia and neighboring countries (Bagley 1990, 459–60).[4]

The discrepancy between Washington's position and Colombia's interests was more apparent during the negotiation of Plan Colombia under the Pastrana administration. As chapter 4 by Camacho illustrates, during the negotiations with the Clinton administration, Plan Colombia was transformed from a development plan emphasizing crop substitution and alternative economic initiatives into a military strategy centered on fighting insurgent groups. The *desencuentro* between Colombia's priorities and the distribution U.S. aid between 1997 and 2003 is reflected in the small percentage dedicated to social and economic development: only 7 percent goes to alternative development, 4 percent to displaced and vulnerable groups, 4 percent to human rights and judicial reform, and 2 percent to the rule of law. The remaining is military and police assistance (see appendix).

It is during the governments of George W. Bush and Álvaro Uribe Vélez that the visions of the two countries have coincided. The unifying factor is the war on terror. But as I demonstrate, in the following section, the war on terrorism undermines prospects for a political solution to the conflict.

Colombia's Domestic Wars and the Problem of Recognition

A main consequence of the war on drugs is the transformation of a political problem into a criminal war. Uribe's war on terrorism has gone further by not recognizing even the presence of a war and leaving the problem as one of terrorism, as it appears in the following statement: "the international community must know that there is no war. Here, we have terrorism by armed groups against the rest of Colombia, and this must be resolved quickly" (Hagen 2002, 25).

Endangering Territory

In Colombia, conflict over territory has always been at the center of the armed confrontation, for political, cultural, and economic reasons. In this section, I argue that the violence linked to territory is a form of the misrecognition of identities. Moreover, ontological structures of recognition, such as race or gender, are constructed around territory. An example from the nineteenth century illustrates how territories were identified according to hierarchies of civilization: some regions were considered as more civilized than others (Rojas 2002). According to this hierarchy of the recognition of identities a "white and enlightened elite" living in the so-called civilized highland regions, took for themselves the power to transform, by force if necessary, the black and indigenous peoples living in lowland regions. The following description by José María Samper in 1861 illustrates this point:

> The European race settled almost entirely in the peak and the mountains slopes; the African race, slaves, were condemned to misery and decolonization in the deepest and hottest valleys; and the indigenous races, exploited and dominated everywhere, remained in their own territory. Therefore, the result was: on the peak, civilization; in the middle, desolation; and in the low land, the violence and horrors of slavery.
>
> As a result of the spatial distribution of races and social conditions, all the work of civilization in the New Granada could be summarized in an ascending and descending movement. Civilization had to spread down to the valleys [. . .] The barbarian should climb towards the plateau and then disappear or to change completely. (Samper 1861, 299)

A similar structure of nonrecognition accompanied the colonization that took place at the beginning of the twentieth century, when the concept of progress was linked to a territoriality based on gender and race. According to Roldán's (1998, 6), the colonization of Uraba was seen as a masculine conqueror taking over a feminine territory populated by indigenous people. The elites divided the department into two territories: Medellín and Urabá. In the former its people were considered genuine "Antioqueños," that is people of a "noble and strong race, wholesome, valiant and hard-working, cradle of liberators and heroes" (Roldán 1998). Uraba, located in the periphery was described as insalubrious, populated by African, indigenous, non-Antioqueñan people. The entrance of Uraba into "modernity" was a violent process, described in the magazine (Progress) in a poem also entitled "*Progress*":

> To progress is to violate. The Indian, the mountain
> The howling waterfall, the virgin forest,
> The blue transparency of the horizon,
> The fauna, the ocean . . . all of this
> In favor of future fleece,
> Suffers the violations of progress.
> Progress is to violate. But nevertheless,
> Welcome to my homeland, you the bitter
> Violator of the murmuring landscape . . . (Roldán 1998, 9–10; my
> translation)

Roldán's study of the period of *La Violencia* in Antioquia also found that the towns with major violence bordered departments perceived as ethnically and culturally different from the imagined "*Antioqueño ideal*" (Roldán 2002, 36).

Territory as a strategy of recognition plays an important role in political resistance. During *La Violencia* armed settlers escaped army attacks by establishing "independent republics" in places like Marquetalia, El Pato, and El Ariari. These peasant positions were defensive in that their purpose was not to take the state but to act as a zone of peasant protection (UNDP 2003, 28). In 1964, the government attacked these independent republics in an operation known as "Plan Lasso," applying counterinsurgency measures similar to the ones used in Vietnam (Safford and Palacios 2002, 356). As a result of this offensive, some communities, under the inspiration of the Communist Party, founded the Fuerzas Armadas Revolucionarias de Colombia (FARC) in 1966.

Territoriality may be used by governments to send signals of peace. During his campaign for presidency of Colombia, Andrés Pastrana proposed two initiatives: the first was a promise to negotiate with the guerrillas in an attempt to end the increasing conflict between the guerrillas and the paramilitaries; the second was a change in U.S. anti-narcotics policy back to its promise of a Marshall Plan for Colombia centered on a social solution to the drug problem. A turning point in the campaign was his visit to FARC territory to meet its leader Manuel Marulanda. The photographs taken at this meeting received wide coverage and in certain way broke the barrier between "official" and guerrilla territorial divide.

After Pastrana's assumed office in August 1998, his attention focused on a demilitarized zone of five municipalities in south/central Colombia. This area was to be known as a peace laboratory and was subsequently seen as a *zona de despeje* (demilitarized territory). The dialogue with FARC was inaugurated in January 1999 in El Caguán, one of the five municipalities, at a ceremony that was attended by government officials, representatives of the international community and a representative of the FARC leader Manuel Marulanda. His speech was primarily a recounting of the history of armed struggle in Colombia, extending back to 1955. The underlying message was the lack of recognition of peasants' claims. According to Marulanda, insurgency resulted from government's deafness and the military response to peasants' demands:

Running away from official repression we settled in the Marquetalia (Tolima) region, where the state expropriated [our] farms, cattle, pigs and chickens, extending this measure to our fellow countryman who did not share the vision of the bipartisan National Front [. . .] We waited eight years to know the results [of the amnesty and pardon], including the compensation of those who lost everything in the provinces of Tolima, Huila, Cauca, Valle and Caldas. The three government powers never did anything to carry out the agreements and even less to produce an environment of peace. In 1964, after the triumph of the Cuban revolution, President Kennedy designed a counterinsurgency plan for Latin America, aimed to contain other revolutions in the continent. These measured designed by the Pentagon were named Plan Lasso, and within this framework President Guillermo León Valencia declared war to 48 peasants of the Marquetalia region, led by Manuel Marulanda Vélez.

Faced with an imminent attack, these 48 men addressed the President himself, Congress, governors, national and international red cross, the church, United Nations, French intellectuals and other democratic organizations, in order to avoid a new armed battled in Colombia with unknown consequences. Unfortunately, no one listen to us, except the church that commissioned the priest Camilo Torres to have an interview with us, but the high commanders of the army did not allow it. Few days later the army started a massive military operations with 16 thousand soldiers using all kind of weapons, even bacteriological arms launched from US pilots, and only now, after 34 years of permanent armed confrontation, the three [governmental] powers and society start to realize the seriousness of the Marquetalia attack.

In those days, the 48 peasants only asked for the construction of roads to take their products to the market, a centre for marketing and schools to educate their children, all of this could be done with and state investment of less than 5 million pesos. (UNDP 2003, 37)

During the peace talks, the demilitarized zone acquired a symbolic connotation. Public spaces of deliberation were opened and, as a result, 25,000 delegates participated in "public hearings" where vast amount of proposals were presented.

The peace process also received international attention through the direct or indirect participation of European, Latin American and Canadian governments as well as representatives of the UN Secretary General and other UN agencies (González Posso, 2004). The climate surrounding the negotiations also impacted the policies of the U.S. government to the point that officials from the Clinton administration meet with representatives of FARC in Costa Rica to discuss the kidnapping of U.S. citizens and the drug problem. AID funds were provided to finance small local initiatives in the *zona de despeje*, although, the abduction and then killing of three U.S. activists weakened U.S. support for the negotiations (Arnson 2001, 10; Tickner 2001, 222).

The opportunity to consolidate peace was missed and the *desencuentro* among the government, FARC, and the United States continued. Plan Colombia, originally conceived as the Marshall Plan, was transformed into an antinarcotics strategy. Domestically, dialogue between the government and the guerrilla stalled on several occasions and collapsed in February 2002. Three important consequences followed from the collapse of the peace talks. First, FARC lost the battle of public opinion. Second, the opportunity for a negotiated peace agreement, opened 20 years earlier, disappeared. As Bejarano (2003, 241) notes, the election of May 2002 was a plebiscite on the role of FARC in the peace process. FARC was blamed for using the *zona de despeje* to strengthen its military power and as a safe heaven for kidnapping, and for the pursuit of the cocaine and arms traffic. Finally, Álvaro Uribe won the presidency with a mandate to restore security.

President Uribe set out a security strategy based on territory to establish state control. Three days after taking office, his government declared a State of Internal Commotion and, one month later, through Decree 2002, established three Rehabilitation and Consolidation Zones (RCZ) in three Departments. RCZ give the military the power to restrict freedom of movement, freedom of assembly and to carry out preventive detentions without judicial orders. Unlike Pastrana's *zona de despeje*, Uribe's zones of rehabilitation became war zones, at least according to the Report of Amnesty International on the Department of Arauca. A department rich in oil, Arauca is one of the most militarized regions in the country, with support from the U.S. government in the form of military resources and "military advisors" (Amnesty International 2004, 5).

According to Amnesty International, violations of human rights by the military and armed opposition groups have increased since the establishment of the RCZ's (Amnesty International 2004, 13). President Uribe's policy of "peasant soldiers" has dragged civilians into conflict. Further, Amnesty has denounced the open policy of stigmatization of human rights activists, and peasant leaders in Arauca. Operations like *pescas milagrosas* (miraculous fishing trawls), detention of civilians in the hope of finding guerrilla "suspects," serve to label communities as subversive, exposing them to paramilitary attacks (Amnesty International 2004, 21). Human rights activists are arbitrarily searched and detained. The Amnesty report also mentions a continuation of collaboration between paramilitary and security forces that has strengthened paramilitary forces in the region (Amnesty International 2004, 30).

Guerrillas have also equally been party to violations of human rights and the use of excessive force in the region. FARC is accused of using disproportionate attacks on military targets using home made mortars and bombs that often kill civilians, of using threats of "reign or die" against mayors and local councilors, and of imposing "war taxes" and conducting kidnappings to raise revenue, estimated at US$14 million annually (Amnesty International 2004, 36–38).

Territory is not only related to structures of recognition in rural or oil-rich regions, it also forms part of the structure of recognition in poor urban neighborhoods as seen in the rivalries between urban militias and juvenile gangs. The extent of this problem is reflected in the high homicide rate for young men. In 1994, it reached 142.5 homicides for every 100,000 habitants (Franco 1999, 83–84). According to Pilar Riaño (2000) in the wars waged between juvenile gangs the enemy is not a person culturally or ideologically different but the one that evokes *another* territory. Young people demarcate social spaces and delimit areas in which circulation is not allowed. According to her, territory is a context, resource and a power symbol in which violence is developed. Areas are renamed according to the memories of death: "the place of sparks" (*el chispero*), "the cave" (*la cueva*), "the passage of hell" (*el callejón del infierno*).

Engendering Violence

An examination of the statistics of violence in Colombia reveals a relationship between gender and violence where men number proportionally higher as victims and perpetrators of homicides and where women are overrepresented as victims of domestic violence and rape during wars and collective violence. It would be erroneous to conclude that men are naturally aggressive and women are, by nature, peaceful. One problem with this view is, as shown by Whitworth (2004, 230), that some men prefer peace and some women are comfortable with violence. One explanation is to see the masculine and the feminine as being relationally formed. While aggressiveness may be seen as a component of manhood and is ingrained in the concept of *machismo*, women are not precluded from the desire to acquire this trait. Viewing women as defenseless also increases the feeling of protectiveness in men's behavior. A complementary explanation is to see gender entrenched in conceptions of power. In the case of colonization of Urabá, mentioned above, the possession of territory by white settlers took place under the vision of a masculine conqueror taking over a feminine and racial territory. The feminine acts as a projection of a masculine desire where violence is naturalized.

This is what happened in Colombia during *La Violencia*, as illustrated by Meertens (2001a, 153). During this time, it was common practice to massacre entire families. According to Meertens, women were more than victims in these massacres; they performed a symbolic role. Combatants viewed women as mothers and as potential procreators of a hated enemy. Besides the assassination of the mother and her children, pregnant women had her fetus ripped out with the objective of "destroying the seed." Rape was conducted to humiliate the enemy and to express hatred for his collectivity.

But women are not only passive victims in situations of conflict. Women may imitate masculine traits by joining combatant's forces. They negotiate with their opponents and push their way into the opposite camp: "to be like them." María Eugenia Vásquez, ex-combatant of the April 19 Movement, M-19, describes this process:

> For women, the decision to participate in insurgent groups was a choice that implied a series of changes, all of them in constant confrontation with existing cultural norms. To be part of an army, even though it was revolutionary, meant to penetrate a masculine world and demanded a process of adaptation. This compelled them to modify their identity to successfully fulfill their role and to survive in a world of men, led exclusively by men, to accept the challenges of competing with them on their own terrain, and to be valued for qualities conceived to belong to masculinity: courage, audacity, toughness, qualities of leadership, willpower, physical strength and bravery. (2001, 26; my translation)

In the guerrilla movement, women were not accepted as equal partners; they had to confront a patriarchal hierarchy. In the case of the guerrilla movement, violence and discrimination against women increased because the heroic image of the male guerrillero (Castellanos 2001, 177). Dora Margarita, an ex-combatant of the National Liberation Army (ELN) and of the M-19, describes her arrival in the ELN camp in the following manner:

> When we arrived, our comrade led us to a very tall man, quite white, with a huge moustache, and long, black, straight hair, tied at the back. He pointed at him and said—"That is Fabio Vásquez, the boss." Fabio made some joke. He seemed happy to see us. A very beautiful woman accompanied him. Later I learned that only he could have a woman in the camp. The rest lived in total abstinence. Fabio took them by turns. He lasted about seven or eight months with each, and when bored he took another. (Lara 2000, 39; my translation)

Women become an interchangeable symbol on which the prestige of the guerrilla combatant rests. However, this feminine presence perturbs masculine self-image. Facing the problem of a fragmented masculine identity, women perform the double role of "comrade" and mother. As Vásquez relates:

> Simultaneously, in discourses and writings of the time, qualities culturally ascribed to women as innate to their condition as women, were recognized and exalted: their generous devotion, unselfish commitment, humility, ability to disassociate, patience, comprehension, and tenderness; all of these were qualities that facilitated the maternal role, exercised towards the comrades of the guerrilla, and strengthening the feminine and maternal roles in the daily war routine. (2001, 63–64; my translation)

Identity is constructed through mutual interaction, revealing its acquired character either as war experts or in their maternal role, as in the following testimony of a guerrillera:

> I did not love arms. As a child, I liked the doll clothes my mother made for me, and the paper boats I made and floated in the puddles formed by rain showers [. . .] But I gradually got used to arms, they turn into your only defense, they slowly become something as important as the worst punishment that can happen to a guerrilla fighter, after the firing squad and disarming. (Lara 2000, 42; my translation)

As a result of this incursion of women into the armed conflict, the homicide rate for women has increased dramatically. In the Department of Antioquia, it reached 26.3 for every 100,000 homicides in 1994 (Franco 1999, 88), higher than rates in Latin America. This figure is also indicative of the changing nature of the relation between gender and conflict:

> From an average of one victim [woman] every day and a half in 1999, it climbed to one victim per day in the year 2000, due to extra-judicial executions and political homicides; one woman every fourteen days was the victim of forced disappearance; one woman died every 50 days as the victim of homicides against socially marginalized persons; every seven days a woman died in combat. This daily average means that in one year, 363 women lost their life due to social-political violence. (CCJ 2001, 3)

Seeing violence as an attempt to destroy the identity of the other also applies to the phenomenon of internally displaced populations (IDP) and, particularly, displaced women, and Afro-Colombians and indigenous populations. For Afro-Colombians and indigenous communities attachment to the land is more than a way of making a living; territory is part of their identity. By being displaced, women live through the triple trauma of having lost a partner, their belongings (home, furniture, animals, crops), and their roots; they arrive in a place where have to adapt from a rural and isolated setting to the anonymity of the city (Meertens 2001a, 140).

This is the situation for nearly 3 million Colombians displaced by the conflict. The disproportionate displacement of minorities coincides with armed actors' rivalry over territory. Areas inhabited by Afro-Colombians and indigenous groups are often rich in natural resources, and have potential for expanding cultivation of illicit crops, and the development of large-scale projects (NRC 2003, 2). Many people have also been displaced by coca-crop fumigations, a situation not widely recognized. While Plan Colombia predicted that 15,000 people would be displaced by fumigations, the figure is 75,597 between 2001 and 2003 (NRC 2003, 10).

Although men and women both suffer from displacement, several studies show that it affects their identities differently (Segura Escobar 2000; Meertens 2001a). Peasant women live in rural settings where rigid separations exist between feminine and masculine spheres; women have limited contact with social organizations and their experience is centered on domestic life. Violence destroys these economic relationships due to the loss of crops and land, as well as their emotional attachments due to the assassination or disappearance of their partners. However, women appear to adapt to the city quickly. In part, this is due to solidarity links with other women, who are generally not displaced, and the formation of self-help organizations. Incorporation into the labor market is faster than with men, resulting in lower unemployment rates and easier labor adaptation since they continue with employment in domestic service. Furthermore, participation in community groups provides them with "new elements for re-constructing their identity, sociability, and social links, and for establishing objectives that did not exist in the countryside" (Meertens 2001a, 144).

If violence is elusive in Colombia, violence against women and girls is even more difficult to capture. On the one hand, a lack of statistics makes it very difficult to measure the extent of the problem. On the other, there is silence surrounding sexual crimes. There is official silence because sexual offences are not investigated by appropriate state agencies (CCJ 2001, 10). More importantly, the authorship of violence against women, children, and the elderly is not publicly recognized. As pointed out by Meertens, (2001a, 155–56) "it is a kind of symbolic resistance to stripping them of their condition as defenseless beings, mothers, citizens, and generators of life and peace."

The silence surrounding violence against women makes the design of policies to address specific gender and reproductive health needs more difficult. For example, it is estimated that about half of displaced women have been physically attacked and about a quarter have been raped. Further nearly one-third of displaced women had either miscarriages or still-births, only 63 percent received treatment (NRC 2003, 11). According to a report from PROFAMILIA (*El Tiempo August 16*, 2001) three of ten displaced girls between the ages of 13 and 19 have been mothers or are awaiting a child.

Women ex-combatants are rejected twice by society, first because they have transgressed the role assigned to women (Castellanos 2001, 178) and then because they have joined the guerrilla movement. Theirs is a personal history of joining the guerrillas to escape from a violent home, abandoning their own children to join the conflict and thus losing their own identity (Castellanos 2001, 178). The lack of a gender perspective of programs of postconflict makes the reinsertion of women to society even more difficult.

Reciprocal Violence: Guerrilla and Paramilitaries

In contemporary violence, war between the paramilitary and the guerrillas is at the center of the armed conflict. The paramilitary, mostly working under the Autodefensas Unidas de Colombia (AUC), has tripled in size since 1998, and may now have as many as 15,000 members (Hagen 2003, 66).

The growth of paramilitary forces is a complex phenomenon exceeding the objectives of this chapter.[5] I will refer only to two aspects, both related to processes of recognition. One is the antagonism between guerrilla and paramilitary, which I characterize as a feud between rivals. A second aspect is that antagonism between guerrilla and paramilitary does not lead to a military confrontation between them; rather the war is directed against a third party: civil society. Both phenomena can be explained as an ontological war of doubles.

There is no doubt that the paramilitary was born out of an alliance with cattle ranchers and local elites interested in halting social and political reforms. The paramilitary identity was forged as a defensive strategy against guerrilla. Carlos Castaño (Aranguren 2001, 96), leader of the paramilitaries, refers to the origin of what he calls "self-defense" group as a "corporation of victims of guerrilla." In his view, it is guerrilla violence that valorizes the paramilitary project:

[W]e aspire to have a self-defense group wherever there is a guerrilla front. And given the way things are going in this country, it will have to be, since on a daily basis, the State, through its Armed Forces, is incapable of controlling the advance of the guerrilla. Therefore, we have to advance as much as our enemy advances. (Segura Escobar 2000, 113; my translation)

Guerrilla organizations have defined their project as being against the state. Despite this difference, guerrillas have converted into the mirror image of paramilitaries. Daniel Pécaut describes this phenomenon as follows:

The armed protagonists cannot appeal to principles of identity. Those to be found within the ranks of the paramilitary and those in guerrilla ranks are no longer distinguishable. The protagonists turn to violence, for the lack of division, producing fragmentation [. . .] (2001, 256)

Violence becomes a substitute for difference and once it is legitimized as a tactic, a cycle of reciprocity and vengeance is produced.

In a situation where one is perceived as the double of the other, the object of rivalry is what the other desires. In this case, their desires converge on the control of the population recognized as belonging to the other. This explains why violence is used against society. Paramilitaries direct their aggression against civilians, killing and torturing those accused of collaborating with the guerrilla. Massacres, in which three or more people are assassinated, are a common practice. During 2001, the number of massacres exceeded 200, and involved the assassination of 493 people (U.S. Department of State 2001, 2). Paramilitary groups are accused of 70 percent of the homicides, and the remainder 15 percent is attributable to the guerrilla and 5 percent to the state (Gallón 2001, 1).

As a paramilitary leader explains, "in war, the notion of unarmed civilians is a relative term. Two-thirds of the members of the guerrilla are unarmed, they function as civilians but they are guerrilla collaborators" (Romero 2000, 66). Their strategy consists of "removing the water surrounding the fish," which means eliminating the support of the civilian population. Anybody can be the enemy. The conflict becomes a "war against society" (Pécaut 2001, 288). In 2003 over 4,000 noncombatants were killed for political reasons (USIP 2004).

Violence and Lack of Political Recognition

Several factors make the constitution of political actors with the capacity to participate in a political dialogue to solve conflict even more difficult. Armed confrontations between paramilitaries and guerrillas have had deleterious effects on political organizations. According to Reyes Posada (1999, 206) peasant movements concentrating on land disputes have disappeared. In his view "peasants are no longer active protagonists of their own conflicts but targets of a polarization between armed actors" (Reyes Posada 1999, 209).

Armed confrontation had a detrimental effect on the constitution of alternative social movements as a result of the assassination of trade unionists, teachers, human-rights activists, and community leaders. The conflict also had disastrous consequences for traditional parties as well. These statistics compiled by USIP (2004) do not need further explanation:

- Four of every five unionists killed in the world are from Colombia. Since 1991, more than 1,800 labor leaders have been killed.
- Of Colombia's 1,098 mayors, 560 were threatened as part of an FARC campaign launched in 2003 against municipal authorities.
- Since June 2002, the FARC have killed 13 mayors and 70 town councilmen, forced the resignation of nearly 400 mayors, and caused hundreds of public employees to flee their posts or resign.
- Some 30 candidates for local office were killed and a dozen others kidnapped in the campaign leading to municipal elections in October 2003.
- In Colombia, in 2002, 3,255 people were reported missing.

Assassination is an extreme way of silencing dissident voices, but, as this chapter demonstrates, a lack of proper recognition of the identity of the other silences and produces invisibility and is therefore a form of violence. One way in which actors are rendered voiceless is by blurring the distinction between political affiliation and criminal activity. This makes it very difficult to differentiate between negotiable and nonnegotiable violence and between political and nonpolitical violence (Sánchez 2001, 10–11). One example is the expression "narcoguerrilla" and "narcodemocracy," both coined by U.S. ambassadors to Colombia. These expressions depoliticize the conflict by equating political identities with criminal activities.

Labeling individuals "guerrilla collaborators" is the justification used by paramilitaries for targeting and assassinating civilians. Collaborators are not only those providing shelter or medical assistance to persons alleged to belong to the armed conflict, but also those attending political meetings, demonstrations or civic events, thus making it dangerous to engage in political activities (Fichtl 2004, 29).

It is in this context of hindering the formation of political actors that I found the major weakness of the policies of "democratic security" implemented by President Uribe. In the first place, the informant and peasant soldier programs blur the distinction between the combatants and the civilian population (USIP 2004; ICG 2003a). Moreover, policies such as peasant soldiers place responsibility for the solution of conflict on all citizens, which exacerbates the problem in a country where private forms of justice, tends to prevail.

The international war on terrorism has strengthened the position of a military solution to conflict and weakened the support for human rights and democracy. This is the case of president Uribe's "state of internal commotion" proposal, which allows for arbitrary arrest, suspension of civil liberties and the granting the judicial power security forces. The constitutional court declared these measures unconstitutional, but some of them continue to be implemented in the RCZs.

Stigmatization of human rights groups also increases the possibility of being targeted by paramilitaries as collaborators. Moreover, President Uribe's well-known speech of September 2003 signaled NGOs as allied of terrorists (Project Counseling Service 2003), hindering their efforts to protect human rights. The Centro de Investigación y Educación Popular (CINEP) and the NGO Justice and Peace documented the killing of 49 activistists, 160 forced disappearances, 144 cases of torture, 573 death threats, and the arbitrary detention of 2,546 individuals during the first year of Uribe's administration (USIP 2003).

Another measure that has the potential of making peace more elusive is the proposed negotiation with paramilitaries. This measure has been denounced because it entails the possibility of closing the doors to the process of reconciliation by granting pardons to individuals responsible of the worst abuses of human rights (ICG 2003b). As Sánchez (2001, 9) explains, the long tradition of armistices and amnesties in Colombian history make exorcising violence difficult and, on the contrary, tend to displace it to a frontier between memory and no memory.

Conclusion: Recognizing Violence, Consolidating Peace

In this chapter, I reject the argument that violence in Colombia is generalized across territory and historical periods. I highlight the chronological, gender, ethnic, and geographical discontinuities that make violence elusive. I contend that a commonality is present in the different situations whereby violence is related to a lack of recognition of the identity of others. The solution to violence lies in the reconstruction of these identities. This is the paradox of violence.

Monological elaboration of policies by holders of positions of unbalanced power such as the United States or the Colombian executive has resulted in a failure to recognize human rights, cultural differences, and alternative solutions to conflict. Processes of identity construction along security and identity threats increase violence by criminalizing identities and territories. Measures such as states of exception, or granting excessive power to security forces and placing territories under military control, silence voices of dissent and violate fundamental rights and restrict democracy.

Violence against indigenous and Afro-Colombian populations, against the homeless, homosexuals, street workers, peasants, and street children have in common the failure to recognize them as equally worthy. An extreme consequence is their physical annihilation as in social cleansing. In the case of Afro-Colombian and indigenous populations, cultural differences have been ignored and, consequently, alternative possibilities of development marginalized or suppressed by force.

Lack of investigation of the causes, authors, and origin of violence have perpetuated conflict. The lack of a fair and inclusive judicial system dilutes responsibility and leads to private justice solutions. Moreover, the failure to identify the authors of violence has enabled those in power to attribute violence to the poor and different (Indians, homosexuals, peasants) and therefore justifying their rule through violent means. Processes of healing and the establishment of truth have rarely taken place in the history of Colombia, making it more difficult to break the circle of violence and to achieve reconciliation.

The stigmatization of actors, by expressions like "narco-guerrilla" and "collaborators" makes peace more elusive. On the one hand, it gives priority to military solutions over political ones; on the other, it disorganizes political actors and makes it more difficult to reach peaceful solutions. The solution to Colombia's elusive violence should come first from the cultural sphere through a process of recognition and valuing of identities. This recognition implies a struggle for valuing identities, territories, alternative forms of development and cultures. Actors with valued identities are then able to enter into dialogue and democratic debates. In Colombia, the reconstitution of identities is an ongoing and difficult process, as the following examples illustrate.

A first and important step is to increase citizens' participation in activities and mobilizations that favor peace and value life. In Colombia this includes public demonstrations, networks supporting peace initiatives like REDEPAZ (Network of Initiatives for peace against War), Long Live Citizenship (*Viva la Ciudadanía*), the National Conciliation Commission and the Permanent Civil Society Assembly for Peace, among others. There are also events like the Children's Mandate for Peace held in 1996, the Citizens Mandate for Peace Process held in 1997, mass demonstrations like No More held against kidnapping, forums like Business for Peace, Media for Peace, and University Network for Peace. Despite the tensions and differences between these perspectives (Fernandez, García, and Sarmiento 2004, 5), they make violence less elusive by creating awareness and solidarity among citizens. They provide a space for public debate, raise political awareness, and contribute to the formulation of peace agendas.

Although centralized strategies of territorial recognition such as the demilitarized zone have failed, there are courageous local initiatives still struggling for recognition. Perhaps the best known internationally is the Program for Development and Peace in the Magdalena Medio Region (PDPMM). PDPMM is participatory and inclusive in nature and, more important, it is committed to processes of rehabilitation, reconciliation and development. It is also a program whereby the transformation of violence starts "from recognition of the other and dialogue" (Katz 2004).

Indigenous *pueblos* are also engaged in the politics of identity, as illustrated in chapter 8 by Jean Jackson. The changing concept of territory has been central to the redefinition of indigenous identities and identity is related to claims of justice and land rights. Ramírez (2002) illustrates some of the difficulties in the process of reconstitution of identities. In her view, the 1991 Constitution recognized cultural diversity but it has been indigenous communities that have struggled to maintain their rights. This includes struggling against reifying views of indigenous groups and the overcoming of internal contradictions between them. But more important, they have had to struggle against views held by the state, settlers, and transnational oil companies, that indigenous groups are obstacles to development. Their rights to cultural difference and to be neutral in the conflict have cost the lives of many indigenous leaders killed by paramilitaries and guerrillas alike.

The struggle for recognition of Afro-Colombian communities includes the right to their identity and territory, to a measure of autonomy, and to their own vision of development (Escobar 2003, 165). As Escobar emphasizes, the displacement of Afro-Colombian and Indigenous communities is not alien to projects of capitalist modernity and extraction and exploitation of natural resources (Escobar 2003, 161). The right to recognition, as understood by Afro-Colombian organizations, implies a moving away from the conventional understanding of capitalist development and the possibility of alternative forms of modernity (Escobar 2003, 165).

Cities have opened room for a new concept of urban citizenship through the creation of spaces of recognition and peaceful coexistence. For example, Bogota, the capital, has enacted a program of citizenship to broaden opportunities for deliberation in decision-making processes (local development plans and participatory budgeting) as well as the respect for cultural norms and the recovery of public space. As a result, the city has reduced the homicide rate by half and provided an example of political inclusion by electing, for the first time in the country's history, a mayor from the left, a trade union leader (Rojas 2003). In poor neighborhoods of the city of Medellin, young people are creating subaltern publics by changing their relationship with their territory. As illustrated by Riaño in the streets of different neighborhoods, "memory communities" are created, often woven around the history of the dead and the elaboration of pain. As Mario Carlos Perea (2000, 21) mentions, in the city the street is a counterpublic space where life and death come together. In the street, the gangs (*pandilleros*), representing "narcissistic madness," meet with rap groups who convert the street into a discourse of possibility, making it feasible to establish new semantics for the conflict.

Women's organizations such as the *Corporación Vamos Mujer* (Corporation Let's Go, Women), the *Ruta Pacífica* (The Pacifist Path), and the *Corporación Mujeres que Crean* (Corporation Women Who Create) are working with peasant movements in programs of land recovery and supporting women's participation in dialogues for peace.

Last but not the least important, the international community has taken a more active role in the solutions to the Colombian conflict. It includes a "Group of Friends," but as Tokatlian's mentions, it is necessary to create a new Contadora for the region and to increase solidarity between Andean countries. The United Nations High Commission for Human Rights office in Colombia (UNHCHR) and the UNDP are playing important roles in putting together proposals and recommendations for the Colombian government and civil society. One of the recommendations of the UNDP (2003) document is the recovery of politics instead of bullets as the alternative for solving the conflict. Just as important is the call to legitimize urban protest and the creation of a culture that accepts and does not stigmatize citizens' organizations and their struggle for rights. I conclude endorsing one of the recommendations of the UNHCHR 2004 report:

> The High Commissioner recommends the Government, the illegal armed groups and representative sectors of civil society to spare no effort in establishing, as soon as possible, contacts for dialogue and negotiation so as to rise above internal armed conflict and achieve lasting peace. Such dialogue and negotiations should from the outset take account of human rights and international humanitarian law, and *should include in their agenda the issue of the right to truth, justice and reparation.* (2003, 40; my emphasis)

Notes

* Associate Professor, Norman Paterson School of International Affairs, Carleton University. For reading this chapter and making excellent comments I am grateful to Olga Abizaid, Arthur Conn, Catherine LeGrand, and Judy Meltzer. Thanks to my research assistant Alison Simonetti. This research has been funded by a grant of the Social Sciences and Humanities Research Council of the government of Canada.
1. The proportion of deaths resulting from political conflict is debated between scholars. The proportion varies from 7% to 15%. For different perspectives on this debate see Rubio (1999) and Pécaut (2001).
2. Feminist groups have begun to break the silence about the violence that women exercise over their female partners. See e.g. Vickers (2002, 229).
3. This account is inspired in Lacan's views of construction of subjectivity as a function of contacts with others. See Shapiro (1997) and Rojas (2002).
4. As documented by Bagley (1990, 459) the military equipment such as the A-37 jets were inappropriate for conducting a war against narcotraffickers; there was no

intelligence equipment, or data collection and radar. Furthermore, a petition of US$14 million for the strengthening of the Ministry of Justice, only received $2 million adducing lack of resources on the part of the Justice Department.
5. The reader can consult the recent book by Mauricio Romero (2003).

References

Amnesty International, 2004. *Colombia A Laboratory of War: Repression and Violence in Arauca*. AI index: AMR23/004/2004. http://web.anmesty.org/library/Index/ENGAMR230042004?open&of = ENG-2AM (consulted on April 26, 2004).

Aranguren, M.M. 2001. *Mi Confesión. Carlos Castaño Revela sus Secretos*. Bogotá: Editorial la Oveja Negra.

Arnson, Cynthia. 2001. *The Peace Process in Colombia and U.S. Policy*. Paper prepared for the conference on Democracy, Human Rights, and Peace in Colombia, University of Notre Dame, Helen Kellogg Institute for International Studies, March 26–27.

Bagley, Bruce M. 1990. Narcotráfico: Colombia Asediada. In *Al filo del caos: crisis política en la Colombia de los años 80*, edited by Francisco Leal Buitrago and León Zamosc, 445–74. Bogota: Tercer Mundo Editores.

Bakhtin, Michael. 1984. *Problems of Dostoevsky's Poetics*. Minneapolis: University of Minnesota Press.

Bejarano, Ana María. 2003. Protracted Conflict, Multiple Protagonists, and Staggered Negotiations: Colombia, 1982–2002. *Canadian Journal of Latin American and Caribbean Studies* 28: 223–47.

Berquist, Charles, R. Peñaranda, and G. Sánchez, eds. 2001. *Violence in Colombia. The Contemporary Crisis in Historical Perspective*. Wilmington: SR Books.

Bonilla, Adrián. 2003. Conflicto en la Región Andina. In *El conflicto colombiano y su impacto en los países andinos*, edited by Álvaro Camacho, 223–49. Bogota: Uniandes.

Castellanos, Gabriela. 2001. Mujeres y conflicto armado: representaciones, prácticas sociales y propuestas para la negociación. In *Sujetos Femeninos y Masculinos, edited by* Gabriela Castellanos and Simone Accorsi, 161–84. Bogotá: Editorial la Manzana de la Discordia.

Comisión Colombiana de Juristas (CCJ). 2001. Preview of the Report on Violence against Women and Girls in the Colombian Armed Conflict. Unpublished document, May, Bogota, 1–17.

Connolly, William E. 1995. *The Ethos of Pluralization*. Minneapolis: University of Minnesota Press.

Council on Foreign Relations. 2004. *Andes 2020: A New Strategy for the Challenges of Colombia and the Region*. http://www.cfr.org/pdf/Andes2020.pdf (consulted on January 8, 2004).

El. Tiempo, August 16, 2001. Mujeres siguen su marcha contra la guerra.

Escobar, Arturo. 2003. Displacement, Development, and Modernity in the Colombian Pacific. *International Social Science Journal* 175: 157–67.

Fernandez, Carlos, M. Garcia-Duran, and F. Sarmiento. 2004. Peace Mobilizations in Colombia 1978–2002. In *Accord An International Review of Peace Initiatives.* http://www.c-r.org/accord/col/accord14/faultindex.shtml

Fichtl, Eric. 2004. The Ambiguous Nature of "Collaboration" in Colombia. http://www. Colombiajournal.org/colombia181.html (consulted on March 30, 2004).

Franco, Saúl. 1999. *El quinto no matar. Contextos explicativos de la violencia en Colombia.* Bogotá: Tercer Mundo/IEPRI.

Fraser, Nancy. 1997. *Justice Interruptus. Critical Reflections on the 'Postsocialist' Condition.* New York & London: Routledge.

Gallón, Gustavo. 2001. *Human Rights: A path to democracy and Peace in Colombia.* Paper presented at Notre Dame University, March 26.

García, Andelfo. 2003. Lucha antiterrorista en la cúspide de la agenda: repercusiones para Colombia. In *El conflicto colombiano y su impacto en los países andinos,* edited by Álvaro Camacho, 35–52. Bogota: Uniandes.

García Márquez, Gabriel. 1978. *La Mala Hora.* Bogotá: Editorial La Oveja Negra.

Girard, René. 1995. *La violencia y lo sagrado.* Barcelona: Anagrama.

González Posso, Camilo. 2004. Negotiations with the FARC. *Accord An International Review of Peace Initiatives* 9. http://www.c-r.org/accord/col/acord14/faultindex.shtml

Hagen, Jason. 2002. New Colombian President Promises more War. *NACLA* 36: 24–6.

———. 2003. Uribe's People: Civilians and the Colombian Conflict. *Georgetown Journal of International Affairs* (Winter/Spring): 65–71.

International crisis group (ICG). 2003a. *Colombia: President Uribe's Democratic security Policy.* ICG Latin America Report No.6. http://www.crisisweb.org/ Library/documents/Latin_America/06_Colombia_Uribe_demsecurity-pdf.

———. 2003b. *Colombia: Negotiating with the Paramilitaries* ICG Latin America Report No.5. Bogota/Brussels. *http://www.intl-crisis-group.org/projects/showreport. cfm?reportid=1123* (consulted on March 10, 2003).

Jelin, Elisabeth. 2003. *State Repression and the Labors of Memory.* Minneapolis: University of Minnesota Press.

Katz Garcia, Mauricio. 2004. A regional Peace Experience: The Magdalena Medio Peace and Development Programme. *Accord an International Review of Peace Initiatives. Colombia's Peace Processes.* Edited by Mauricio García-Duran. http://www.c-r.org/accord/col/accord14/faultindex.shtml

Lara, Patricia. 2000. *Las mujeres en la guerra.* Bogotá: Planeta.

Meertens, Donny. 2001a. Facing Destruction, Rebuilding Life. Gender and Internally Displaced in Colombia. *Latin American Perspectives* 28 (January): 132–48.

Norwegian Refugee Council (NRC). 2003. Profile of Internally Displaced: Colombia. May 14. NRC/Global Internally Displaced Project. http://www.db. idpproject.org/Sites/IdpProjectDb/idpSurvey.nsf/wCountries/Colombia/$File/ Colombia% 20-May%202003.pdf?OpenElement (consulted on May 20, 2003).

Oquist, Paul. 1980. *Violence, Conflict, and Politics in Colombia.* New York: Academic.

Pécaut, Daniel. 1987. *Orden y Violencia en Colombia, 1930–1954.* Bogotá: Siglo XXI editores.

————. 1999. Las violencias y su interpretación. Entrevista a Alberto Valencia Gutiérrez. *Ensayo y Error* 4: 152–67.

————. 2001. *Guerra contra la sociedad.* Bogotá: Espasa.

Perea, Carlos Mario. 2000. Juventud y subjetividad. *Letrazas* (September): 19–21.

Project Counselling Service. 2003. Se deterioran las relaciones entre el Presidente Uribe y las ONG Colombianas. *Colombia Brief* (September 26), Bogotá.

Ramírez, María Clemencia. 2002. The Politics of Identity and Cultural Difference in the Colombian Amazon: Claiming Indigenous Rights in the Putumayo Region. In *The Politics of Ethnicity: Indigenous Peoples in Latin American States,* edited by David Maybury-Lewis, 135–66. Cambridge: Harvard University Press.

Reyes Posada, Alejandro. 1999. La cuestión agraria en la guerra y la paz. In *Armar la paz es desarmar la guerra,* edited by Álvaro Camacho and Francisco Leal Buitrago, 205–26. Bogotá: Fescol/Instituto de Estudios Politicos de la Universidad Nacional/CEREC.

Riaño, Pilar. 2000. La memoria viva de las muertes: lugares e identidades juveniles en Medellín. *Análisis Político* 41 (September): 23–39.

Rojas, Cristina. 2002. *Civilization and Violence: Regimes of Representation in Nineteenth-century Colombia.* Minneapolis, MN: University of Minnesota Press.

————. 2003. *Forging A Culture of Citizenship in Bogotá City.* Unpublished manuscript, Ottawa.

Roldán, Mary. 1998. Violencia, colonización y la geografía de la diferencia cultural en Colombia. *Análisis Político* 35 (September–December): 3–25.

————. 2002. *Blood and Fire. La Violencia in Antioquia, Colombia, 1946–1953.* Durham and London: Duke University Press.

Romero, Mauricio. 2000. Changing Identities and Contested Settings: Regional Elites and the Paramilitaries in Colombia. *International Journal of Politics, Culture and Society* 14 (Fall): 51–69.

————. 2003. *Paramilitares y Autodefensas 1982–2003.* Bogotá: IEPRI/Editorial Planeta Colombiana.

Rubio, Mauricio. 1999. *Crimen e impunidad. Precisiones sobre la violencia.* Bogotá: Tercer Mundo Editores/CEDE.

Safford, Frank and Marco Palacios. 2002. *Fragmented Land, Divided Society.* New York and Oxford: Oxford University Press

Sánchez, Gonzalo. 2001. Introduction. Problems of Violence, Prospects for Peace. In *Violence in Colombia,* edited by Charles Berquist, Ricardo Peñaranda and Gonzalo Sánchez. Washington: SR Books.

Samper, José María. 1861. *Ensayo sobre las revoluciones políticas y la condición social de las Repúblicas Colombianas.* París: Imprenta de E. Thunot y C.

Sarmiento, Alfredo. 1999. Violencia y equidad. In *Armar la paz es desarmar la guerra,* edited by Álvaro Camacho and Francisco Leal, 227–61. Bogota: FESCOL/IEPRI/CEREC.

Segura Escobar, N. 2000. Colombia: A New Century, an Old War, and More Internal Displacement. *International Journal of Politics, Culture and Society* 14 (Fall): 107–27.

Shapiro, Michael J. 1997. *Violent Cartographies. Mapping Cultures of War.* Minneapolis: University of Minnesota Press.

Stratfor Strategic Forecasting Inc. 2004. Plan Colombia: Nearsighted Solution to Long Term Problem? http://www.stratfor.biz/Print.neo?storyId = 229878 (consulted on February 4, 2004).

Taylor, Charles. 1994. The Politics of Recognition. In *Multiculturalism,* edited by A. Gutmann. Princeton: Princeton University Press.

Tickner, Arlene B. 2001. La "guerra contra las drogas": las relaciones Colombia-Estados Unidos durante la administración Pastrana. In *Plan Colombia. Ensayos críticos,* edited by Jairo Estrada Alvarez, 215–34. Bogota: Universidad Nacional de Colombia.

Todorov, Tzvetan. 1984. *Mikhail Bakhtin. The Dialogical Principle.* Minneapolis: University of Minnesota Press.

United Nations Development Programme (UNDP). 2003. *El Conflicto. Callejón con Salida. Informe Nacional de Desarrollo Humano para Colombia—2003.* Bogotá: Colombia.

United Nations High Commissioner for Human Rights Office in Colombia. 2004. Report of the United Nations High Commissioner for Human Rights on the Human Rights Situation in Colombia. E/CN.4/2004/13.

United States Institute of Peace. 2004. *Civil Society under Siege in Colombia.* Special Report No. 114 (February). http://www.usip.org/pubs/specialreports/sr114.html (consulted on April 7, 2004).

U.S. Department of State. 2001. Country Reports on Human Rights Practices, Colombia. http://www.state.gov/g/drl/rls/2001/wha/8326.html (consulted March 8, 2001).

Vásquez, María Eugenia. 2001. Entre la guerra y la paz: resignificación del proyecto de vida en las mujeres excombatientes. *En Otras Palabras* 8 (January–July): 61–68.

Vickers, Jill. 2002. Thinking about Violence. In *Gender, Race, and Nation: A Global Perspective,* edited by Vanaja Dhruvarajan and Jill Vickers, 222–46. Toronto: University of Toronto Press.

Whitworth, Sandra. 2004. *Men, Militarism and UN Peacekeping: A Gendered Analysis.* Boulder Co.: Lynne Rienner Publishers.

Young, Iris Marion. 1990. *Justice and the Politics of Difference.* Princeton: Princeton University Press.

Appendix

Center for International Policy, Adam Isacson*

U.S. Assistance to Colombia 1997–2004

Long before George W. Bush entered the White House, critics of the U.S. approach to Colombia contended that it was too focused on drug–war priorities and relied too heavily on the country's troubled security forces. The policy, they argued, ignored the complicated, deep-rooted origins of Colombia's conflict. In a weakly governed country with stark social inequalities and historically abusive and corrupt security forces, focusing U.S. largesse on the police and military to fight drugs—a symptom more than a cause for the country's problems—would have grave consequences. "It will lead to the escalation of the social and armed conflict, fail to solve the drug-trafficking problem, endanger the peace process, attack indigenous populations' culture and life styles, seriously hamper the Amazon eco-system, worsen the humanitarian and human rights crisis, promote forced displacement and further worsen the social and political crisis," warned a June 2000 letter from 73 Colombian NGOs. These warnings went unheeded. Between 1999 and 2002, the United States gave Colombia $2.04 billion. Of that amount, 83%—$1.69 billion, or nearly $1.2 million per day over four years—has gone to Colombia's military and police. This pattern continues in the Bush Administration's aid request for 2003 and 2004.

This statistical appendix provides an overview of:

- U.S. military and police aid to Colombia, 1997–2004 (requested);
- U.S. social and economic assistance programs, 1997–2004 (requested);
- Coca cultivation in the Andean Region;
- U.S.–Colombia 2003: A look at the numbers.

U.S. assistance to Colombia has increased dramatically since Bill Clinton's second term in office (1997–2001). Assistance to Colombia's military and police has grown particularly rapidly, multiplying by a factor of seven between 1997 and 2003. Aid to the Colombian security forces spiked upward in 2000, with the passage of the U.S. contribution to Plan Colombia (funds which, though appropriated in 2000, were largely spent in 2001), and has remained similarly high ever since.

From 2000 to 2003 alone, Washington provided Colombia with $2.44 billion, of which $1.97 billion—80.5%—went to Colombia's armed forces and police. This money has paid for the transfer and maintenance of dozens of helicopters; an ambitious aerial herbicide-spraying program; riverine and aerial antidrug activities; the training of over 20,000 Colombian military and police personnel; and an effort to protect an oil pipeline from guerrilla attacks.

Figure A.1 indicates a projected reduction in aid for 2004; it is not clear, though, whether this will come to pass. In mid-2003, through an emergency request for "war on terror" funds, the Bush Administration added $105 million in military aid for Colombia; a similar supplemental request could take place again in 2004, bringing aid to comparable or greater levels (Isacson 2003).

Though all seem to agree that bringing peace, security, and reduced drug production to Colombia requires more than a military approach, U.S. assistance has overwhelmingly favored military programs (see table A.1). Far less resources have

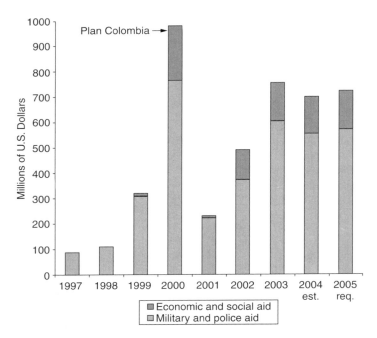

Figure A.1   U.S. Aid to Colombia 1997–2005

Table A.1 U.S. Aid to Colombia Since 1997: Summary Tables (Data in Millions of Dollars)

	Military and Police Assistance Programs								
	1997	1998	1999	2000	2001	2002	2003	2004, estimated	2005, requested
International Narcotics Control (INC) State Department-managed counterdrug arms transfers, training, and services	33.45	56.5	200.11	688.05	46.35	254.2	431.0	313.0	334.0
Foreign Military Financing (FMF) Grants for defense articles, training and services	30	0	0.44	0.02	4.49	0	17.1	110	108
International Military Education and Training (IMET) Training, usually not counterdrug	0	0.89	0.92	0.9	1.04	1.18	1.17	1.8	1.7
Emergency Drawdowns Presidential authority to grant counterdrug equipment from U.S. arsenal	14.2	41.1	58	0	0	0	0	0	0
"Section 1004" Authority to use the defense budget for some types of counterdrug aid	10.32	11.78	35.89	68.71	150.04	84.99	136	110.5	110.5
"Section 1033" Authority to use the defense budget to provide riverine counterdrug aid to Colombia	0	2.17	13.45	7.23	22.3	4	13.2	13.2	13.2

Table A.1 Continued

	Military and Police Assistance Programs								
	1997	1998	1999	2000	2001	2002	2003	2004, estimated	2005, requested
Anti-terrorism Assistance (ATA) Grants for anti-terrorism defense articles, training and services	0	0	0	0	?	25	3.28	0	3.92
Excess Defense Articles (EDA) Authority to transfer "excess" equipment	0.09	0	0	0.41	0.46	2.37	3.40	2.89	2.89
Discretionary Funds from the Office of National Drug Control Policy	0.5	0	0	0	0	0	0	0	0
Subtotal	88.56	112.44	308.81	765.32	224.68	371.74	605.10	551.33	574.15

Note: Numbers that are italicized are estimates taken by averaging previous two years.

	Economic and Social Assistance Programs (millions of dollars)								
Economic Support Funds (ESF) Transfers to the recipient government	0	0	3	4	0	0	0	0	0
Development Assistance (DA) Funds for development projects	0	0.02	0	0	0	0	0	0	0
International Narcotics Control (INC) State Department managed funding for counterdrug economic and social aid	0	0.5	5.75	208	5.65	120.3	149.2	150	150
Subtotal	0	0.52	8.75	212	5.65	120.3	149.2	150	150
Grand Total	88.56	112.96	317.56	977.32	230.33	492.04	754.2	701.33	724.15

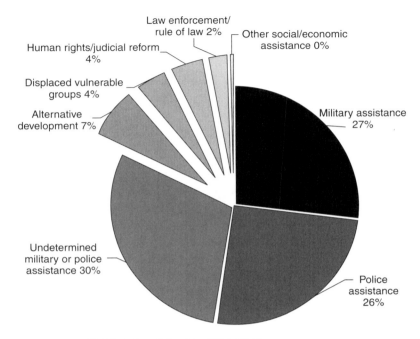

Figure A.2   All U.S. Aid to Colombia, 1997–2003

gone to other efforts needed to solve the structural causes of Colombia's violence and lawlessness, such as emergency aid to displaced persons, efforts to end impunity and improve the judicial system's functioning, or programs to integrate rural areas into the national economy and make legal crops profitable (see figure A.2) (Isacson 2003).

U.S. contractors sprayed 254,586 herbicides over hectares of Colombian territory in an effort to eradicate coca between 2000 and 2002. Yet by the end of 2002, the U.S. Department of State reports 144,400 hectares of coca remained under cultivation in Colombia—more than was grown in 2000. After nearly a decade, aerial fumigation has proven to be effective only at reducing coca-growing in a specific area for a limited time. New cultivations constantly appear in lightly governed zones where spraying is not occurring—an unsurprising consequence, given the high-profit margins the drug trade offers. Departments of Colombia that had never seen coca before—from the southeastern jungles to the hard-hit coffee-growing region—now contain thousands of hectares of illicit crops. At the same time, Colombia's neighbors, particularly Peru and Bolivia, are experiencing increases in their own coca cultivation as fumigation intensifies in Colombia (see figure A.3). Throughout the Andean region, the net effect is that coca cultivation has not budged from a total of roughly

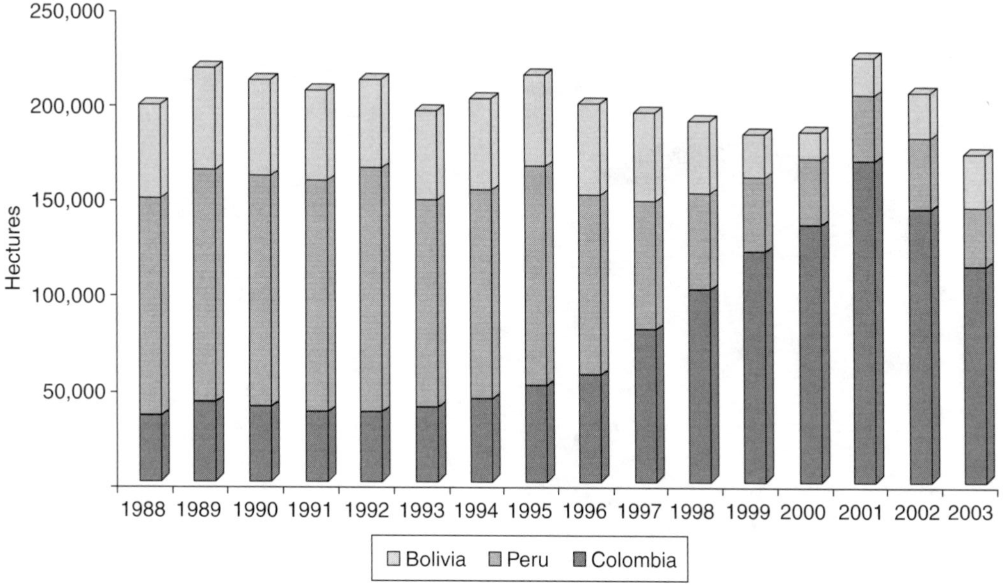

	1988	1999	1990	1991	1992	1993	1994	1995	1996	1997	1998	1999	2000	2001	2002	2003
Colombia	34,000	42,400	40,100	37,500	37,100	39,700	44,700	50,900	57,200	79,500	101,800	122,500	136,200	169,800	144,400	113,850
Peru	115,530	121,685	121,300	120,800	129,100	108,800	108,600	115,300	94,400	68,800	51,000	38,700	34,100	34,000	36,600	31,150
Bolivia	48,925	52,900	50,300	47,900	45,500	47,200	48,100	48,600	48,100	45,800	38,000	21,800	14,600	19,900	24,400	28,450
Total	198,455	216,985	211,700	206,200	211,700	195,700	201,400	214,800	199,700	194,100	190,800	183,000	184,900	223,700	205,400	173,450

Figure A.3 Andean Coca Cultivation, 1988–2003

Source: U.S. State Department, *International Narcotics Control Strategy Reports* 1996–2002.

200,000 hectares, while the price of cocaine on North American streets has not registered any increase (Isacson 2003).

Center for International Policy: Colombia Project

The United States and Colombia, 2003: A Look at the Numbers (http://www.ciponline.org/colombia/031028stat.htm)

U.S. Aid to Colombia Since 2000

1. Overall U.S. aid to Colombia, 2000–2003[1]: $2.44 billion
2. U.S. aid to Colombia's military and police, 2000–2003[2]: $1.97 billion (80.5%)
3. Overall U.S. aid to Colombia requested for 2004, including estimated defense-budget counternarcotics funds[3]: $688.29 million ($567.8 million through Foreign Operations)
4. U.S. aid to Colombia's military and police requested for 2004[4]: $552.59 million (80.3%) ($432.1 million through Foreign Operations)
5. U.S. funds for maintenance of Colombian military and police aircraft, 2003 estimate[5]: $191.01 million
6. Number of UH-60 "Blackhawk" helicopters granted to Colombia since 1999[6]: 22
7. Cost of operating a Blackhawk for one hour[7]: nearly $3,000
8. U.S. military, police, and fumigation funds paid to 16 private contractors, 2002[8]: $150.38 million
9. U.S. funds appropriated since August 2002 to help Colombia's military protect the Caño Limón-Coveñas oil pipeline[9]: $99 million
10. Share of oil in this pipeline belonging to U.S.-based Occidental Petroleum[10]: 43.75%
11. Guerrilla bombings of Caño Limón pipeline in 2001[11]: 170
12. Guerrilla bombings of Caño Limón pipeline in 2002, before the pipeline-protection program's inauguration[12]: 41

Fighting Drugs

1. Coca grown in Colombia, 2000[13]: 136,200 hectares (336,600 acres)
2. Coca sprayed with herbicide in Colombia, 2000–2002[14]: 254,586 hectares (629,096 acres)
3. Coca grown in Colombia, 2002[15]: 144,400 hectares (356,820 acres)
4. Increase in Colombian coca-growing, 2000–2002[16]: 8,200 hectares (+6.0%)
5. Coca grown in Colombia, Peru, and Bolivia combined, 2000[17]: 184,900 hectares (456,898 acres)
6. Coca grown in Colombia, Peru, and Bolivia combined, 2002[18]: 205,400 hectares (507,554 acres)
7. Increase in Andean region coca-growing, 2000–2002[19]: 20,500 hectares (+11%)

8. Total Andean coca cultivation in 2002, as a percentage of Rhode Island's land area[20]: 75.9%
9. Combined land area of Colombia, Peru, and Bolivia, as a multiple of Texas' land area[21]: 5.19
10. Colombian counties where a UN study detected coca, 2000[22]: 178
11. Colombian counties where a UN study detected coca, 2002[23]: 162
12. Price of a gram of powder cocaine, survey of 20 U.S. cities, fall 2000[24]: $30–200
13. Price of a gram of powder cocaine, survey of 20 U.S. cities, summer 2002[25] : $28–150
14. Price offered for a kilogram of coca paste in southern Colombia, 2000[26]: $600–800
15. Price offered for a kilogram of coca paste in southern Colombia, 2003[27]: $600–800

Human Rights
1. Murders, disappearances, or combat deaths as a result of political violence in Colombia, October 1, 1999 to September 30, 2000[28]: 6,067
2. Murders, disappearances, or combat deaths as a result of political violence in Colombia, July 1, 2002 to June 30, 2003[29]: 6,978
3. Of four groups (the U.S. State Department, UN High Commissioner for Human Rights, Human Rights Watch and Amnesty International), number whose 2003 human rights reports maintain that many Colombian military and police personnel collaborate with paramilitaries on the U.S. terrorist list[30]: 4
4. Date that Colombia's United Self-Defense Forces (AUC) paramilitary group declared a cease-fire, thus fulfilling President Álvaro Uribe's precondition for starting peace talks: December 1, 2002
5. Paramilitary killings of civilian noncombatants during the first six months of 2003[31]: 603
6. Colombian military personnel under investigation or awaiting trial for human rights abuse or collaboration with paramilitaries as of June 2003[32]: 27
7. Among the above individuals, those above the rank of sergeant[33]: 10
8. Those above the rank of major[34]: 1
9. Percentage of violent crimes that went unpunished in Colombia, 1995 (and likely 2003)[35]: 97

Alternative Development
1. Percentage of Colombian coca plots that are "family-size" (less than 3 hectares)[36]: 62%
2. Colombian families helped by U.S.-funded alternative development programs, as of October 2003[37]: 33,000

3. Colombian families estimated to have been displaced from their homes by fumigation since 1999[38]: 35,000
4. Price of a pound of Colombian coffee, October 2003[39]: 67 cents
5. Approximate price of a pound of coca leaves in rural Colombia[40]: $1.35
6. Miles of paved roads in Putumayo, a Maryland-sized province with extensive coca cultivation, June 2002[41]: 55
7. In three Putumayo counties, percentage of signers of alternative development assistance pacts who claim that their crops were sprayed with herbicides[42]: 32%
8. Percentage of rural Colombians living in poverty, 2001[43]: 80%

Colombia's Contribution

1. Colombia's defense budget—excluding police expenditure—as a percentage of GDP, 2003 estimate[44]: 3.2%
2. U.S. defense budget as a percentage of GDP, 2003 estimate: at least 4%
3. Annual income of wealthiest 10% of Colombians, as a multiple of the income of the poorest 10%[45]: 42
4. Annual income of wealthiest 10% of Americans, as a multiple of the income of the poorest 10%[46]: 17
5. Colombia's tax collection as a percentage of GDP, 2002[47]: 13.3%
6. U.S. tax collection as a percentage of GDP, 2000[48]: 29.6%
7. Percentage of Colombian recruits with high school degrees legally excluded from service in combat units[49]: 100%
8. Recommended ratio of armed forces to insurgents, according to counterinsurgency doctrine[50]: 10:1
9. Colombian military personnel available for combat, excluding those in training or support roles, mid-2002[51]: 60,000–80,000
10. Colombian insurgents and paramilitaries combined, estimate[52]: 37,000

U.S. Involvement

1. Ratio of U.S. military and police assistance to Colombia's own military and police budget, 2003[53]: 1: 6
2. Ratio of U.S. military and police assistance to El Salvador's own military and police budget, 1984[54]: 4: 7
3. U.S. military personnel on Colombian soil, November 2001[55]: 117
4. U.S. military personnel on Colombian soil, May 2003[56]: 358
5. Private contractors who have died on the job in Colombia since 1998[57]: 11
6. Months that three U.S. contractors have spent in custody of FARC guerrillas since their plane crash-landed in southern Colombia: $8^1/_2$ months

* Senior Associate, Center for International Policy—Colombia Project. This statistical Appendix consists of select data compiled by the Center for International Policy (CIP) (ciponline.org)

Notes

1. From numerous sources cited at <http://ciponline.org/colombia/aidtable.htm>. (includes estimates for 2003).
2. Ibid.
3. Ibid.
4. Ibid.
5. United States, Department of State, Bureau of International Narcotics and Law Enforcement Affairs, Fiscal Year 2004 Budget Congressional Justification (Washington: Department of State: June 2003) <http://www.state.gov/g/inl/rls/rpt/cbj/fy2004/>.
6. Statement of Rand Beers, Assistant Secretary of State for International Narcotics and Law Enforcement Affairs, Senate Caucus on International Narcotics Control (Washington: February 28, 2001): <http://www.ciponline.org/colombia/022801. htm>. Conference Committee report 105-825 on P.L. 105–277, the Omnibus Consolidated Appropriations bill which contains the Western Hemisphere Drug Elimination Act (Washington: U.S. Congress, October 19, 1998) <http://thomas. loc.gov/cgi-bin/cpquery/R?cp105:FLD010:@1(hr825):>.
7. Rep. Bob Barr, The Barr Report on Plan Colombia and the War on Drugs (Washington: House Government Reform Committee, January 2003): 8.
8. United States, Department of State, Report on Certain Counternarcotics Activities in Colombia (Washington: Department of State, April 2003) <http://ciponline.org/colombia/03041401.htm>.
9. United States, Department of State, Office of Resources, Plans and Policy, Congressional Presentation for Foreign Operations, Fiscal Year 2004 (Washington: February 2003) <http://www.state.gov/m/rm/rls/cbj/2004/>. United States Congress, Public Law No: 107-206 (Washington: August 2, 2002) <http://thomas.loc.gov/cgi-bin/query/z?c107: H.R.4775.ENR:>.
10. United States, Department of State, Report to Congress: Colombia: Cano Limon Pipeline (Washington: December 2002) <http://www.ciponline.org/colombia/02120001.htm>.
11. Ibid.
12. Marc Grossman, under secretary of State for Political Affairs, press conference (Bogota: March 5, 2003) <http://ciponline.org/colombia/03030501.htm>.
13. United States, Department of State, International Narcotics Control Strategy Report (Washington: Department of State, March 2003) <http://www.state.gov/g/inl/rls/nrcrpt/>.
14. Ibid.
15. Ibid.
16. Ibid.
17. Ibid.
18. Ibid.
19. Ibid.
20. United States Census Bureau (2003).
21. Ibid.
22. Government of Colombia, Dirección Nacional de Estupefacientes, Proyecto Sistema Integrado de Monitoreo de Cultivos Ilícitos -SIMCI- Estadísticas Cultivos de Coca Consolidadas por Municipio (Bogota: DNE, site visited October 2003) <http://www.cultivosilicitoscolombia.gov.co/aux_estadisticas1.htm>.

23. Ibid.

24. United States, White House, Office of National Drug Control Policy, *Pulse Check: Trends in Drug Abuse* (Washington: ONDCP, March 2001) <http://www.whitehousedrugpolicy.gov/publications/drugfact/pulsechk/midyear2000/index.html>.

25. United States, White House, Office of National Drug Control Policy, *Pulse Check: Trends in Drug Abuse* (Washington: ONDCP, November 2002) <http://www.whitehousedrugpolicy.gov/publications/drugfact/pulsechk/nov02/index.html>.

26. Center for International Policy, interviews with community leaders in Putumayo, Colombia, March 2001.

27. Center for International Policy, interviews with community leaders from Putumayo, Colombia and Sucumbíos, Ecuador, September 2003.

28. Colombian Commission of Jurists, "Panorama de violaciones a los derechos humanos y al derecho humanitario en Colombia abril a septiembre del 2000" (Bogotá: CCJ, October 2000) <http://ciponline.org/colombia/040001.htm>.

29. Colombian Commission of Jurists, "Alerta Frente a las Cifras Gubernamentales Sobre Derechos Humanos en Colombia" (Bogotá: CCJ, July 2003) <http://ciponline.org/colombia/030709ccj.htm>.

30. United States, Department of State, Country Reports on Human Rights Practices—2002 (Washington: Department of State, March 31, 2003) <http://www.state.gov/g/drl/rls/hrrpt/18325.htm>. United Nations, High Commissioner for Human Rights, Informe Anual del Alto Comisionado sobre Derechos Humanos en Colombia (Geneva: UNHCHR, February 24, 2003) <http://www.hchr.org.co/documentoseinformes/informes/altocomisionado/informe2002.html>; Human Rights Watch, World Report 2003 (New York: HRW, January 2003) <http://www.hrw.org/wr2k3/americas4.html>; Amnesty International, Amnesty International Report 2003 (London, AI, 2003) <http://web.amnesty.org/report2003/col-summary-eng>.

31. CINEP and Justicia y Paz, Banco de Datos sobre Derechos Humanos y Violencia Política, *Revista Noche y Niebla* 27 (Bogotá: CINEP and Justicia y Paz, 2003) <http://www.nocheyniebla.org/27/index.html>.

32. United States, Department of State, Memorandum of Justification Concerning Human Rights Conditions with Respect to Assistance for Colombian Armed Forces (Washington: Department of State, July 8, 2003) <http://ciponline.org/colombia/030708cert.htm>.

33. Ibid.

34. Ibid.

35. United States, Department of State, Country Reports on Human Rights Practices for 1995 (Washington: Department of State, March 1996) <http://www.usis.usemb.se/human/1995/west/colombia.html>.

36. Government of Colombia, Dirección Nacional de Estupefacientes, Proyecto Sistema Integrado de Monitoreo de Cultivos Ilícitos -SIMCI- Estadísticas Cultivos de Coca Consolidadas por Municipio (Bogotá: DNE, site visited October 2003) <http://www.cultivosilicitoscolombia.gov.co/documentos/mapa_colombia_02.pdf>.

37. Testimony of Adolfo Franco, assistant administrator, Bureau for Latin America and the Caribbean, U.S. Agency for International Development, Hearing of the House International Relations Subcommittee on the Western Hemisphere (Washington: October 21, 2003) <http://www.house.gov/international_relations/108/fran1021.htm>.

38. Marcela Ceballos, CODHES, Plan Colombia: Contraproductos y Crisis Humanitaria (Bogotá: Consultancy for Human Rights and Internal Displacement, October 2003): 26 <http://www.codhes.org.co/Documentos/10/boletinfumigaciones.pdf>.

39. "Indicadores económicos," *El Tiempo* (Bogotá: October 28, 2003) <http://eltiempo.terra.com.co/>.

40. Center for International Policy, interviews with community leaders from Putumayo, Colombia and Sucumbíos, Ecuador, September 2003.

41. Government of Colombia, Transportation Ministry, Instituto Nacional de Vías, Estado de la Red Vial Nacional (Invías, June 2002) <http://www.invias.gov.co/programas/red_vial/red_vial.asp>.

42. Ceballos, Plan Colombia, 36.

43. Government of Colombia, Departamento Nacional de Planeación, La economía Colombiana: del ajuste económico a la reactivación (Bogotá: DNP, 2002) <http://www.dnp.gov.co/ArchivosWeb/Direccion_General/Presentaciones/revista_cambio.ppt>.

44. "Presupuesto defensa de Colombia de este año será de 3.600 millones de dólares," EFE Spanish News Agency, February 20, 2003 <http://www.terra.com/actualidad/articulo/html/act134781.htm>. All currency conversions are based on 2,800 pesos to the dollar. Economist Intelligence Unit, Country Report: Colombia (London: January 2003).

45. United Nations Development Program, Human Development Report 2003 (New York: UNDP, 2003) <http://www.undp.org/hdr2003/>.

46. Ibid.

47. Government of Colombia, Centro de Noticias del Estado, "Superadas Metas de Recaudo de Impuestos en el 2002," January 20, 2003 <http://www.presidencia.gov.co/cne/2003/enero/20/08202003.htm>.

48. Organisation for Economic Co-operation and Development, Revenue Statistics 1965–2001 (Paris: OECD, 2002) <http://www.oecdwash.org/DATA/STATS/taxrevenue.pdf>.

49. Gabriel Marcella, The United States and Colombia: "The Journey from Ambiguity to Strategic Clarity," The Dante B. Fascell North-South Center Working Paper Series 13 (Miami: University of Miami, March 2003): 10 <http://www.miami.edu/nsc/publications/pubs-WP-pdf/WP13.pdf>.

50. Ibid., 25.

51. Ibid., 8.

52. Ibid., 25.

53. From numerous sources cited at <http://ciponline.org/colombia/aidtable.htm>. Includes estimates for 2003. "Presupuesto defensa de Colombia de este año será de 3.600 millones de dólares."

54. Richard A. Haggarty (ed.), El Salvador: A Country Study (Washington: Library of Congress, November 1988) <http://memory.loc.gov/frd/cs/svtoc.html>. United States, Arms Control and Disarmament Agency, World Military Expenditures and Arms Transfers 1995 (Washington: ACDA, 1996): 72.

55. United States, White House, Presidential Letter to U.S. Congress (Washington: June 24, 2002) <http://www.whitehouse.gov/news/releases/2002/07/20020703–14.html>.

56. United States, White House, Presidential Letter to U.S. Congress (Washington: June 20, 2003) <http://www.whitehouse.gov/ news/releases/2003/ 06/20030620– 22.html>.

57. Barr, The Barr Report, 9.

Index